Locating Classed Subje

Locating Classed Subjectivities explores representations of social class in British fiction through the lens of spatial theory and analysis. By analyzing a range of class-conscious texts from the nineteenth, twentieth, and twenty-first centuries, the collection provides an overview of the way British writers mobilized spatial aesthetics as a means to comment on the intricacies of social class. In doing so, the collection delineates aesthetic strategies of representation in British writing, tracing the development of literary forms while considering how authors mobilized innovative spatial metaphors to better express contingent social and economic realities. Ranging in coverage from early-nineteenth-century narratives of disease to contemporary writing on the working-class millennial, *Locating Classed Subjectivities* offers new perspectives on literary techniques and political intentions, exploring the way class is parsed and critiqued through British writing across three centuries. As such, the project responds to Nigel Thrift and Peter Williams's claim that literary and cultural production serves as a particularly rich yet unexamined access point by which to comprehend the way space and social class intersect.

Simon Lee is Assistant Professor of English at Texas State University where he researches and teaches post-war British literature with a particular focus on working-class writing and culture. He has published a range of scholarship on British writing, specifically authors like Alan Sillitoe, Shelagh Delaney, Colin MacInnes, Nell Dunn, and John Osborne.

Locating Classed Subjectivities

Intersections of Space and Working-Class Life in Nineteenth-, Twentieth-, and Twenty-First-Century British Writing

Edited by Simon Lee

Routledge
Taylor & Francis Group

NEW YORK AND LONDON

First published 2022
by Routledge
605 Third Avenue, New York, NY 10158

and by Routledge
4 Park Square, Milton Park, Abingdon, Oxon, OX14 4RN

Routledge is an imprint of the Taylor & Francis Group, an informa business

© 2022 selection and editorial matter, Simon Lee; individual
chapters, the contributors

Library of Congress Cataloging-in-Publication Data
A catalog record for this book has been requested

ISBN: 978-0-367-63510-7 (hbk)
ISBN: 978-0-367-63514-5 (pbk)
ISBN: 978-1-003-11942-5 (ebk)

DOI: 10.4324/9781003119425

Typeset in Sabon
by Apex CoVantage, LLC

Contents

Contributors

Chloé Ashbridge is Lecturer in Modern and Contemporary Literature at Newcastle University, where her research concerns the interplay between literature and politics in Britain. Cholé is currently preparing her first monograph, *Rewriting the North: Contemporary British Fiction and the Politics of Devolution* (Routledge, 2023), which situates Northern England at the center of a new devolutionary approach to the twenty-first-century British literary culture. Elsewhere, her publications explore class and geography in literary responses to Brexit, and the political identity of the North in Sarah Hall's fiction.

Nick Bentley is Senior Lecturer in English Literature at Keele University, UK. He is the author of *Martin Amis* (2015); *Contemporary British Fiction* (2008); *Radical Fictions: The English Novel in the 1950s* (2007); editor of *British Fiction of the 1990s* (2005); and co-editor of *The 2000s: A Decade of Contemporary British Fiction* (2015), *Teenage Dreams: Youth Subcultures in Fiction, Film and Other Media* (2018), and *The 1950s: A Decade of British Fiction* (2018). He is currently writing a monograph, titled *Making a Scene: Youth Subcultures in Postwar and Contemporary Fiction*.

Ben Clarke is Associate Professor of English at the University of North Carolina, Greensboro. He is the author of *Orwell in Context* (Palgrave, 2007), co-author of *Understanding Richard Hoggart* (Wiley-Blackwell, 2011), and co-editor of *Working-Class Writing* (Palgrave, 2018). He has written on authors, including Jack Hilton, Malcolm Lowry, Edward Upward, H. G. Wells, and Virginia Woolf, and subjects such as public houses, ideas of Englishness, and Western representations of Taiwan. He is currently editing the *Routledge Companion to Working-Class Literature*.

Elizabeth Floyd completed her PhD in English at the University of California, Santa Barbara, in 2019. Her dissertation examined the physical reconstruction of London after WWII, the political attempt to create a modernized middle class through new public architecture, and the reaction to this project through the gendered, "middlebrow" literature of the period. Her work analyzes realist novels, film, and architectural and design archival materials from the late 1940s until the mid-1960s. She currently teaches literature at Anacapa School.

Nick Hubble is Professor of Modern and Contemporary English at Brunel University London, UK. They are the author of *Mass-Observation and Everyday Life: Culture, History, Theory* (2006) and *The Proletarian Answer to the Modernist Question* (2017). Nick is the co-editor of *Working-Class Writing: Theory and Practice* (2018) and six volumes of British Fiction: The Decades Series: *The 1970s* (2014), *The 1990s* (2015), *The 2000s* (2015), *The 1950s* (2018), *The 1930s* (2021), and *The 2010s* (forthcoming 2023).

Patricia E. Johnson is Professor Emerita of English and Humanities at Penn State Harrisburg. She has published articles on Carnie Holdsworth's poetry and fairy tales and has edited an edition of her poems. She is also the author of *Hidden Hands: Working-Class Women and Victorian Social Problem Fiction* (Ohio University Press, 2001) as well as articles on Charles Dickens, Charlotte Bronte, Elizabeth Gaskell, and Pat Barker.

Meghan Jordan is the diversity, equity, and inclusion project and program manager at Utica College. Her work appears in *Neo-Victorian Studies* and *Studies in English Literature, 1500–1900*. She was an Associate Professor of English, teaching courses in composition and literature, for many years. Her latest research projects include a monograph on notions of selfhood, the rise of the realist novel, British life writing, bodily mutilation, gender, and global religious culture.

Simon Lee is Assistant Professor of English at Texas State University where he researches and teaches post-war British literature with a particular focus on working-class writing and culture. He has published a range of scholarship on British writing, specifically authors like Alan Sillitoe, Shelagh Delaney, Colin MacInnes, Nell Dunn, and John Osborne.

Cornelia Photopoulos earned her doctorate in English from Tufts University in 2020. Her dissertation, "'Home Is Where You Feel a Welcome': Homemaking as National Belonging in 20th and 21st c. Black British Novels," explores the intersection of the affective ideologies of "home" and the material realities of housing as shaped by the history and present of British imperialism, colonialism, and white supremacy.

Matthew L. Reznicek is Associate Professor of Nineteenth-century British and Irish Literature at Creighton University, where he also holds a joint appointment in the Department of Medical Humanities. He currently serves as vice president for the American Conference for Irish Studies.

Molly Slavin is Marion L. Brittain Postdoctoral Fellow at the Georgia Institute of Technology, where she teaches and researches contemporary British, Irish, and post-colonial literature. She has published widely on the subject of contemporary literatures, urban spaces, and figurations of crime, with articles in the *Journal of the Midwest Modern Language Association*, *C21 Literature: Journal of 21st Century Writings*, the *Journal of Commonwealth Literature*, and *Global South*. She holds a PhD from Emory University.

Introduction

Simon Lee

The Problem of Genre

In terms of analyzing social class and working-class life, Marxism and cultural studies have generally operated as the most customary points of academic inquiry. Yet, class theorized in the abstract fails to account for the nuances of lived experience. *Enter literature*. British literature foregrounds the *feeling* of social class, partly because social class in British culture is an unavoidable reality—a tangible formation felt most distinctively through the experience of "knowing one's place." It can be said that literature grants access to a more textured recognition of such feelings by shrinking the gap between the abstract and the tangible. It helps render immaterial social formations concrete through the use of narrative methods and the particulars of representation. Yet, despite the recognition and ubiquity of social class in Britain, the very idea of "working-class literature" has proven evasive in literary scholarship. This is due, in part, to the fact that canonicity is deeply rooted in class distinction and tied to cultural capital. To this day, institutions associated with literature and the arts actively exclude swathes of working-class people. In essence, this volume deals primarily—although not exclusively—with literary depictions of working-class life and their relationship to social formations. Attempts to galvanize working-class writing as a genre have encountered a range of definitional difficulties such as problems of authorial legitimacy, representational veracity, and questions of aesthetic and ethical intent. Even so, working-class writing continues to be a veritable subject of analysis. Sherry Lee Linkon, one of the founding figures of the field of working-class studies, has addressed such concerns by suggesting how class consciousness and an attuned familiarity with working-class life can serve as a perceptive lens. For Linkon, what this means is that a text does not need to be written by or for working-class people, per se, but that it lends itself to analysis that prioritizes working-class concerns or tends to issues pertinent to the lives of working-class people (2010). A question may be asked as to how an analysis of working-class representation might differ from more traditional forms of Marxist analysis.

DOI: 10.4324/9781003119425-1

While a thorough consideration of such a distinction is beyond the purview of this volume, it might be said that the kinds of texts explored here are predominantly invested in representing the lived experience of socioeconomic inequality rather than simply emphasizing the processes that occasion such experience. While Linkon's approach does indeed reflect the challenge of defining a working-class canon of literature or even tracing a veritable lineage of genre development, it also speaks to the fluid, homeostatic nature of class formations in addition to the shifting contexts in which literature is produced and consumed.

Despite definitional difficulties, working-class themes and topics are readily identifiable in British literature across a broad range of nineteenth- and twentieth-century texts, with twenty-first-century texts signifying sustained investment in the topic despite the splintering of tripartite class delineations. By focusing on such themes, critics have determined a body of work that while perhaps not "working-class" by design, is, at least, deeply class conscious and committed to exploring the lived realities and concerns of socio-economic inequality. For instance, nineteenth-century Chartist texts are generally considered to be the first sustained instance of recognizably class-conscious writing, drawing on Romantic tropes and narrative techniques to advance an explicitly political message about the plight of workers and their subjugation in British society. The consonant rise of urbanization and industrialization positioned the ensuing "social novel" as a genre grounded in realist techniques that document issues of poverty and harrowing working conditions in the hopes of enacting social change. The 1920s and 1930s saw a range of new texts detailing the impact of the Great Depression, and literature of the late 1950s indexed a shift from post-WWII austerity to the consensus era—a period of relative affluence in which an increase in disposable income coincided with the advent of consumer culture. Throughout such cases, working-class life is highlighted in captivating ways. Still, a definable category of proletarian fiction remains tenuous, in that class-conscious literature reflect shifts in cultural conditions as well as changes in the reading habits of the British populace. The tropes and motifs used to represent working-class life in British writing are, for all intents and purposes, bound to their cultural moment and are therefore highly contingent. There is no discernible value, for example, to write in the propagandistic manner of the Chartists today, just as a contemporary text that mirrors the aesthetics of the Victorian social novel might seem anachronistic or likely to be pigeonholed as historical fiction. So, if a definable genre of working-class writing could ever exist, it is one that is marked by its own indefinability because of its obligation to a particular cultural context. That is not to deny the existence of working-class texts that have indeed become canonized or have helped establish a lineage of recognizable devices. In fact, texts like Robert Tressell's *The Ragged-Trousered Philanthropists* (1914), Ethel Carnie Holdsworth's *This Slavery* (1925), and Walter Greenwood's

Love on the Dole (1933) hint at what might be considered a coherent and categorical body of working-class fiction. Yet, the problem of definition remains: class-conscious writing, by design, is almost always tethered to a contextual moment, which, in turn, is rarely stable. The result is a genre that is near impossible to codify through stable characteristics; in fact, it might be argued that working-class writing is a genre in which discursivity serves as its most tangible through line. That said, recent years have registered an uptick of interest in working-class writing due, in part, to the increased visibility of class as an intersectional vector as well as the increased scapegoating of working-class voters in the political realm. Scholarship on the topic has also increased, with criticism exceeding de facto modalities of Marxism or cultural studies. Furthermore, academic institutions historically indifferent to socio-economic inequality have begun to consider working-class culture as not just a legitimate subject of inquiry but as a meaningful component of diversity. And yet the question of "Where are the working-class voices?" persists. The irony, of course, is that such voices have been present for centuries, but perhaps this question can be forgiven in light of the fact that the genre of working-class writing actively resists its own formulation.

Perhaps most instrumental in cementing a somewhat stable notion of working-class literature are non-fiction texts that deploy narrative structures and forms of characterization ordinarily associated with imaginative writing. The most prominent of these texts is Richard Hoggart's *The Uses of Literacy* (1957), a book that explores the nature of working-class culture in Britain. It is perhaps not surprising, then, that his work is frequently cited in this volume. Influenced by George Orwell's *The Road to Wigan Pier* (1937), Hoggart traces the particulars of working-class life with fidelity. In doing so, he questions the way such life can withstand shifts in a cultural sphere shaped by the advent of new media forms and rising commodification. Generally considered a classic of British cultural studies, what Hoggart's text emphasizes more than anything is the mercurial nature of class experience in Britain, the necessity of recursive writing, and the challenge of describing what is essentially a moving target: working-class life. In his own attempt to pin down such definitions, Raymond Williams characterized working-class writing as "internal"—writing by and for working-class people, or as a body of work that prioritizes "internal relations, at once interlocking and in tension" (1978, 132). This collection affirms such problems of categorization but arguably leans more toward Linkon's notion of a "working-class reading" in which representations of class difference are parsed as a way to better apprehend historical context in addition to issues specific to working-class people. Central to this volume, though, is concern for the way class-conscious literature is preoccupied with representations of space and place, be it as a method to depict a working-class environment or as a way to explain how aspects of working-class identities are informed by spatial relations. The essays reveal how spatial motifs and engagements with the environment serve as a trope that, in part, help define an otherwise-stubborn working-class canon. Therefore, an increased focus on such features helps to offer one particular response to the problem of genre definition, affirming that working-class writing operates more as a shifting composite of techniques and approaches rather than as a fixed and closed entity. In fact, it might be said that spatialized representations of social class act as the most consistent trope of what we might understand as "working-class writing."

The Spatial Turn as Method

The "spatial turn in the humanities" is generally viewed as an annex of traditional Marxist analysis, a moment in which power relations and social dynamics are theorized as a consequence of geography and environment. Sometimes referred to as the "spatialization of Marxism," the "turn" began in the 1970s with texts such as Williams's *The Country and the City* (1973) and Henri Lefebvre's *The Production of Space* (1974). It was not until the 1980s and 1990s, though, that "the turn" crystalized with writers such as Frederic Jameson (1991), Edward Soja (1996), and David Harvey (2006), expanding Lefebvre's concepts and ideas in ways that emphasize his interdisciplinary reach. According to Reingard Nethersole (1990), the formation of the spatial turn and the expansion of Marxist analysis beyond economics correlates with an analogous impulse for academic fields and disciplines to innovate. Nethersole identifies the spatial turn as an organic development in cultural criticism, suggesting how concepts and frameworks associated with spatial analysis arise from discourse around theoretical methods more broadly (63). In this regard, the spatial turn transpires as an analytical inevitability, the drive to extend Marxist thought across disciplines. In addition, the spatial turn's crystallization represents a much-needed intervention into a largely abstract analytical method, an intervention that spotlights lived experience. Put differently, the spatial turn suggests a move from theory to praxis: a form of critical inquiry in which subjectivity prevails.

Lefebvre's *The Production of Space* offers a systematic approach, to analyzing social relations through spatial structures. Serving as a response to 1973's *The Survival of Capitalism*, Lefebvre's text advances a framework as a means to grasp the nature of power relations and social inequities. In this model, a site is considered as a composite of three states in tension: conceived space (the intent of the space's design), perceived space (how the space appears in reality), and lived space (how the space functions). According to Lefebvre, spatial analysis must consider all three components, focusing on imbalances and strains as a method by which to recognize differential power relations in society. The result is a system of analysis that offers a more substantial, experiential understanding of the impact of economic forces ordinarily explored through traditional Marxist methods. In the years preceding Lefebvre's text, Michel Foucault also considered notions of spatial analysis through his 1967 lectures on heterotopic space, a kind of discursive realm that both mirrors and disturbs material reality. Heterotopic space, as Foucault has it, operates similar to that of Lefebvre's spatial triad, in that analysis of a site reveals hidden layers of social production and power dynamics through a process of alterity. But of interest to this volume is Foucault's discussion of narrative, seen most powerfully in 1986's "Of Other Spaces: Utopias and Heterotopias," in which he maps out the concept. Here, Foucault begins by arguing that narratives of all forms have played a role in the subordination of space to chronological time; the notion of the heterotopia emerges as an attempt to reignite interest in the analysis of space alongside more traditional temporal methods of parsing the world. As Leo Mellor writes, "Conceptualizing any aesthetic in terms of locale can be useful, since it gives texture to particularity, specificity and the happenstance juxtapositions of geography that could remain obscured" (2011, 3). Therefore, the importance of centering space and place in literary analysis offers ways of discerning culture and cultural dynamics too easily misunderstood or overlooked. For Nethersole, the hope is that an increased emphasis on spatial awareness will impact the way we read and write, in that "stories will no longer begin with 'Once upon a time . . .' but with 'Once upon a place . . .'" (1990, 63).

The advent of the spatial turn can be understood as a fine-tuning of the initial concept advanced by Lefebvre and Foucault, which, in turn, elucidates its intervention into Marxist modes of thought. Perhaps the most notable example is David Harvey's expansion of Lefebvre's triad into what he deems a "nine-way matrix." For Harvey, spatial analysis has always played a key role in understanding the socio-economic makeup of an environment, rendered most explicit in terms of mapping economic shifts seen, for example, in regions of deindustrialization and sites of known inequality. But Harvey's adoption of Lefebvre's method suggests an equal commitment to the exploration of social relations often unclear or intangible. In his 2004 lecture, "Space as a Keyword," Harvey multiplies Lefebvre's dialectical triad to include "absolute," "relative," and "relational space" in ways that intersect with Lefebvre's "conceived," "perceived," and "lived space." The goal, for Harvey, is to complicate the notion of lived experience by reintroducing a temporal element of analysis that heightens awareness of the way a space is experienced over time. In what is perhaps his most lucid example, Harvey discusses the area of Manhattan that once held the Twin Towers and now serves as the 9/11 memorial, emphasizing the contingent nature of spatial signification. Edward Soja, on the other hand, builds more on Foucault's "heterotopia" in his *Thirdspace* while keeping Lefebvre's discursive triad in mind. For Soja, "thirdspace" is a conceptual endeavor with "firstspace" most proximal to Lefebvre's perceived space (the apprehension of material reality) and "secondspace" operating akin to conceived space (the intellectual comprehension of a space's function). "Thirdspace" reflects inquiry into the way a space operates via "firstspace" and "secondspace." That is to say that Soja's conceptualization of "thirdspace" is akin to Lefebvre's larger project of parsing social relations as a dynamic triad in tension. But for Soja, the analysis has an effect akin to the heterotopia, in that it unmasks dimensions of otherness while championing utopian *potentiality* as an alternative to the material reality that exists. The term "spatial turn" was coined by Soja, and these two texts (among others) demonstrate the way the burgeoning spatial analysis of the 1970s took hold in the decades that followed in a form that would lay the foundation for literary studies and adjacent fields to incorporate models of spatiality that generate elevated interpretations.

As noted by Nethersole and others, the rise of the spatial turn in the humanities mirrors an increase in interdisciplinary scholarship as well as an increased commitment to the expansion of humanistic inquiry beyond the contours of academic institutions. Consequently, the spatial turn can appear orphaned as a theoretical field, one with peripheral ties to geography but perhaps less tethered to other disciplines. Given its proximity to Marxist analysis, the major texts of the spatial turn take literary works as cultural artifacts, but their analytical focus veers more toward culture at large. In more recent years, though, productive affiliations have materialized between spatial analysis and literature, forming discrete disciplines such as literary geographies and spatial literary studies. According to Sheila Hones, distinctions can *and should* be drawn between these two categories based on their unique disciplinary origins. Literary geographies, Hones argues, is marked by a "double interdisciplinarity" (2018, 146)—a balanced merger of geography and literary studies. Spatial literary studies, conversely, is centered in English departments and literary practices while making reference to a range of geographical ideas and concepts. Hones points out that the separation is often rendered unclear and that geographers associated with literary geographies often rely more heavily on literary analysis than on traditional geographical methods aligned with the social sciences. Yet, Hones's concern is based more on the way the fields themselves emerge, noting that spatial literary studies is a fairly recent endeavor, with literary geographies traceable over almost four decades (149). Whether such territoriality is helpful or not is an argument beyond the purview of this particular introduction, but Hones's claims highlight the fact that both literature and geography benefited from the spatial turn, which itself surfaced from critical concepts grounded in Marxist thought.

The practices that Hones relegates to spatial literary studies (as opposed to those associated with literary geographies) have led to critical approaches that help expand the discipline, be it through the interdisciplinary practices that might be considered literary geography or through practices that prioritize literary analysis as a method by which to expand geographical and space-based knowledge. By way of illustration, Bertrand Westphal's innovative *Geocriticism: Real and Fictional Spaces* centers on literary analysis but in the service of contributing to research in the social sciences by spotlighting fact in fiction. More pointedly, Westphal argues that the process of mapping urban space should exceed traditional cartographic forms. To wit, a geocritical map might also consider various cultural factors alongside traditional mapping practices, one example being imaginative narrative portrayals of space. Westphal notes that the representational strategies identifiable in literature offer imaginative and paralogical details absent in material analysis. In his words, this nuanced articulation of place is rendered rich through its composite of the real with the fictional, in that "fiction does not mimic reality, but that it actualizes new virtualities hitherto unexpressed, which then *interact* with the real according to the hypertextual logic of interfaces" (2011, 103). The result, Westphal contends, is that "fiction detects possibilities buried in the folds of reality" (103). Westphal's method validates the kind of lineage central to spatial studies more broadly, showing how its development not only branches across disciplines but also takes root within them. The approach also highlights how singular texts and concepts emerge in a manner similar to that of Lefebvre's and Foucault's proposals alongside those whose theories built on their original concepts and positions.

In recent decades, spatial literary studies has grown to offer more fixed, definitive modes of analytic inquiry in contrast to the malleable, loose interdisciplinarity of the early spatial turn. The result is that what Hones would deem spatial literary studies has led to new ways of understanding a text through the application of spatial and cartographic methods. For instance, GIS technology is now used to map certain narrative accounts and sequences in ways that mark locations and regions as most likely to beget certain kinds of stories. Lancaster University, for example, deployed such methods for their "Mapping the Lakes" project as a way to articulate the attraction of specific sites and regions for the first generation of Romantic poets. Similar analysis can be seen in the work of Sten Pulz Moslund whose "topopoetics" aims to articulate links between landscape and language. For Moslund, speech patterns emerging in regions and dialects are driven, in part, by the form of the land itself, allowing connections to be made between the physical terrain and the images used in a text (2011, 37). Robert T. Tally Jr., perhaps one of the most notable figures in spatial literary studies, is responsible for not just an editorial series on this precise topic, but copious monographs advancing new concepts and approaches to textual analysis through spatial categories. Tally's *Spatiality* (2012) offers a clear-minded overview of the formation of spatial literary studies, especially the spatial turn's impact on the way literature can be viewed as a legitimate mode of site-specific analysis. Tally goes on to define spatial literary studies as

> a multiform critical practice that would include almost any approach to the text that focuses attention on space, place, or mapping, whether within the confines of the text, in reference to the outside world, or some combination of the two.
>
> (2014)

Tally's more recent notion of "topophrenia"—a response to Yi-Fu Tuan's "topophilia" (1974)—highlights much of what spatial literary studies entails. For Tally, "topophrenia" connotes a specific kind of "placemindedness" in fiction in which "the persistence of place and the subject's relation to it must be taken into account" (2018, 23). Such considerations reinforce the development of spatial studies over time, from Lefebvre's augmentation of Marxist analysis and Foucault's phenomenological thinking, to the notion of the spatial turn as a new interpretive paradigm across a range of disciplines, to the fine-tuning and discipline-specific concepts emerging in spatial literary studies. On the one hand, such developments reflect a neat and linear path; on the other, they represent a complex network of concepts and ideas best enumerated through geographic terms or the process of mapping.

Class Representation as a Spatial Concern

In their introduction to *Class and Space: The Making of Urban Society*, Nigel Thrift and Peter Williams make a plea for research that merges class with space. Opening with a survey of traditional approaches in which social stratification is rendered abstract through economics, the authors imply that such rigid methods breed unstable results due to the shifting nature of the subject itself. Furthermore, the authors show that no single theorization can take precedence over another. They reference David Stark's consideration of class discursivity, in which Stark notes how "it becomes apparent that a class never exists as a single collectivity-in-struggle but as a multiplicity of collectivities-in-struggle," with him adding that "[t]he study of the forms and dynamics of these groups is the task of class analysis" (1980, 98). By offering an overview of the way methods of class analysis prove to be as convoluted and mercurial as the dynamics of class itself, Thrift and Williams promote spatial analysis as a viable and more defined category of class knowledge akin to traditional economics-driven methods, reiterating their frequently repeated claim that the study of class formations has overlooked the productive potential of geography and spatial understanding (2014: xiii).

Rather than situate spatial analysis as a replacement for "hard" objective analysis, Thrift and Williams suggest that "soft" data can help augment more traditional modes of class inquiry by illuminating the subjective. Considering that social class is "felt," it can be said that the most tangible notions of class are experienced materially, understood by individuals as their lived reality. As the authors grant, attempts to analyze such perspectives are manifold, but the fact that spatial analysis is not widely considered in class analysis does indeed seem like an oversight. Their volume surveys three general areas in which a modicum of space-class analysis can be recognized: urbanism and the ties between sites of industry and class formation; individual communities and the formation of classed identities within them; and class capacity and the tendency for working-class regions to subdivide under pressure. For Thrift and Williams, then, a spatial comprehension of social class seeks not to streamline analysis but to complicate existing models by prioritizing the lived experience they believe critical yet so deficient. The essays that follow align with Thrift and Williams's contention, drawing on existing scholarship around spatio-class analysis but also turning to earlier, more phenomenological aspects of spatial comprehension as a means to flesh out possible approaches. In doing so, this volume validates the role of cultural production in the analysis of lived experience by positioning fictional texts as condensed, compressed accounts of working-class realities. Fiction, then, can be unpacked in ways that reflect the kinds of ethnographic accounts and narratives central to research in the social sciences; fiction begets fact and vice versa.

So Thrift and Williams advocate for richer analysis in terms of forging links between space and class, acknowledging that there is much to be done and considerable room to expand the approaches and methods they propose. Subsequent research across the social sciences reflects an attempt to address these issues. But, in general, it is mostly aligned with sociological and anthropological modalities, in which human geography is elevated as the dominant framework. For example, there appears to be an uptick in the sociological study of gentrification, in which space and class are unified along the lines of Thrift and Williams's initial discussion. Gary Bridge, for instance, argues for modes of analysis that sidestep the abstraction of traditional economic analysis to modes in which social forces are spatialized. For Bridge, class analysis that overlooks lived experience and material reality fails to account for the "multiple determinations" of structuration (1995, 236). Although Bridge's account does not produce a specific set of claims about such links, it does affirm the need to study social class in more nuanced and granular ways. In a similar manner, Gerry Veenstra considers how space and class intersect in terms of health and access to certain social resources. Drawing on Pierre Bourdieu's conceptualization of "habitus," Veenstra advocates for a structuralist approach to class analysis to underscore the experiential component lacking in abstract and hypothetical methods. Challenging the more economically centered modes of class analysis associated with Max Weber, Veenstra concludes that "[a] relational interpretation of social space encompasses or even transcends these dichotomies by identifying the real with relations rather than with substances" (2007, 29–30). Following a similar line of thinking that contrasts social inequality with access to resources, Emil Israel and Amnon Frenkel also draw on Bourdieu's work as a way to demonstrate how classed identities emerge as the upshot of spatial dynamics. For these authors, lived experience understood through spatial analysis can lead to results that help enable social change, or what they refer to as "a normative turn in spatial studies that advances the exploration of avoidable human suffering" (2020, 1). Building on the relationality emphasized by Veenstra, Israel and Frenkel restate the importance of mapping how "[l]iving environments manifest the political agendas of different communities, concealing power relationships within the social space" (3). Such approaches to identifying power relations that operate through spatial means are the province of Lefebvre's spatial triad and Harvey's nine-way matrix. Arguably, these methods work toward the same goal: to better acknowledge how space is socially constructed and how such a production might increase our understanding of social inequality as it pertains to social class and stratification.

Put differently, much of the work centering on the intersection of space and class still builds on the foundational ideas pioneered by Lefebvre and, to a lesser degree, Foucault. Therefore, the spatial turn can almost always be seen as a project rooted in Marxist principles and as a development intimately tied to the study of power dynamics. In a manner that reflects the kind of social justice–centered analysis of Veenstra—as well as that of Israel and Frenkel—the spatial turn questions the efficacy of existing economic systems, or as J. Richard Peet puts it in his "Introduction to Marxist Geography," a spatial approach to Marxist analysis "is a mode of understanding and action suited to the present stage of the human endeavor" (1985, 6). For Peet, then, Marxist critique should move beyond an analysis of social and economic relations in order to quantify the impact of late-stage capitalism on the environment writ large. He argues that analysis must address the shifting material forms of its subject in addition to highlighting practical, palpable experiences. As such, the kinds of methodologies developed as part of the "spatial turn" by figures like Lefebvre and Foucault, later refined by Harvey, Soja, and others, are Marxist in nature yet offer greater nuance in terms of comprehending material realities in ways that open up new possibilities of interdisciplinary practice by merging abstraction with concrete, lived experience.

Fiction as Consensus of Lived Experience

If a reasonable argument against analysis that prioritizes class in the abstract exists, it is that lived experience is minimized in ways that render class conditions largely hypothetical. The problem, of course, is how to combine large-scale, objective metrics and economic data with discrete, subjective narratives and sentiments. Arguably, literature provides one plausible way of addressing this problem through an exploration of what Williams has termed "structures of feeling." For Williams, "structures of feeling" refer to a broadly felt affective state identifiable across a range of writers of a specific time period. It offers a way to understand the abstract in more concrete, tangible terms, in that "relationships, institutions and formations in which we are still actively involved are converted, by this procedural mode, into formed wholes rather than forming and formative processes" (1978, 128). Williams notes that such an approach demarcates dominant ideological positions of a particular time from the lived experience of writers and their subjects, most perceptible by the use of "feeling" over something more akin to "belief" (132). As John Kirk clarifies, Williams's intention was to highlight a shared, cumulative sense of an experienced reality as the upshot of social or ideological formations while simultaneously acknowledging productive forces (2007, 45). Kirk adds that imaginative literature plays a vital role in what is ultimately a dialectical enigma, noting how

> there is something resolutely dialogic bound up with the concept of "structure of feeling"; we get the sense that art and/or literature represents something more than the author's individual expression, or "vision," as it necessarily engages with wider historical structures or events.
>
> (45)

Extending this logic, literature can surely serve as a hypothetical solution to the problem of class analysis in the abstract; it can open a window into the world of lived experience as an upshot of social formations and ideological temporalities. Yet, one concern that arises through such an approach is that while Williams's concept can potentially organize and reiterate general sentiments of working-class life, it also freezes them in time by articulating dominant feelings associated with a particular historic moment and rendering them static rather than dynamic. This is what Williams refers to as a "knowable community"—a concept that he would develop in later work and one that suggests that literature can function as a kind of snapshot. The fact that such an experience emerges through narrative form reveals some of the challenges associated with parsing class through art, or—put differently—facts through fiction.

That is not to say that the hypothetical use of literature as plausible data in class analysis should be jettisoned; as part of the spatial turn, critics have indeed drawn on imaginative fiction as a way to gain a consensus of lived experience. In this regard, literature does indeed function as a viable tool by which to augment other forms of class analysis, specifically by adding nuance and granularity in the absence of lived experience. Kirk adds how "art constitutes an area of knowledge, a place of 'cognitive mapping'" (61), and such an approach can be seen as a logical extension of developments made through the spatial turn. For example, literature plays a key role in the kind of spatial mapping associated with Westphal's notion of geocriticism mentioned prior—a mode of analysis in which affective summations of cultural production serve to augment traditional forms of cartography and spatial mapping. While Westphal restricts analysis to sites with ample, sanctioned cultural production (such as major cities frequently documented in narrative form), other figures have built on geocritical concepts to suggest how this approach can consider *types* of space in addition to physical spaces. As an example, Eric Prieto (2011) has extended Westphal's thinking to include sites like shanty towns, proving that literature written about particular *types* of space might open the door to a broader application of geocritical methods in class analysis. In this sense, cultural production (and its attendant analysis through a spatial lens) can be understood in three ways: as an element of "mapping" that helps flesh out our appreciation of a specific place, as a tool to take the cultural pulse of a specific time and environment, and as a way to consider how literature can act as a broad consensus of experience. Given this, it is possible to see how literature expresses the missing element of more abstract modes of class analysis—that of lived experience determined not simply by historical or ideological conditions, but as the direct result of environmental interactions and negotiations made with material reality. Returning once more to a claim made at the outset of this essay, literature and the arts operate as a site where abstract notions of social class are transposed into articulations of classed experience. This collection hopes to further concretize this possibility by demonstrating how authors over the course of three distinct centuries not only engage with spatial motifs as part of their technical agenda but also capture certain sentiments of working-class life felt broadly by a wide swathe of the population as well.

As Thrift and Williams suggest, a careful analysis of the mutually constitutive nature of class and environment serves as a rich and unheeded point of inquiry. Furthermore, an emphasis placed on literature as a way to access lived experience highlights the importance of elevating class analysis beyond abstraction while also maintaining objectivity through sanctioned storytelling. In fact, the recent *Routledge Handbook of Working-Class Studies* (2021) emphasized the importance of anecdotes in class-centered scholarship, articulated by Linkon in her "Class

Analysis from the Inside: Scholarly Personal Narrative as a Signature Genre of Working-Class Studies." While the personal anecdote may provide rhetorical ethos, a number of recent critics have turned to literature as a kind of representative working-class spirit, drawing on fiction's imaginative possibilities and helping to illuminate the conceivable directions such approaches might take. For instance, Nicola Wilson's *Home in British Working-Class Fiction* (2015) examines representations of domestic space in a range of class-conscious texts across time and genres. Wilson's text centers on the home's role in the formation of class identity, looking specifically at issues of gender and developments in material culture. As she suggests, a scrutiny of the way specific sites operate in working-class life can help distill discernment of working-class writing more broadly, which, in turn, illuminates the way class is experienced in relation to specific sites. Kim Duff's *Contemporary British Literature and Urban Space: After Thatcher* (2014) makes the case that late-twentieth-century literature emphasizes how conservative political thought operates through modes of spatial strategies. In this regard, texts such as J. G. Ballard's *High Rise* (1975) and Irvine Welsh's *Trainspotting* (1993) cohere around a spatial politics rendered clear through the form of the novel itself. Such analysis sheds light on the way endeavors like urban development and gentrification are critiqued through fiction in ways that elucidate links between classed experience and spatial negotiations. Sonali Perera's *No Country: Working-Class Writing in the Age of Globalization* (2014) veers more toward the abstractions associated with Marxist critique but includes spatial analysis as a way to contour the impact of a global movement associated with post-colonial migration. While recent years have suggested a renewed interest in class-conscious writing, the examples above come closest to spatio-class analysis as a viable mode of literary criticism. In neighboring disciplines, texts have explored similar links between space and class but from positions less driven by literature and imaginative fiction. For example, Sally Munt's edited volume, *Cultural Studies and the Working Class* (2000) features a section named "Class, Taste, and Space," with three distinct essays, all investigating aspects of the topic. Although perhaps more sociological in nature, the text highlights ways of thinking about the formation of classed identities as an upshot of spatial negotiation. Similarly, Yvette Taylor's *Classed Intersections: Space, Selves, Knowledge* (2010) uses more traditional sociological and ethnographic approaches to show how specific environments are associated with classed stigma. While Munt and Taylor's collections sidestep imaginative fiction, tending to draw their analysis from more sociological forms of storytelling, both offer clear ways of thinking about spatio-class analysis that can assist in approaches to literary scholarship. But what such approaches inadvertently confirm is that narrative and storytelling—be it imaginative or otherwise—offer a unique perspective on lived experience, what Westphal refers to as a form of "paralogical discourse" that stresses the significance of space and place in the formation of classed identities and their subsequent articulation. Given the literary imagination's capacity to uncover certain truths about the world otherwise unrecognized, the essays that follow all stress the importance of such analytical methods by highlighting not just how British class-conscious writing has deployed spatial motifs over time, but how authors over the course of three centuries have engaged spatial concepts in a manner that presupposes and anticipates analysis associated with the spatial turn.

The Structure of the Collection

The essays in this volume run chronologically, beginning with Matthew L. Reznicek's study of the way early-nineteenth-century novels by writers like Jane Austen, Maria Edgeworth, and Walter Scott reflect the intersections of urban planning and public health. The chapter considers how the lower orders of society were marked as diseased and the way such demarcations produced spatial borders, boundaries, and divisions. Reznicek argues that the fiction of the era shed light on biopolitical imperatives, in which relative health and wellness were used to justify social stratification. Meghan Jordan turns to Charles Dickens's *Little Dorrit* to show how the novel's famous Circumlocution Office—as well as representations of the Marshalsea Prison—helps to emphasize the value of space-class awareness. The essay considers not just the implications of bureaucratic space for British citizens, but their role in British colonialism at the height of empire. Patricia E. Johnson turns to a figure generally recognized as the first British working-class woman novelist: Ethel Carnie Holdsworth. Focusing on two of Holdsworth's novels—1913's *Miss Nobody* and 1929's *Barbara Dennison*, Johnson examines this radical writer's desire to identify spaces for working-class women beyond their social designation. Drawing on Deleuze and Guattari's notion of nomadicization, Johnson explores the idea of "play" in working-class life in Carnie Holdsworth's writing.

As the twentieth century continues, the collection registers an uptick in class-conscious writing by tracing developments in the way novelists used spatial metaphors and environmental awareness to articulate the nuance of socio-economic disparity. Nick Hubble focuses on the expansion of British proletarian fiction in the 1930s, arguing that such texts helped establish the groundwork for what would become a culturally democratized post-war Britain. Turning to the mining novels of Harold Heslop, Lewis Jones, and Walter Brierley, Hubble explores key spaces associated with mining communities such as the coalfield, miners' homes, and—of course—the mine itself. Their essay clarifies the way such spaces reinforce rigid gender roles often attributed to twentieth-century working-class communities. By contrast, Elizabeth Floyd considers a post-WWII emphasis on social mobility, focusing on the way government propaganda promoted urban planning and middle-class life as a viable path for working-class people. Floyd contrasts the 1945 film *Proud City: A Plan for London* with Graham Greene's 1951 novel, *The End of the Affair*, to demonstrate how architecture and urbanism interact with articulations of classed subjectivity. Greene's novel, Floyd argues, helps make clear inherent tensions between post-WWII redevelopment plans and the anxieties of a middle class whose primacy over the working classes contours their identity. Ben Clarke draws on pioneering texts in the field of cultural studies to examine John Braine's use of spatial representation. The essay suggests that Braine aligns with contemporary figures such as Hoggart in his desire to understand that meaning is generated and contested in everyday spaces and practices. Clarke shows how the significance of the ordinary is founded on working-class forms of thought characterized, as Hoggart argues, by an emphasis on "the personal, the concrete, the local." My own contribution considers the shift away from the period of relative affluence and access to disposable income of the post-WWII years to the late 1970s and early 1980s, in which Thatcher's conservative policies decimated working-class communities by closing mines and factories while moving work overseas. Turning to Pat Barker's 1982 novel *Union Street*, I consider the text's implicit question: What happens to a working-class subjectivity in spaces where work no longer exists? My essay centers on the way new articulations of identity emerge in response through the use of class signifiers. In turn, though, such signifiers carry a valence of stigma in a manner that reiterates Reznicek's study of nineteenth-century fiction, and I read *Union Street* as commentary on what Loïc Wacquant has termed territorial stigmatization.

Moving into the twenty-first century, Nick Bentley discusses Ross Raisin's *Waterline* (2011) and Martin Amis's *Lionel Asbo: State of England* (2012). Echoing Lefebvre's spatial triad, Bentley posits a triangular relationship of working practices, space, and identity that are co-dependent and that changes in any one of these areas cause a subsequent shift in the others. With reference to critics such as Tim Edensor, the essay outlines how the contemporary working-class novel offers a complicated adaptation of realist approaches with a turn toward the gothic as a genre particularly suited to express the ghostly relationship between past and present caused by the deindustrialization of urban landscapes. Molly Slavin's essay centers on Zadie Smith's *NW* (2012) and *Swing Time* (2016)—two novels that use spatial metaphors to triangulate the intersection of class with other social identities. As Slavin observes, *NW* is invested in the way movement through urban centers is predicated on cultural and economic capital; *Swing Time* builds on similar principles with global movement in mind. The essay explores the way space and time intersect in relation to multi-racial working-class identities, particularly as experienced as part of the post-Thatcher era.

Building further on discussions of intersectionality, Cornelia Photopoulos reads Bernardine Evaristo's *Mr. Loverman* (2014) and *Girl, Woman, Other* (2019) to show how racialized classed space is engendered and regulated by multiple ideological and political structures, including white supremacy and neoliberalism. The essay argues that Evaristo writes against the history of Black social exclusion by representing Black British characters asserting their control over private property and public space. Photopoulos comments that, in depicting Black characters achieving national belonging through their ability to assert ownership and control over privileged private and public spaces, Evaristo reinscribes the exclusionary practices of neoliberalism as a metric of social value. Last, Chloé Ashbridge brings the volume up to the present by focusing on the under-theorized notion of the working-class millennial as seen in Jessica Andrews's 2019 novel, *Saltwater*. Here, Ashbridge reminds us of the difficulty of defining "working-class" in spaces and environments no longer commensurate with such notions. The essay explores transitional modes of class signification, in particular how the classed body acts as an alternate to classed space. In this regard, Ashbridge's focus on Andrews's protagonist reflects Johnson's discussion of Carnie Holdsworth's deterritorialized working-class subject, demonstrating how texts written almost a century apart address ongoing concerns relative to their cultural moment. In a sense, Ashbridge's essay helps us to understand not just the productive potential of spatio-class analysis but also its limits as well.

It goes without saying that a volume of this kind cannot be all things to all readers, and its development revealed elisions and areas for further attention. The hope is that the volume's guiding premise—that literature acts as a particularly fruitful interface between conceptions of class and material formations—will be taken up by subsequent scholars who find this line of thinking productive. This volume emerged from a panel held at the 2018 Modern Language Association Convention in New York City—a convention and organization whose commitment to working-class literature has proven inconsistent. Somewhat mythologized now, at least in the field of working-class studies, is Janet Zandy's 1993 attempt to establish a permanent home for the study of working-class literature at the MLA. The attempt was denied—disingenuously so, according to Sharon O'Dair—on the supposition that "her proposal did not offer a definition of class that could clearly identify a set of working-class literary texts" (2000, 8). The irony of the refusal is that, once more, it reflects working-class literature's resistance to categorization. Since that time, efforts to establish regular programming about working-class writing and working-class life at the annual convention have faced similar challenges.

It should also be noted that the development of this collection encountered an array of hurdles, one in particular being a global pandemic that impacted access to research materials and upended scholarly work in general. While this collection offers a broad range of coverage and a rich representation of working-class subjectivities in literature, there is more work to be done on this particular topic. The hope is that these essays will serve as a point of departure for future analysis of class in British literature in which space is foregrounded as a determining factor. This introduction seeks to provide a general overview of the way space and class intertwine in literary representations while advocating for subsequent projects that build on some of the volume's main ideas. As noted at the outset of this chapter, British literature tells a rich and storied history of social inequality. Such stories continue to emerge in ways that provide access to insights and experiences of classed life, sidestepping fixed ideas about genre and, ideally, offer new perspectives on the way British subjecthood continues to evolve.

References

Ballard, J. G. 1975. *High-Rise*. London: Jonathan Cape.

Bourdieu, Pierre. 1984. *Distinction: A Social Critique of the Judgement of Taste*. Translated by Richard Nice. Cambridge, MA: Harvard University Press.

Bridge, Gary. 1995. "The Space for Class? On Class Analysis in the Study of Gentrification." *Transactions of the Institute of British Geographers* 20 (2): 236–47. https://doi.org/10.2307/622434.

Duff, Kim. 2014. *Contemporary British Literature and Urban Space: After Thatcher*. Basingstoke, UK: Palgrave Macmillan.

Evaristo, Bernardine. (2013) 2014. *Mr. Loverman*. New York: Akashic Books.

———. 2019. *Girl, Woman, Other*. New York: Black Cat.

Foucault, Michel. 1986. "Of Other Spaces." *Diacritics* 16 (1): 22–27. https://doi.org/10.2307/464648.

Greenwood, Walter. 1933. *Love on the Dole*. London: Jonathan Cape.

Harvey, David. (2006) 2004. "Space as a Keyword." In *David Harvey: A Critical Reader*, edited by Noel Castree and Derek Gregory, 270–93. Maiden, MA: Wiley-Blackwell.

Hoggart, Richard. (1957) 2009. *The Uses of Literacy: Aspects of Working-Class Life with Special Reference to Publications and Entertainments*. London: Penguin Classics.

Holdsworth, Ethel Carnie. 1925. *This Slavery*. London: Labour Publishing Company.

Hones, Sheila. 2018. "Literary Geography and Spatial Literary Studies." *Literary Geographies* 4 (2): 146–49.

Israel, Emil, and Amnon Frenkel. 2020. "Justice and Inequality in Space: A Socio-Normative Analysis." *Geoforum* 110: 1–13. https://doi.org/10.1016/j.geoforum.2019.12.017.

Jameson, Fredric. (1991) 1992. *Postmodernism, or, the Cultural Logic of Late Capitalism*. Durham, NC: Duke University Press.

Kirk, J. 2007. *Class, Culture and Social Change: On the Trail of the Working Class*. Basingstoke, UK: Palgrave Macmillan.

Lefebvre, Henri. 1973. *The Survival of Capitalism: Reproduction of the Relations of Production*. New York, NY: St. Martin's Press.

———. (1974) 1992. *The Production of Space*. Malden, MA: Wiley-Blackwell.

Linkon, Sherry Lee. 2010. "Why Working-Class Literature Matters." *Working-Class Perspectives* (blog), February 22, 2010. https://workingclassstudies. wordpress.com/2010/02/22/why-working-class-literature-matters/.

———. 2021. "Class Analysis from the Inside: Scholarly Personal Narrative as a Signature Genre of Working-Class Studies." In *Routledge International Handbook of Working-Class Studies*, edited by Michele Fazio, Christie Launius, and Tim Strangleman. New York, NY: Routledge.

Mellor, Leo. 2011. *Reading the Ruins: Modernism, Bombsites and British Culture*. Cambridge, UK: Cambridge University Press.

Moslund, Sten Pultz. 2011. "The Presencing of Place in Literature: Toward an Embodied Topopoetic Mode of Reading." In *Geocritical Explorations: Space, Place, and Mapping in Literary and Cultural Studies*, 29–43. Basingstoke, UK: Palgrave Macmillan.

Munt, Sally, ed. 2000. *Cultural Studies and the Working Class: Subject to Change*. London and New York: Cassell.

Nethersole, Reingard. 1990. "From Temporality to Spatiality: Changing Concepts in Literary Criticism." In *Space and Boundaries: Proceedings of the XIIth Congress of the ICLA*, edited by Roger Bauer and Douwe Fokkema, Vol. 5, 59–63. München, DE: Iudicium.

O'Dair, Sharon. 2000. *Class, Critics, and Shakespeare*. Ann Arbor, MI: University of Michigan Press.

Orwell, George. (1937) 1972. *The Road to Wigan Pier*. San Diego, CA: Mariner Books.

Peet, J. Richard. 1985. "An Introduction to Marxist Geography." *Journal of Geography* 84 (1): 5–10. https://doi.org/10.1080/00221348508979261.

Perera, Sonali. 2014. *No Country: Working-Class Writing in the Age of Globalization*. New York, NY: Columbia University Press.

Prieto, Eric. 2011. "Geocriticism, Geopoetics, Geophilosophy, and Beyond." In *Geocritical Explorations: Space, Place, and Mapping in Literary and Cultural Studies*, edited by Robert T. Tally Jr, 13–27. Basingstoke, UK: Palgrave Macmillan.

Smith, Zadie. 2012. *NW*. New York: The Penguin Press.

———. 2016. *Swing Time*. New York: The Penguin Press.

Soja, Edward W. 1996. *Thirdspace: Journeys to Los Angeles and Other Real-and-Imagined Places*. Malden, MA: Wiley-Blackwell.

Stark, David. 1980. "Class Struggle and the Transformation of the Labour Process." *Theory and Society* 9 (1): 89–130. https://doi.org/10.1007/BF00158894.

Tally Jr, Robert T. 2012. *Spatiality*. London: Routledge.

———. 2014. "Textual Geographies: Real-and-Imagined Spaces in Literature, Criticism, and Theory." *Reconstruction* 14 (3).

———. 2018. *Topophrenia: Place, Narrative, and the Spatial Imagination*. Bloomington, IN: Indiana University Press.

Taylor, Yvette, ed. (2010) 2016. *Classed Intersections: Space, Selves, Knowledge*. London and New York, NY: Routledge.

Thrift, Nigel, and Peter Williams. (1987) 2014. *Class and Space (RLE Social Theory): The Making of Urban Society*. London: Routledge and Kegan Paul.

Tressell, Robert. 1914. *The Ragged Trousered Philanthropists*. Ware, UK: Wordsworth.

Tuan, Yi-Fu. 1974. *Topophilia: A Study of Environmental Perception, Attitudes, and Values*. Eaglewood Cliffs, NJ: Prentice-Hall.

Veenstra, Gerry. 2007. "Social Space, Social Class and Bourdieu: Health Inequalities in British Columbia, Canada." *Health & Place* 13 (1): 14–31. https://doi.org/10.1016/j.healthplace.2005.09.011.

Welsh, Irvine. 1993. *Trainspotting*. New York, NY: W. W. Norton & Company.

Westphal, Bertrand. 2011. *Geocriticism: Real and Fictional Spaces*. Translated by Robert T. Tally Jr. Basingstoke, UK: Palgrave Macmillan.

Williams, Raymond. (1973) 1975. *The Country and the City*. Oxford, UK: Oxford University Press.

———. (1977) 1978. *Marxism and Literature*. Oxford, UK: Oxford University Press.

Wilson, Nicola. 2015. *Home in British Working-Class Fiction*. London: Routledge.

1 Fevered Anxieties
Public Health, Urban Infrastructure, and Infectious Classes in Austen, Edgeworth, and Scott

Matthew L. Reznicek

In *Discipline and Punish*, Michel Foucault lays out two distinctly spatial "ways of exercising power" in the wake of illness: the leper "gave rise to rituals of exclusion, which to a certain extent provided the model for and general form of the great Confinement," while the seventeenth-century plague produced "the utopia of the perfectly governed city," a city "traversed throughout with hierarchy, surveillance, observation, writing" (1995, 198). Over the course of the eighteenth century and into the early years of the nineteenth century, Foucault traces the way in which these two projects merge. This occurs primarily through "an intensification and a ramification of power" felt and seen in the development of modern urban infrastructure (198). The primary spaces Foucault notes are "the psychiatric asylum, the penitentiary, the reformatory, the approved school and . . . the hospital" (199). Each of these spaces functioned in order to extend the logic of exclusion to "beggars, vagabonds, madmen and the disorderly," while also instituting "the technique of power proper to disciplinary partitioning" more broadly throughout the city (199). According to Mary Poovey, this process of cultural formation depended upon an ambiguity that allowed society in the long eighteenth century to "treat one segment of the population as a special problem at the same time that they could gesture toward the mutual interests that (theoretically) united all parts of the social whole" (8). This ambiguity enables and enacts the Foucauldian premise of exclusion and segregation so that the offending segment of society can be identified as a special problem "needing both discipline and care" in order to be reintegrated into the broader social whole.

Foucault's turn to prisons, asylums, and hospitals, as well as Poovey's focus on workhouses and factories, reveals the degree to which this system of integration and surveillance spread throughout the nineteenth-century city. To borrow from Pamela Gilbert, the surveillance and control of "the city's and citydwellers' bodies" are essential to the experience of modernity (2004, 110). Urban infrastructure, then, became key not only to the surveillance that allowed the "perfectly governed city" to identify those segments that are not perfectly governed but

DOI: 10.4324/9781003119425-2

also to provide the spaces of exclusion necessary to reinstating the perfect governmentality.[1] The development of urban infrastructure in the eighteenth and nineteenth centuries reveals a class-based anxiety that reflects and draws upon a health-based anxiety amplified by geographic demarcation. By attending to the representation of urban infrastructure and its intersection with public health in novels of the early nineteenth century, this chapter argues that the metaphors of contagion and sight reveal a biopolitics that reflect an anxiety that seeks to exclude and segregate those impoverished and contagious parts of society that might infect the wider public. Novels of the early nineteenth century reveal the metropolitan developments that seek to contain the threat of class and health contamination. Jane Austen's *Sense and Sensibility* (1811), Maria Edgeworth's *The Absentee* (1812), and Walter Scott's *The Heart of Midlothian* (1818), all employ urban infrastructure as a way of both revealing and excluding the threat posed by specific populations of the poor, the ill, or the criminal. Indeed, these literary representations of urban development emphasize the way that space and infrastructure within the metropolis can be used to achieve a class-based social segregation under the rubric of public health.

Fundamental to the type of exclusion and segregation that Foucault and Poovey lay out is an eighteenth-century obsession with the development of an urban and spatial technology of sight—a sight that enables us to see society as a whole and a sight that enables us to see completely and thoroughly the individuals who make up that whole. Governing society through the literal and metaphorical vehicle of sight was key throughout this period of urban development. Central among these theories is Adam Smith's works of moral philosophy, in which he famously argues that the individual functions as a microcosm for the larger self-governing society through an internal mechanism of observation and sight. Famously, Smith claimed that "[w]e endeavour to examine our own conduct as we imagine any other fair and impartial spectator would examine it" (2009, 133). This construction identifies the moral gaze and spectatorship of society at large as the "mirror" and "looking glass" that enables the individual to view "the propriety and impropriety of his own passions, the beauty and deformity of his own mind" (134–35). As Poovey makes clear in her interpretation of Smith, the image of society as a mirror that reflects back the individual's propriety or impropriety is key to his understanding of "the larger self-governing society," precisely because the metaphor of sight and observation functions as a type of the internal discipline that Foucault describes (1995, 33). However, even as Smith's conception of society "depended upon (literally or imaginatively) being seen" (Poovey 1995, 33), he acknowledges that

as soon as he comes into a great city, he is sunk in obscurity and darkness. His conduct is observed and attended to by nobody, and he

is therefore very likely to neglect it himself, and to abandon himself
to every sort of low profligacy and vice.

(Smith 2008, 440)

In order to counteract this effect of modern society, Poovey notes that
Smith believed these urban citizens had "to be governed from above"
since "their literal bodies could no longer be seen, the former had to
be conceptualized as an aggregate; because they could not govern themselves" (1995, 34). If society depends upon the gaze of others to instill
a moral critic in each individual, but modern cities particularly disrupt
the ability of the gaze to penetrate into each individual, then society
must govern through a more totalizing vision of the social body. It must
develop a more complex and authoritative capacity to see and, thus, to
enforce its disciplinary gaze—a process that, in the late eighteenth and
early nineteenth centuries, occurs through urban renovations, literally
reshaping the space of the city so that it is easier to govern.

The city, for Smith, both provides the ideal form of self-government
through the constant gaze of others and undermines the ability to govern
by its impenetrability. This contradiction helps to explain the intervention of urban infrastructure and public health in order to better govern
and better see the bodies that, unobserved, could fall into profligacy and
vice. Public health infrastructure was "increasingly related to intervention by a state that came to be seen as the proper guardian of public
health," marking the "body and its health" as a social issue (Gilbert
2004, XVII). The extension of this observation occurred through the
development not only of asylums, prisons, and hospitals but also new
thoroughfares, housing developments, and the management of impoverished neighborhoods. These urban infrastructural developments reflect
an "insistence on order, efficiency, and social discipline, and a concern
with the conditions of men" (Rosen 2015, 71). Demonstrating an anxiety over the disorder, inefficiency, lack of discipline, and impoverished
conditions of, especially, the poor, these urban renovations provide an
essential framework for understanding the representation of social and
political attitudes toward the poor and the sick. Thus, the imbrication
of metaphors of sight, illness, poverty, and urban development in the
early-nineteenth-century novels of Jane Austen, Maria Edgeworth, and
Walter Scott demonstrate the fear that their moral and physical ills posed
a "threat to the larger social body" (Gilbert 2004, 111).

"No Family of Ton Can Breathe Eastward of Berkeley Square": Urban Planning and Health in *Sense and Sensibility*

E. J. Clery has recently argued that Jane Austen's *Pride and Prejudice*
(1813) is "a product of London," despite the novel's overwhelmingly

rural mise-en-scène (2018, 156). The novel's "metropolitan orientation," Clery notes, "goes beyond its status as a literary commodity"
produced in London; London's brief appearances in *Pride and Prejudice* impress upon both the content and form of Austen's novel in a
way that "exposes changes and tensions characterizing the topography
of the metropolis" (159). I argue that the topography of the metropolis
plays a similar role in Austen's first published novel, *Sense and Sensibility*. This is not simply because "more of the action of *Sense and Sensibility* takes place in London than in any of [Austen's] other works";
rather, it is because of the way London's geography in the novel reveals
a narrative of concern over illness and social contamination (159).
Focusing explicitly on the overlap of the Dashwood sisters' trip to Mrs.
Jennings's house in "one of the streets near Portman-square," with
Marianne's contracting a "putrid fever," and the historical topography
of John Nash's development of Regent Street as a way of "screening the
fashionable West End from déclassé quarters" (Porter 1995, 127), I argue
that the illness narrative central to Austen's novel provides a lens through
which we can better understand the redevelopment of the physical urban
landscape as a manifestation of Regency anxieties of the threat posed to
public and individual health by social mixing.

In *Pride and Prejudice*, Austen reveals the overlay of geography and
class in London through Caroline Bingley's attitude toward the Gardiners, the Bennett sisters' aunt and uncle, because they reside "somewhere
near Cheapside" (2008, 26). Far from Grosvenor Street in the fashionable West End, the Gardiners' address in Gracechurch Street in the City
of London lies "in so different a part of town, all our connections are so
different . . . that it is very improbable [Jane Bennett and Mr. Bingley]
should meet at all, unless he really comes to see her" (109). To emphasize
the degree of social separation, Elizabeth Bennett acknowledges that this
is "quite impossible" since Mr. Bingley is

> now in the custody of his friend, and Mr. Darcy would no more suffer
> him to call on Jane in such a part of London. . . . Mr. Darcy may have
> *heard* of such a place as Gracechurch Street, but he would hardly
> think a month's ablution enough to cleanse him from its impurities,
> were he once to enter it.
>
> (109–10)

The language of "impurities" and "cleanse" reinforce not only the class-
based and spatial division of the capital but also alert us to the threat that
such cross-class relations pose. Indeed, the threat of contamination from
appearing in Gracechurch Street is enough that a month's "ablution"
would rid Bingley of the threat posed by such low-class environs. Ablution, in particular, invokes both a physical and a spiritual form of contamination; its religious connotations of ritualistic cleansing, especially

in the Judeo-Christian tradition, signify a deep-seated infection of the body as well as the soul. To borrow from William A. Cohen, society characterizes people "as filthy when they are felt to be unassimilably other, whether because perceived attributes of their identities repulse the onlooker or because physical aspects of their bodies do" (2005, IX—X). In Elizabeth's understanding of Darcy's and Caroline Bingley's disgust at her Cheapside relatives, the mark of filth is simply their relationship to trade, which is to say that the threat is one of Cohen's "perceived attributes," rather than something inherently physical about the Gardiners.

However, as Clery has noted, the assumption of "abjection invoked here, the horror of contamination Elizabeth attributes to Mr. Darcy, is her recognition of the taboo of intermarriage between alien tribes" (2018, 163). The fact that this taboo is expressed in terms of "contamination," to use Celery's phrase, obviously marks the residents of the City, those who engage in trade, as capable of spreading their filth to anyone with whom they come into contact. They are, to put it another way, *infectious*. And this language of infection reveals an important element of the Bingleys' and Darcy's anxiety—one that is rooted in historical realities of the English capital at the time and one that shaped the geography of Austen's narratives. The threat that the Gardiners and Gracechurch Street might infect Mr. Bingley and Grosvenor Street situates this class anxiety in a broader context of public health. It is important to draw attention to the way that Elizabeth Bennett's characterization of Cheapside and the City more broadly reflect the concerns around public health that shape the geography of London and, especially, the development of infrastructure in order to maintain class separation specifically for the purpose of maintaining individual and social health.

The clearest example of public health infrastructure is the development of Regent Street by John Nash, which Parliament approved in 1813, the same year that *Pride and Prejudice* was published. Part of a larger redevelopment that would connect the royal residence Carlton House in Pall Mall with the Prince Regent's estates beyond Oxford Street, John Nash "envisaged one long, majestic south-north street, leading up from Carlton House through Lower Regent Street to a Quadrant (just north of the present Piccadilly Circus), and then along Regent Street and into Portland Place" (Porter 1995, 126–27). While this redevelopment of London's West End was designed around the Prince Regent's desire, Regent Street functions "unmistakably [as] a *cordon sanitaire*" by leaving the West End's "airy fabric of straight wide streets and squares intact while demolishing the outer edge of the unsavory, heterogeneous district of Soho" (2018, 164). In his history of *Georgian London*, John Summerson describes the street as a "'biologically' correct line" (171), while Clery describes it as possessing "surgical" precision (2018, 164). Indeed, even during its building, Regent Street was discussed in terms of maintaining public health by separating out "the fashionable West End from *déclassé* quarters" when the *World* magazine declared that "[n] o family of ton can breathe eastward of Berkeley Square" (Sutherland 1995, 127). Even John Nash himself assured the parliamentary commissioners that "in the whole extent from Piccadilly to Oxford Circus there will be but four crossings on either side of the street" so that the "New Street," as it was supposed to be called, effectively formed "a boundary and complete separation between the streets and squares occupied by the nobility and gentry, and the narrow streets and houses occupied by mechanics and the trading parts of the community" (1814, XLVIII). The development of the West End and, especially, Regent Street during Austen's era reflects an instance of "epidemiological town-planning" that uses urban infrastructure to achieve public health aims by separating the filthy classes from the fashionable families of Berkeley Square, Marylebone, and Mayfair (Clery 2018, 164).

It is this fashionable geography that Austen's first published novel occupies. Early in Volume II of *Sense and Sensibility*, Mrs. Jennings's son-in-law and daughter, Sir John and Lady Middleton, announce "their arrival in Conduit-street . . . requesting the company of her mother and cousins the following evening" (2017, 124). As Laurie Kaplan notes, Conduit Street connects the fashionable Bond Street, where John Willoughby lives when he is in London, with Swallow Street, which itself forms the western edge of Soho, the outer limit of the *cordon sanitaire* of the new Regent Street (2018, 178). Moreover, Conduit Street's connection to Swallow Street emphasizes the "epidemiological town-planning" that Clery notes in reference to *Pride and Prejudice* precisely because a large portion of Swallow Street is destroyed in John Nash's efforts to construct this new boundary between the area of nobility and working-class corruption (Clery 2018, 164; Kaplan 2018, 179). Indeed, playing with the semantic meaning of their street's name, Sir John Middleton "contrive[s] to collect around him, nearly twenty young people, and to amuse them with a ball," which "Lady Middleton did not approve" because it "was risking too much" of the Middletons' "reputation of elegance" (2017, 124). The threat Lady Middleton perceives in Sir John's sociability, according to Kaplan, reveals "the wealthy's fear of such social mixing," which was one of the motivating factors "for the demolition of Swallow Street in 1814, and its replacement with Regent Street" (2018, 179). It is important to connect Lady Middleton's perceived threat to her "reputation for elegance" with her concern that it might be known "that Lady Middleton had given a small dance of eight or nine couple, with two violins, and a mere side-board collation" because it demonstrates a class-based anxiety of not appearing elegant enough in the eyes of Mayfair on the eve of its cordoning off the lower classes through Regent Street. Lady Middleton's anxieties about elegance, interclass mingling, and the looming presence of Nash's urban and public health infrastructural reforms link Austen's representations of London in *Sense and Sensibility* with the intertwined concerns around social boundaries, class purity, and, especially, health and contamination. This is made especially clear through the way the novel associates the metropolis with observation, illness, community, and exclusion.

From their arrival in London with Mrs. Jennings, Elinor Dashwood often uses the threat of illnesses like "head-aches, low spirits, and over fatigues; and of everything to which she could decently attribute her sister's behaviour" (Austen 2017, 118). In this way, Elinor uses illness to allay class-based anxieties over propriety. In doing so, she enacts a version of the processes that Priscilla Wald describes as "constitut[ing] a community" based on the "interactions that make us sick" (2008, 2). Elinor, appealing to non-threatening illness that are importantly non-communicable, attempts to place Marianne's improper behavior behind the veil of understandable and relatable illness in a way that both excuses Marianne and solicits sympathy for her. She identifies her sister as suffering in a way that does not threaten those with whom she comes into contact—Marianne's sufferings, thus, become understandable in a Smithian framework, but do not pose the risk of contamination.[2]

In the pivotal scene at a party in London where Marianne finally observes Willoughby, Elinor once again uses a specific performance of illness in order to excuse Marianne in the face of public scrutiny over improper behavior. This scene, especially, functions as a microcosm for the novel's representation of its urban anxieties through its emphasis on the room being "quite full of company, and insufferably hot," while the "croud" itself seems omnipresent and at the very least an "inconvenience" (Austen 2017, 128). In his discussion of public health in eighteenth-century London, Roy Porter notes the capital was "notorious for its crush of humanity . . . and thus became the breeding-grounds of flyblown noisomeness and disease" (1991, 63). Indeed, in order to overcome this crowding associated with illness and disease, the Georgian city developed "gracious, spacious, leafy squares spread north and west, across Bloomsbury, Soho, and Marylebone," the exact geography in which the Dashwood sisters move in London (66). So, then, the overcrowding in this elite space clearly blurs the lines of distinction between the spacious squares that connote wealth and health and the crowded rookeries and lanes that Nash will seek to obscure. This ball, with its emphasis on crowding and heat, poses the threat of contamination—both social and physiological. Thus, when Marianne is rebuffed by Willoughby and turns "dreadfully white, and unable to stand, sunk into her chair," Elinor again attempts "to screen her from the observation of others, while reviving her with lavender water" in order to prevent her being seen as either socially or physiologically contagious (Austen 2017, 129). Unsure of her sister's ability to maintain control and the appearance of belonging, Elinor informs Lady Middleton "that Marianne was unwell," as a way of separating her from the urban crowd (130). In effect, this mirrors the urban development that separates the wealthy from the potentially infectious poor; as the physician Gilbert Blaine noted in his *Observations on the Comparative Prevalence, Mortality and Treatment of Different Diseases*, the "thinning of the population" produces "the most beneficial effects upon health" (1813, 17).

Of course, this begins a long bout of illness for Marianne that, as John Wiltshire has argued, "is articulated as a sequence of quite specific, and physiologically plausible reactions," not simply as a manifestation of sensibility (1992, 45). But it cannot be ignored that Marianne's illness begins in a metropolitan environment that is so rife with similarities to the perceived unhealthy elements of the broader urban landscape. In this way, the city, its class-based divisions, and the threat of contagion posed by the various classes becomes central to understanding Austen's London and its geography. Indeed, it is only by putting *Sense and Sensibility* in the context of the urban spatial developments that immediately followed its publication and the public health concerns that predate these renovations can we truly recognize the way that Marianne's "excessive affliction" and "restless pain of mind and body" might be attributable to the metropolitan crowd and the underlying contagion it suggests (2017, 131, 139). If, as Gilbert has argued, the nineteenth-century understanding of the social body depended upon "compulsively mapp[ing]" urban spaces like London in order to police poverty and vice, then *Sense and Sensibility* demonstrates the ways in which redeveloping the city's map responds to and shapes attitudes about infectious cross-class contamination.

"Not to Make the Remedy Worse Than the Disease": Dublin, Disease, and Development in Maria Edgeworth's Novels

The threat of infectious contamination that I have traced in *Sense and Sensibility* takes on an even greater social danger and, as a result, impresses itself more obviously in the representation of space in Maria Edgeworth's Ireland. In a letter dated 1834, a mere two years after the outbreak of cholera in Britain and Ireland, Edgeworth claimed that it is "impossible to draw Ireland as she is at present in any book of fiction" because "a fever" has distorted nature on the island (2018, 335).[3] While this comment has most often been taken as a critical framework for the supposed failure of Irish realism in the nineteenth century, placing the comment in a history of medicine and illness reveals a much broader pattern within Edgeworth's fiction that demonstrates the relationship between illness and urban development in the Georgian period and, especially, in the wake of the Act of Union of 1801.

Edgeworth's connection between fever and Ireland "as she is at present" reflects an historical awareness in which the repeated outbreaks of fever on the island were attributable to specific socio-economic conditions that were most concentrated in the metropolitan environment of Dublin. During the cholera outbreak of 1832, roughly 40 percent of those who contracted the disease died and, in some places on the island, the death rate was as high as 76 percent (O'Neill 1973, 16). In the crowded spaces of Ireland's cities, the spread of the disease was profound: by May 2, 430 people had died of cholera in Dublin; by July 5, nearly 1,524 had died; by Christmas, the number of deaths in Dublin was estimated at 4,478 (16). It is estimated that in the first nine months of the epidemic, Ireland lost more people than did England and Wales; Dublin, alone, lost more people than London (23). That so much of the death resulting from cholera was felt in cities is not surprising, considering the concentration of cholera cases in London; what is remarkable is Dublin outpacing London. This suggests that Dublin's socio-economic and infrastructural conditions exacerbated the spread of the outbreak. The groundwork for these conditions was laid not simply in the wake of the Act of Union of 1801, but in the urban infrastructural developments and their alignment with public health in the years that precede Edgeworth's representations of the Irish capital.

Diarmuid Ó Gráda has argued that reformers in Georgian Dublin understood that "the health of the poor was the security of the rich" (Ó Gráda 2015, 152). Recalling Gilbert's claims that poverty was reconfigured as stemming from "the perversion of human nature through unnatural circumstances, such as living in the conditions contingent upon urban poverty," we can recognize the security of the rich depending upon "[h]ealthy subjects acting rationally" and using the metropolitan space "in appropriate ways" (2004, xiv). This biopolitical governance led to an overlapping in the development of Georgian Dublin's urban infrastructure with its "agenda of social control," attempting to "confine the poorest people to identified quarters so as to contain epidemics" (Ó Gráda 2015, 152). As we will see in Edgeworth's representation of urban and suburban Dublin, there was a noticeable "decline of the established quarters" near the city center; the streets radiating from High Street "were described as one continuous mass of ruin" (102). Jacinta Prunty has argued that "decay spread out from the Liberties," a long-established industrial quarter noted for its "dense population" and association with poverty (2011, 45). An 1822 report, "Inquiry into the Causes and Character of the Diseases of the Lower Orders in Dublin," noted that "habit, occupation and character" associated with the city itself exerted "distinct and decided effects on our physical frame" as well as "powerful and peculiar influences" on the production of "*city disease*" (Speer 1822, 162–63, emphasis in original). Late-eighteenth- and early-nineteenth-century public health reforms focused on "the 'nests' of fever which were the city slums," which were noted for "predisposing persons to disease" (Prunty 2011, 62). "Noted for their narrow streets numerous lanes and alleys, and crowded houses," Prunty adds, these decrepit and impoverished "ancient parts of the city" became increasingly described as "turbulent" and threatening to public order (2011, 21; Dickson 2014, 210).

The threat of disorder and contagion generated by these urban slums increasingly drove two facets of urban renovation in Dublin—the movement of the wealthy to suburban areas "out as far as the coastline" and a competing attempt to curb this urban sprawl by "[d]emands for better infrastructure" (Ó Gráda 2015, 90, 98). As with the development of London, the movement to the suburbs and the redevelopment of the urban infrastructure are tied to concerns around public health—both in terms of preventing contagion from exposure to the impoverished areas and also in seeking areas more beneficial to the health of the wealthy. As evidenced by a 1750 thesis from an Irish-educated physician, medical publications encouraged the movement to the seaside villages on the north and south coast of Dublin Bay as providing "a cleaner environment . . . out of the city" (91–92). As a result, suburban locations such as Clontarf, Ringsend, Blackrock, and Dunleary developed reputations for "the genteelest society," with hotels, assembly rooms, and increased postal services (93, 101). With the Dublin suburbs and coastal town an increasing draw for the fashionable members of society, there was a parallel movement to develop the city's inner geography. As David Dickson puts it in *The First Irish Cities*, the Wide Streets Commission, along with the development of the College Green, the Fitzwilliam estate along with Merrion Square, helped to produce "an unexpectedly powerful centrepoint for the city . . . rival[ing] Dublin Castle as the hub of Dublin fashionable society" (2021, 156). Dickson noted previously in his study of Dublin how this "principal corridor for luxury shopping" slowly moved eastward, following the development of the Fitzwilliam estate and the adjoining Merrion Square (2014, 186). He adds that, although the Merrion estate "took over fifty years for all ninety-two sites in the square to be converted into terraced houses," the square "became the real epicentre for fashion by the end of the century" (2021, 157). The geographic location of, as well as the commitment to openness in, Merrion Square reflects a diametric opposition to the cramped and closed quarters that characterized the Liberties and other areas associated with poverty and disease.

This geography, unsurprisingly, shapes Maria Edgeworth's representation of Dublin in her Irish novels, especially in *The Absentee*. As the narrator explains, Dublin provides "positively good company, and positively bad; but not, as in London, many degrees of comparison" (2000, 79). This bifurcation of society, leaving none "of that confusion of ranks or predominance of vulgarity," reveals a notable gap that is crucial to understanding the largely absent lower orders in Edgeworth's representation of Dublin (79). Just as the urban geography and, especially, the public health developments of Georgian Dublin would suggest, places for interaction with the urban poor are relatively rare and the majority of Colambre's time in the capital is spent in the presence of the upper class. Noting the lack of "confusion of ranks" emphasizes the degree to which Dublin society was able to maintain a class-based and health-based separation of the fashionable from the threat of contagion. Indeed, the only representation of the urban poor in *The Absentee* occurs near the Customs House, in an area defined by its connection to commerce.

The separation between classes becomes even clearer in the discussion of the city's urban sprawl. Following the Act of Union and the removal of the Irish Parliament to Westminster, the "hereditary authority" of the "nobility and many of the principal families . . . either hurried in high hopes to London, or retired disgusted and in despair to their houses in the country" (80). Edgeworth's Anglo-Irish principal families even engage in the fashion of seaside villas in an attempt to escape from the "incursions of the vulgarians" (81). The representation of the villa, "called Tusculum, situate near Bray," emphasizes the degree of urban sprawl, spreading beyond the realm of Dublin City and, indeed, County Dublin, into the northern edge of County Wicklow (83). Mirroring the actual site of Lord Powerscourt's estate in County Wicklow, Tusculum pretends to the picturesque discourse associated with these suburban estates, providing "a charming tour in the county of Wicklow, where the beauty of the natural scenery, and the taste with which those natural beauties had been cultivated, far surpassed the sanguine expectations lord Colambre had formed" (84). This estate, however, becomes an object of ridicule for its "mixture . . . of taste and incongruity, ingenuity and absurdity, genius and blunder, by the contrast between the finery and vulgarity" (84). Though this estate recalls the flight of the aristocracy out of Dublin's crowded city center, its vulgarity and absurd mixture reminds us of the threat posed not only by heterogeneity and mixing social classes but also of the rise of the *nouveaux riches* in the wake of the Union. Indeed, Mrs. Raffarty, the lady of Tusculum, admits "she hated every thing straight, it was so formal and *unpicturesque*. 'Uniformity and conformity,' she observed, 'had their day; but now, thank the stars of the present day, irregularity and deformity bear the bell, and have the majority'" (85, emphasis in original). In this condemnation of "every thing straight" and praise of "irregularity and deformity," Raffarty reveals a disregard for the type of urban renovations that helped keep separate the fashionable classes and the lower classes; the urban renovations like the widening of Dame Street and the construction of Merrion Square that are associated with a flight from the threat of contagion and of a concentration of fashionable society in certain parts of Dublin here reveal Raffarty's own vulgar status. This "desire to appear what they were not," in fact, demonstrates the ongoing mixture of classes that produced the need for the urban renovations of Dublin to reinforce social segregation (85).

While Edgeworth's Dublin reflects the "great but transit change" that occurred following the Act of Union and the movement of the Irish parliament to Westminster with a critical irony, there remains an underlying anxiety about the mixture of classes that ought to be tied to questions and concerns regarding public health. That *The Absentee* concentrates its representation of Dublin in "an excellent hotel" and in the developing suburbs along the Dublin coast, omitting the "'nests' of fever" and the city's slums, ought not occlude the fact that these urban renovations were established in order that the wealthy and fashionable society might avoid these same areas. Edgeworth's Dublin, then, reveals a growing metropolis that is highly segregated by class in order to maintain the health and governance of the city.

"In the Cells at Edinburgh": Madness, Riots, and Social Order in Scott's *The Heart of Midlothian*

Although most consistently associated with his representation of the romantic, antiquarian Scottish Highlands in his poetry, fiction, and especially the *Waverley* novels, Walter Scott's *oeuvre* also reveals an important awareness of the imposition of social order through urban infrastructure, particularly the prison and the asylum. As John Sutherland's biography makes clear, Scott's early life was itself intimately shaped by the overlapping of urban infrastructure and public health that this chapter has sought to trace, just as Edgeworth's experience of the cholera outbreak in 1832 shaped her later thought on Ireland. Following a fever that deprived him of the power of his right leg when he was around eighteen months old, Scott was "removed to his other grandparents at Sandy Know, to recuperate in the countryside's 'free air and liberty', some thirty miles from the city" (1995, 12). This is, at least partially, attributable to the "famously insanitary" Old Town of eighteenth-century Edinburgh, despite attempts as early as 1701 to ban "[d]irty water thrown from windows" and 1726 requirements that the streets "[be] cleaned every day except Sunday" (11; Pittock 2019, 56). The type of overcrowding that characterized Edinburgh's "explosive growth in the 1750–80 period" necessitated the extraordinary urban development that is most clearly signified by "the draining of the Nor Loch and the emerging of the New Town across its dried-out bed" (Sutherland 1995, 11). Compared to the Closes and Wynds of his parents, the Edinburgh in which Walter Scott lived was remarkable for its "new forms of urban sociability" as well as its "urban improvement . . . reformatting the urban landscape to take account of the new commercial realities and pressures" (Harris 2011, 1099). What is surprising, then, is that the Edinburgh Scott presents in his arguably most urban novel, *The Heart of Midlothian*, presents instead an

Edinburgh characterized by disorder, chaos, riots, and madness. In its representation of the city, *The Heart of Midlothian* demonstrates the danger of an uncontrollable lower class, associated specifically with the threat of madness and infanticide. This necessitates the restoration of order not only through royal intervention but also the threat of the titular prison as well as the asylum.

When three convicted smugglers attempt to escape from the Tolbooth Prison in the center of Edinburgh's Old Town, the city's

> magistrates thought it their duty to provide against the possibility of disturbance. They ordered out, for protection of the execution of the sentence [against the prisoners], the greater part of their own City Guard, under the command of Captain Porteous.
>
> (Scott 2008, 32)

Porteous, Scott notes, was "useful in his station, and his harsh and fierce habits rendered him formidable to rioters and disturbers of the public peace" (33). In this representation of 1736 Edinburgh, the urban landscape sits on the verge of disorder and depends upon the threat of "harsh and fierce" habits of policing to maintain social order. While this also reflects the type of anxiety about social mixing that I have demonstrated in both Austen and Edgeworth, Scott's representation of the prison and the police exacerbates the threat posed by this sort of urban mixing and chaos. In order to maintain order, the city's magistrates

> requested the assistance of part of a regular infantry regiment, not to attend upon the execution, but to remain drawn up on the principal street of the city . . . in order to intimidate the multitude in case they should be unruly, with a display of force which could not be resisted without desperation.
>
> (36)

The overt connection between Porteous's City Guard, the "regular infantry," and the need to intimidate the "multitude" into order reveals the severity of the anxiety around social order in this novel. Indeed, the outbreak of the riot does not so much prove the magistrates correct as further underscore the novel's disciplinary mechanism of urban policing as a means of enforcing social order.

While the city magistrates, the City Guard, and the infantry may see these forceful mechanisms as establishing and maintaining public order, it becomes clear that these forces of discipline cannot withstand the assault of disorder posed by Edinburgh's citizenry. The "mob of Edinburgh," as Scott describes them, "had been at all times one of the fiercest which could be found in Europe; and of late years they had risen repeatedly against the governments, and sometimes not without temporary success" (41). The opposition Scott creates between the citizenry and the government reinforces the threat between the populace and the civil authorities; he goes so far as to declare that, while there is a "natural feeling, on the part of all members of government, for the general maintenance of authority," "the lower part of the rabble" are associated not with authority or order, but with chaos and madness (41–42). Indeed, just before the mob breaks into the Tolbooth to seize Porteous and kill him, Scott emphasizes their "deep and agitating murmur, which . . . begins to howl," "the unsettled state of their minds, [which] fluctuated to and fro without any visible cause of impulse," and their "minds [which] had been wound up to the pitch which we have described" (42). The assembled crowd is repeatedly represented in terms of mental disorder and mental agitation; moreover, because it is a dynamic group, it seems to be contagious, affecting not merely an individual but the entire collective body of the poor that soon "filled the principal street of the city" (60). Just as their madness and agitation overwhelm the bounds of reason, the collective body of the mob soon overwhelms the streets and urban infrastructure that is meant to impose order. They seize "[t]he Netherbow Port," which "divided Edinburgh, properly so called, from the suburb named the Canongate," in order to prevent "a regiment of infantry . . . which might have occupied the city by advancing through this gate" (60). In order to control the city, the mob overruns the very mechanisms designed to enforce civil and social order.

The association of a contagious madness and social disorder becomes central to the novel's representation of the riot through the fact that the mob's assault on the Tolbooth in order to seize Porteous is led by the figure of Madge Wildfire, the preeminent figure associated with madness in the novel.[4] Wildfire, who "has been insane ever since [George Staunton] abandoned her with child," functions as a "challenge to nineteenth-century British ideology" not only of rationality and reason, but especially of containment and order (Thompson 1987, 188). If the figure of Madge leads the wild charge against the Tolbooth and against the rational order of municipal justice in the beginning of the novel, her insanity and, more importantly, her history of incarceration in asylums reveals the public health infrastructure that is itself meant to contain these contagious threats to the wider public and to social order. As Emrys Jones has argued, Madge signifies an unspooling of order that blurs the boundaries between "prisons and asylums," making it "impossible for the 'sane' reader, let alone the madwoman, to tell where incarceration of criminals ends and care fore the mad begins" (2016, 545). Thus, the strategy of containment embedded within the novel's representation of urban authority and infrastructure again gives way to confusion.

Confronting the novel's protagonist, Madge wonders aloud "Were ye ever in Bedlam" and, upon hearing that Jeanie had never in fact been in Bedlam, Madge exclaims, "Never in Bedlam! . . . But ye'll have been in the cells at Edinburgh" (Scott 2008, 287). Once again, Jeanie insists she has never been "in the cells at Edinburgh," which prompts Madge to insist "the magistrates send naebody to Bedlam but me—they maun hae an unco respect for me, for whenever I am brought to them, they aye hae me back to Bedlam" (287). It is, as Jones notes, "extremely difficult" to pinpoint the specific reference Madge is making to Bedlam. On the one hand, Edinburgh "did not have a recognisable, public madhouse in 1736," but the "Bristo Bedlam was founded in the 1740s as an offshoot of the Charity Workhouse" (2016, 544). There was some provision for the mentally ill in a "small asylum in New Grayfriars churchyard," as part of a network of "private houses, the House of Correction and the city's jails" that cared for the mentally ill before the establishment of "the first separate repository exclusively for the insane" (Jones 2016, 544; Houston 2003, 12). Before the construction of the new workhouse and Bedlam, Edinburgh's mentally ill were placed in "Correction Houses for idle beggars and vagabonds," established under a 1672 Act of the Scottish Parliament (Houston 2003, 13). The confusion of jail and asylum reveals the underlying logic of containment and threat with which figures like Madge were perceived. Indeed, as the opening of the novel demonstrates, the boundary between urban disorder, criminality, and madness was understood to be remarkably fluid.

While Jones is correct to emphasize the passages where Jeanie Deane's "own mental firmness is called into question," what I want to underscore is the way that the urban infrastructure within *The Heart of Midlothian* not only mirrors the historical development of Edinburgh's public health institutions like the Bedlam but also lays bare the anxiety around urban disorder through the confusion of class and madness. If *The Heart of Midlothian* begins with urban confusion, disorder, and the threat of madness, it also reveals the ongoing anxiety over the relationship between public health and urban infrastructure that gives shape to early nineteenth-century novels. Demonstrating repeatedly the threat of contagion that comes from social mixing, these novels, ultimately, provide a geography of health, class, and social order.

"A Pattern of Exclusion": A Conclusion

Franco Moretti opens his foundational study of urban geography in the European novel with a discussion of the general topography of Austen's novels, noting that "a pattern does indeed emerge here: of exclusion, first of all. No Ireland; no Scotland; no Wales; no Cornwall. . . . And not even all of England: Lancashire, the North, the industrial revolution—all missing" (1999, 13). Despite this supposed pattern of exclusion, representations of urban development in nineteenth-century fiction reveal less the emergence of the nation state than that of metropolitan attempts to manage and govern the social body. Reading novels by Austen, Edge-worth, and Scott through the framework of the urban developments and infrastructure that reshaped the nineteenth-century metropolis demon-strates the way that class anxiety, illness, and urban renovation func-tioned as "tools for understanding the environment of the population [and] paralleled a spatialization of governmental knowledges (*savoirs*) of the social body" (Gilbert 2004, XV). It can be said that such novels provide a map for understanding the overlapping systems of urban space, class, and public health.

Notes

1. Pamela Gilbert notes that Foucault's studies of power, medicine, and the body demonstrate "the move toward modern liberal government is marked by 'gov-ernmentality'—the development of bodies of knowledge that are also prac-tices, particularly in regard to biopolitics (the management of populations) through public health, the census, and the like. These knowledges, which were also practices, enabled governments both to know about the movements and living habits of their subjects and to mobilize consent among those subjects to governmental aims, rather than relying on brute power" (2004, 3–4).
2. In *The Theory of Moral Sentiments*, Smith argues that the sufferer "can only hope to obtain [sympathetic relief] by lowering his passion to that pitch, in which the spectators are capable of going along with him. He must flatten, if I may be allowed to say so, the sharpness of its natural tone, in order to reduce it to harmony and concord with the emotions of those who are about him" (2009, 28).
3. Terry Eagleton has famously argued that this letter demonstrates "[a] unifying mode of representation, which is just what the look-glass image signifies, is no longer able to capture a contradictory reality. For Edgeworth, however, what is twisted out of decent proportion is not the signifier but the referent—not the glass itself, but the feverish masses it fails to reflect. The people are now refus-ing to peer into this mirror. . . . The truth has finally pulled the fiction asunder, shattering the means of representation" (1995, 177).
4. It is important to note that George Staunton is here impersonating Madge. As Helen Small argues, this act of crossdressing "sum[s] up the displacement of political insurgency on to the figure of the madwoman, as her private, familiar tragedy becomes the costume for a political drama enacted by men" (1996, 121).

References

Austen, Jane. (1811) 2017. *Sense and Sensibility*. Edited by John Mullan. Oxford, UK and New York, NY: Oxford University Press.

———. (1813) 2008. *Pride and Prejudice*. Edited by James Kinsley. Oxford, UK and New York, NY: Oxford University Press.

Blaine, Gilbert. 1813. *Observations on the Comparative Prevalence, Mortality and Treatment of Different Diseases*. London: G. Woodfall.

Clery, E. J. (2017) 2018. "'That Is Capital': Views of London in Pride and Preju-dice." In *Jane Austen's Geographies*, edited by Robert Clark, 156–74. New York, NY: Routledge.

Cohen, William A. 2005. "Locating Filth." In *Filth: Dirt, Disgust, and Modern Life*, edited by William A. Cohen and Ryan Johnson, VII–XXXVII. Minneapolis, MN and London: University of Minnesota Press.

Dickson, David. 2014. *Dublin: The Making of a Capital City*. Cambridge, MA: The Belknap Press of Harvard Press.

———. 2021. *The First Irish Cities: An Eighteenth Century Transformation*. New Haven, CT and London: Yale University Press.

Eagleton, Terry. 1995. *Heathcliff and the Great Hunger: Studies in Irish Culture*. London: Verso.

Edgeworth, Maria. (1812) 2000. *The Absentee*. Edited by Heidi Thomson. New York, NY: Penguin.

———. 2018. "Letter from Maria Edgeworth to Pakenham Edgeworth, February 10, 1834." In *Maria Edgeworth's Letters from Ireland*, edited by Valerie Pakenham, 334–36. Dublin, IE: The Lilliput Press.

Foucault, Michel. (1975) 1995. *Discipline and Punish: The Birth of the Prison*. New York: Vintage Books.

Gilbert, Pamela K. 2004. *Mapping the Victorian Social Body*. Albany, NY: State University Press of New York.

Harris, Bob. 2011. "The Enlightenment, Towns and Urban Society in Scotland, c.1760–1820." *The English Historical Review* 126 (522): 1097–136. https://doi.org/10.1093/ehr/cer259.

Houston, R. A. 2003. "Care of the Mentally Disabled in and Around Edinburgh, c. 1680–1820." *Journal of the Royal College of Physicians of Edinburgh* 33 (12): 12–20.

Jones, Emrys D. 2016. "'Never in Bedlam?' Madness and History in Sir Walter Scott's the Heart of Mid-Lothian." *Studies in Romanticism* 55 (4): 537–58. https://doi.org/10.1353/srm.2016.0003.

Kaplan, L. (2017) 2018. "Jane Austen's Allusive Geographies: London's Streets, Squares, and Gardens." In *Jane Austen's Geographies*, edited by Robert Clark. New York, NY: Routledge.

Moretti, Franco. (1997) 1999. *The Atlas of the European Novel, 1800–1900*. London: Verso.

Nash, John. 1814. "Appendix III." In *Some Account of the Proposed Improvements of the Western Part of London . . .*, XXI–LXII. London: W & P Reynolds.

Ó Gráda, Diarmuid. 2015. *Georgian Dublin: The Forces That Shaped the City*. Cork, IE: Cork University Press.

O'Neill, Timothy P. 1973. "Fever and Public Health in Pre-Famine Ireland." *The Journal of the Royal Society of Antiquaries of Ireland* 103: 1–34.

Pittock, Murray. 2019. *Enlightenment in a Smart City: Edinburgh's Civic Development, 1660–1750*. Edinburgh, UK: Edinburgh University Press.

Poovey, Mary. 1995. *Making a Social Body: British Cultural Formation 1830–1864*. Chicago, IL: University of Chicago Press.

Porter, Roy. 1991. "Cleaning up the Great Wen: Public Health in Eighteenth-Century London." *Medical History* 35 (S11): 61–75. https://doi.org/10.1017/S0025727300071118.

———. (1994) 1995. *London: A Social History*. Cambridge, MA: Harvard University Press.

Prunty, Jacinta. (1997) 2011. *Dublin Slums 1800–1925: A Study in Urban Geography*. Dublin, IE: Irish Academic Press.

Rosen, George. 2015. *A History of Public Health*. Revised and Expanded Edition. Baltimore, MD: Johns Hopkins University Press.

Scott, Walter. (1818) 2008. *The Heart of Midlothian*. Edited by Claire Lamont. Oxford, UK and New York, NY: Oxford University Press.

Small, Helen. 1996. *Love's Madness: Medicine, the Novel, and Female Insanity, 1800–1865*. Oxford, UK: Clarendon Press.

Smith, Adam. 2008. *An Inquiry into the Nature and Causes of the Wealth of Nations*. Edited by Kathryn Sutherland. New York, NY: Oxford University Press.

———. (1759) 2009. *The Theory of Moral Sentiments*. Edited by Ryan Patrick Hanley. New York, NY: Penguin.

Speer, T. C. 1822. "Medical Report Containing an Inquiry into the Causes and Character of the Diseases of the Lower Orders in Dublin." In *The Dublin Hospital Reports and Communications in Medicine and Surgery Volume III*, 161–200. Hodges and M'Arthur.

Summerson, John. (1845) 1988. *Georgian London*. London: Barrie & Jenkins.

Sutherland, John. 1995. *The Life of Walter Scott: A Critical Biography*. Cambridge, MA: Blackwell.

Thompson, Jon. 1987. "Sir Walter Scott and Madge Wildfire: Strategies of Containment in The Heart of Midlothian." *Literature and History* 13 (2): 188–99.

Wald, Priscilla. 2008. *Contagious: Cultures, Carriers, and the Outbreak Narrative*. Durham, NC: Duke University Press.

Wiltshire, John. 1992. *Jane Austen and the Body: The Picture of Health*. New York, NY: Cambridge University Press.

2 Spaces of *Little Dorrit,* or the Global Marshalsea

Meghan Jordan

In Chapter X of his later novel *Little Dorrit* (1855–1857), Charles Dickens describes the "Whole Science of Government," by which he means the decidedly ineffective Circumlocution Office. Much has been said in earlier and recent scholarship about Dickens's satire—what, exactly, he is satirizing, being the most pressing question—but Dickens seems to take care to present an amorphous and changeable space, a location shaped by the perception of the beholder. The interior of the Office is never clearly defined. It is a space of writing utensils, paperwork, stamps, glass partitions, hallways, and doors, but not one fully defined *in space*, although it is unaccountably formidable. The Office and Mr. Tite Barnacle, the "man of great power" who runs it, "quite crushed" the eponymous Amy Dorrit whenever its name, or Barnacle's, was mentioned, but she is not certain from whence this "awful impression" comes (Dickens 1998, 113). The Circumlocution Office is, rather, a dream-space signaling to the characters and the reader the inescapable labyrinth within. In *Little Dorrit*, the structure of the Circumlocution Office is an individualized dream of forbidden and formidable space that translates to a collective idea of power, wealth, and institutional might. The Office is bureaucracy defined by the individual and, subsequently, by the British nation. It functions as a representation and an extension of British local and global power: citizens can access a partial vision of power's extension over their lives and the lives of others but cannot realize a complete and accurate picture of this determinacy.[1] Space is a social product, contingent on architectural planning, history, cartography, and, perhaps most importantly, the ways in which it is experienced. In Dickens's novel, the spaces of the Marshalsea Debtors' Prison and the Circumlocution Office—sites on the European continent, especially London—and intimate, familiar areas, like Arthur Clenham's childhood home, are sites of urban planning and psychological imprisonment, at the same time that they are or contain physical structures. In a pseudo-Marxist critique, Dickens contrasts drastic limitations on freedom and social mobility because of class to "the priority of product over process; the cultivation of efficiency, functional specificity, and thrift; and the maximization of profits through

DOI: 10.4324/9781003119425-3

the production of surplus value," which Mary Poovey enumerates as "the inherent logic" of the "modern form of abstraction" (1995, 30). National "efficiency" is a facade obscuring dire poverty; exploitative relations; and, on the one hand, bureaucratic indifference; and on the other, bureaucratic machinations.

Recent studies of *Little Dorrit* have focused on space in the novel and its relationship to guilt, secrecy, and imprisonment. Not as much, however, has been done to examine the relationship between institutional spaces, psychological interiors, *and* metropolitan/colonial transactions. That is, to make connections among the kinds of space represented in the novel—psychological and physical, metropolitan and foreign—and the institutions that bind the characters into specific relationships with themselves and with each other. For example, in Grace Moore's excellent article, "Turkish Robbers, Lumps of Delight, and the Detritus of Empire: The East Revisited in Dickens's Late Novels," she explores British anxieties over "the growing presence of imperial waste and oddments," but does not mention the novel at all in her study (2009, 79). For scholars like Moore, *Little Dorrit* is not a colonial or imperial novel. Yet the novel's obsession with bureaucratic expansion and England's relationship to the commerce of the world—Russia, for example—demonstrate a text concerned with England's economic policies and their failure, both at home and abroad. Jesse Rosenthal writes about the networks of the novel, finding a text that attempts to "navigate a tricky terrain between the public and the private: one in which personal relations between intimates are mediated and facilitated by strangers" (2017, 289). Elaine Hadley (2016) describes Dickens as "pro-order" and anti-bureaucracy, focusing on counting, statistics, and accountability in *Little Dorrit*.[2] Sajni Mukherji (1981), Lillian Nayder (1992), and Alex Tickell (2013) use Dickens's other writings to discuss the author's class consciousness as relates to his pro-imperialist and racist ideology.[3] In *Little Dorrit*, I argue, worldly concerns are central to the psychological development and spatial oppression of the characters. And the intrusion of foreign "detritus" or "excess" disrupts the hierarchical social arrangements so carefully constructed and maintained through the incomprehensible metropolitan mechanism of the Circumlocution Office. In the novel, the "unseen" landscape is the foreign or colonial outpost, and conceptions of the foreign exist in shorthand as ciphers for race, class, nationalism, and bureaucratic inefficiency throughout its nearly 1,000 pages. Similar to the operations of power within government—as evidenced in descriptions of the Circumlocution Office—imperial sites and continental Europe and Asia are also spaces where bureaucratic power operates.

Little Dorrit is the story of Arthur Clenham, who returns home to London after twenty years working for the family business in China. Upon his father's death, he decides to quit the business and leave it to his invalid mother, who engages her longtime servant, Jeremiah Flintwinch, as a partner. Clenham becomes interested in his mother's seamstress, a diminutive woman only introduced as Little Dorrit. Little Dorrit (Amy), it turns out, was born in the Marshalsea debtors' prison, where her father still resides. Through Clenham's intervention and aid, the Dorrit family discovers that they are the inheritors of a large fortune. William Dorrit's, Little Dorrit's father's, debts are paid, and the family attempts to begin a new life in society by traveling abroad. William, quite unfortunately, invests all his money with his eldest daughter's, Fanny's, father-in-law— the ruthless speculator Mr. Merdle. He dies, and Merdle commits suicide. The family is left penniless, but Little Dorrit discovers that she, in fact, is the benefactress of Arthur Clenham's father's will. Arthur was Mr. Clenham's illegitimate child, raised in forced penitence by Mrs. Clenham. On his biological mother's deathbed, his father created a will to restore some money to herself or her patron, who, it turns out, is Amy Dorrit's uncle, also deceased. Amy burns her copy of the will and marries Arthur, with whom she has fallen in love. She keeps the secret of her inheritance from even her new husband. Arthur's business partner returns from Russia, having patented a successful invention there, and pays Arthur's debts to release him from the Marshalsea Prison, where Arthur went of his own volition after investing all of the company's money with Merdle. The novel ends with the main characters financially secure or dead after their dreaded secrets have come to life.

The complicated plot and family indiscretion at the heart of *Little Dorrit* reflect the labyrinthine spaces of London, the intricate web of British power, and the tentacles grasping spaces across the globe through imperial conquest, colonial settlement, and foreign trade. There is, indeed, something rotten at the heart of British colonialism and imperial enterprise. England's industrial expansion, and the gravity with which the members of the emerging middle class of the early nineteenth century began to see themselves and their status, was due in large part to the country's continued expansion overseas. As a colonial power, England required its colonies to provide lucrative resources for sale in European markets and to purchase the exports from Great Britain's own factories. Much of the country's middle class profited from this system, expanding its own wealth and imperial territory in a symbiotic relationship of power. Thus, the "unspoken law" of colonial and metropolitan space, enforced by institutions like the British East India Company, was an uneven distribution of wealth veiled by patriotism, territorial expansion and conquest, and social norms. Colonialism, of course, did not create British social and racial hierarchies, but it sustained and reinforced their importance to the nation and its conception of the British body politic. What colonialism did accomplish on its own, however, was, as Hannah Arendt (1976) and others have convincingly written, the proliferation of middle-class ideals and the expansion of middle-class wealth.[4] Colonial outposts and foreign sites are just part of the bureaucratic "empire" of which Dickens writes in *Little Dorrit*. The proverbial red tape that mires some of the characters in debt or poverty, for example, is part of the same tangle of incomprehensible practices that causes mismanagement of the empire. In the novel, disorganized, ineffective, or bureaucratic space relates to racial, class, and social hierarchies. There is a clear distinction between the spaces where decisions are made and the spaces where those decisions play out—usually in lower-class or working-class spaces, like Bleeding Heart Yard. The final arena in which power demonstrates itself is in uncounted, "inconsequential" space—imperial or foreign sites, like Russia and China—where spaces thought to be less progressive or "developed" intrude into "real" or "acknowledged" spaces like England.

The ability of the system to replicate itself while remaining mysterious and incomprehensible, the novel tells us, allows it to maintain its constant power over citizens. Mr. Plornish, an old friend of the Dorrit family, tells Arthur Clenham as they travel to the Marshalsea Prison that "[t]hey was all hard up there" in Bleeding Heart Yard, where Plornish lives (Dickens 1998, 157). Yet, Plornish

> couldn't say how it was; he didn't know as anybody *could* say how it was; all he know'd was, that so it was. When a man felt, on his own back and in his own belly, that poor he was, that man (Mr. Plornish gave it as his decided belief) know'd well that he was poor somehow or another, and you couldn't talk it out of him, no more than you could talk Beef into him.
>
> (157, emphasis in original)

Although Plornish describes the social immobility often inherent in poverty and lower-class status, Bleeding Heart Yard began as an aspirational neighborhood, according to the narrator. Unfortunately, having "exhausted" its possibility for advancement,

> the ground had so risen about Bleeding Heart Yard that you got into it down a flight of steps which formed no part of the original approach, and got out of it by a low gateway into a maze of shabby streets, which went about and about, tortuously ascending to the level again.
>
> (150)

The original aspirational character of the neighborhood and its inhabitants having disappeared, the citizens of the Yard descended into it, never able to rise out again, except through a "maze" of successes and failures.

It is also fitting that the world of the novel knows neither debtor William Dorrit's reason for imprisonment nor Mr. Merdle's source of wealth. The mysterious bureaucracy that winds its way through the novel, causing the downfall of one character and the rise of another, has as its main symbol the Circumlocution Office. Dickens famously writes of this Office:

> The Circumlocution Office was (as everybody knows without being told) the most important Department under government. No public business of any kind could possibly be done at any time, without the acquiescence of the Circumlocution Office. . . . Whatever was required to be done, the Circumlocution Office was beforehand with all the public departments in the art of perceiving—HOW NOT TO DO IT. . . . It is true that How not to do it was the great study and object of all public departments and professional politicians all round the Circumlocution Office.
>
> (119)[5]

Arthur Clenham, the protagonist of the novel, disrupts an ordinary series of days at the Office by asking questions about William Dorrit's debt. His questions are disruptive, not because his interlocutor, Barnacle Junior, has any disconcerting answers to relay, but because Clenham simply "mustn't come into the place saying you want to know, you know" (128). Junior's other concern is that Clenham may have *international* commercial concerns to discuss. As he says to Arthur, "taking heed of his visitor's brown face, 'Is it anything about—Tonnage—or that sort of thing?'" (123). For, being the very masters of government and the two most important families in British and British colonial society, the Barnacles and Stiltstalkings, who control the Circumlocution Office and Parliament, are also to be found "wherever there was a square yard of ground in British occupation, under the sun or moon, with a public post upon it" (422). Indeed,

> [n]o intrepid navigator could plant a flag-staff upon any spot of earth, and take possession of it in the British name, but to that spot of earth, so soon as the discovery was known, the Circumlocution Office sent out a Barnacle and a dispatch-box. Thus, the Barnacles were all over the world, in every direction—dispatch-boxing the compass.
>
> (422)

The sheaves of dispatches circulate around the globe as they do in the Office itself, each sheet or dispatch part of the imperial archive and the system of power inherent in bureaucracy. Each sheet is an official statement or form of correspondence containing no real information. Each dispatch box is a flag planted in foreign soil, representing British power.

Dickens's witty discussion of nepotism in domestic and imperial relations and the inability of government to effect legitimate rule at home or abroad is not an anarchic or anti-imperial sentiment. From Dickens's other writings, it is very clear that he was pro-empire; he just wanted imperial and domestic law to run more smoothly and with more real "progress." The Barnacles in this case represent ineffective laws that are extended to soils where they do not belong. Thus, the bureaucratic office extended its bureaucracy to the colonies, with the effect that nothing could be done at home, nothing could be done in the colonies, and as a result, the progress of the "great empire" was stalled. The inventor Daniel Doyce, whose important invention cannot be patented because of the Office's machinations, goes to Russia, where he knows his work will be valued. On the other hand, the freed murderer and domestic abuser Rigaud comes to England, where he is certain he will be taken for a gentleman and his plot will succeed. Rather than effecting any kind of real change or promoting any sort of valuable system of management, the Circumlocution Office in London and abroad simply produce documents ("dispatches") that contain little valid information and little useful or proactive methods for improving the state of the nation, specifically the body politic suffering under the rule of How Not to Do It. As diffuse as their own dispatches distributed worldwide, the Barnacles were "dispersed all over the public offices, and held all sorts of public places" (122). The Barnacles, however, do not consider themselves members of the public. Instead, they believe each position their just due and that "the nation was under a load of obligation to [them]" instead of the reverse (122). When Clenham finally has his meeting with Tite Barnacle after being sent back and forth between the chambers of the Circumlocution Office, Barnacle speaks about the Public "as his natural enemy"; he "was always checked a little by that word of impertinent signification" (127–28). Barnacle believes, "The Department is accessible to the—Public" . . . "if the—Public approaches it according to the official forms; if the—Public does not approach it according to the official forms, the—Public has itself to blame" (128). In fact, the Office itself is distributed into public and private spaces. The public spaces are the entryways on the first floor, the waiting rooms where all manner of people are dissuaded from pressing their claims. Clenham, however, barges into the private chambers of the Office, looking into offices where, for example, Barnacle Junior "was eating mashed potatoes and gravy behind a partition by the hall fire," believing he has got rid of Clenham at last (128).

As the enclosed office of a powerful member, Tite Barnacle's office, where Clenham finds Barnacle Junior, is one of the only fully described spaces within the Circumlocution Office. Thus, Barnacle's office is not really a "dream" space, but rather a space whose objects indicate the Barnacle family's power, wealth, and status in an exploitative system. When sent again to meet with Barnacle Junior after meeting with the Barnacle patriarch, Clenham is ushered into the office, where the "lesser star" is holding court in his father's absence (123). Previously, Clenham has "awaited that gentleman successively in a hall, a glass case, a waiting room, and a fire-proof passage where the Department seemed to keep its wind" (122). He finds Barnacle Junior "singeing the calves of his legs at the parental fire, and supporting his spine against the mantel-shelf" (123). We learn:

> It was a comfortable room, handsomely furnished in the higher official manner; and presenting stately suggestions of the absent Barnacle, in the thick carpet, the leather-covered desk to sit at, the leather-covered desk to stand at, the formidable easy-chair and hearth-rug, the inter-posed screen, the torn-up papers, the dispatch-boxes with little labels sticking out of them, like medicine bottles or dead game, the pervad-ing smell of leather and mahogany, and a general bamboozling air of How not to do it.
>
> (123)

The "handsome" furnishings suggest not only wealth and class status but also the colonial sources of the Barnacles' wealth. The dispatch boxes most likely contain dispatches from those very Barnacle outposts across the globe, where medicines were produced and game hunting abounded. The "thick carpet" and leather and mahogany goods also imply colonial and foreign products. Although many nineteenth-century carpets were produced in England, in towns like Kidderminster, Persian and Afghan carpets and rugs were highly prized by the wealthy. In fact, in an effort to revitalize traditional crafts, during the Qajar Dynasty of Persia, rulers encouraged a return to carpet-making in the late nineteenth century, and Persian-style rugs were produced in many of the locations named in *Little Dorrit*, including Russia, India, and, eventually, China. Although leather goods were still manufactured fairly traditionally in English factories, which resisted mechanizing leather production until the 1860s, valonia, sumac, and divi-divi were types of bark imported from the English and currently and formerly occupied Spanish colonies to replace scarce and costly oak bark, once exclusively used in English leather production (Church 1971, 550). Elaine Freedgood has also written extensively about mahogany production, slavery, and English literature, specifically in the novel *Jane Eyre*.[6] The only fully described space in the Circumlocution Office—brief as the description is—evokes layers of material wealth and intangible power extrapolated from colonial land, colonial peoples, the enslaved, the British working classes, and the British middle classes.

Exploitation through ineffective government is also the theme of some of Dickens's non-fiction essays, collected as *The Uncommercial Trav-eller* (1860), but first published as a series in his journal *All the Year Round* just a couple of years after the serial publication of *Little Dorrit*. His semi-autobiographical writing persona, an "innocent" traveler, writes of the treatment of soldiers leaving the "Pagoda Department" of the foreign Circumlocution Office, "on which the sun never sets and the light of reason never rises" (Dickens 1900, 37). Dickens's criticism of the Crimean War and its mismanagement parallels his criticism of metropolitan mismanagement in *Little Dorrit*. Although the traveler sees many deserters, he hopes this is a sort of accident, for, of course, the Department

> will have been particularly careful of the national honour. It will have shown these men, in the scrupulous good faith, not to say the generosity, of its dealing with them, that great national authorities can have no small retaliations and revenges. It will have made every provision for their health on the passage home, and will have landed them, restored from their campaigning fatigues by a sea-voyage, pure air, sound food, and good medicines.
>
> (37)

Yet, when the traveler visits the returned soldiers in Liverpool, he finds:

> Their groans and pains during the performance of this glorious pageant, had been so distressing, as to bring tears into the eyes of spectators but too well accustomed to scenes of suffering. The men were so dreadfully cold, that those who could get near the fires were hard to be restrained from thrusting their feet in among the blazing coals. They were so horribly reduced, that they were awful to look upon. Racked with dysentery and blackened with scurvy, one hundred and forty wretched soldiers had been revived with brandy and laid in bed.
>
> (37)

To defend the claims of the dying Ottoman Empire and preserve Turkey from Russian expansion, the British entered into the unpopular Crimean conflict. Criticism of the military administration in the British press was repeatedly juxtaposed with sadness over the vain sacrifice of the soldiers. The national offices sending the soldiers to death or allowing them to fall prey to disease are racially inflected and denigrated as part of the "Pagoda Department." Its dispatches, evidence of imperial conquest but not logic or reason, are the same ineffective, and downright dangerous, dispatches sent across the globe by the Barnacles and Stiltstalkings. It does not seem an accident that Daniel Doyce emigrates to Russia to patent his game-changing invention: if Britain was defending itself against the possibility of a Russian empire, the fact that one of the country's most important minds in the novel finds recognition there shows how dangerously myopic the British powers that be have become.

British domestic and colonial bureaucracy also has much to do with William Dorrit's imprisonment, his ignorance of the fortune he has inherited, and his loss of fortune in the second half of the novel.[7] Dorrit's creditors seem aligned with the patriarch Tite Barnacle, but it is not clear if Barnacle is one of the creditors or if the interests of Dorrit's creditors are simply concentrated in this one powerful man (Dickens 1998, 125). When Clenham seeks to ascertain if Dorrit's debt may be set right after these twenty-five years, the only answer given from the Office is "possibly," repeated throughout the scene (125). Arthur puts his two friends Mr. Pancks and Mr. Rugg on the case, and they are the men who discover that Dorrit has inherited an unclaimed fortune from a distant relative. So much red tape has forestalled any adjustment of William's situation that the Office is content as usual to simply not do anything in the case. It is William's connection with the thief and forgerer Merdle that leads to the loss of his fortune. Thus, the Dorrit story is heavily contingent on how bureaucracy and capitalism affect citizens in ways that at first appear highly randomized—a product of chance—but are upon inspection clearly the result of negligence and the policy of How Not to Do It. In his article, "On the Financial Crisis, 1825–26," Alexander J. Dick writes,

> It was in the wake of the 1825 crisis that economists realized not only that Britain had a fully commercial society but also that commerce operated according to rules and principles in which individuals had little direct, moral influence either as legislators or as managers.
>
> (2012, np)

According to Dick,

> Cultural commentators and literary writers began to conceive of the market economy not as something distinct from the self or its communities but rather as the condition in which all selves and communities exist and to which, paradoxically, they owed that existence (np).

Similarly, Ben Parker argues,

> [T]he logic of recognition presumes an ultimate knowability: the truth of subjectivity requires a detour through otherness. But . . ., the epistemological rupture of capitalist crisis refuses and obstructs this recognition, remaining intractably other, forbiddingly unrepresentable by the same brush.
>
> (2014, 132)

Bourgeois subjectivity demands the recognition of selfhood through wealth and property, but the tangled web of global markets obscures economic relationships and positions.

Imagined wealth gives Merdle power and social position, but it also hides the pyramid scheme he supports through the persona of a rich man. The national treasury personified in Dickens's novel congratulates Merdle on being "one of England's world-famed capitalists and merchant-princes" (1998, 269). "To extend the triumphs of such men," says Treasury, "was to extend the triumphs and resources of the nation"—it was "patriotic," in fact (269). Merdle's money makes him unquestionable royalty in the eyes of the country's legislators. He can produce prodigious wealth for all—and if some should lose, it was most important that the majority of the bureaucracy's functionaries gain. The personification of the law in the novel, Bar, goes so far as to say that Merdle is capable of "convert[ing]" "the root of all evil into the root of all good" (269). Yet we ultimately learn that Merdle's wealth is as alchemical and exploitative as the other relationships of economic power and dominance in *Little Dorrit*. He "converts" speculative wealth into "good" for the wealthy who can afford to gamble with their money, and saved pennies into loss and poverty for those already struggling or unable to afford such risk, like Pancks and Clenham. Like his mysterious (and ultimately non-existent) wealth, Merdle lives in a fashionable house that mirrors his own facade: "The expressionless uniform twenty houses, all to be knocked at and rung at in the same form, all approachable by the same dull steps, all fended off by the same pattern of railing, all with the same impracticable fire-escapes" (265). And in the same neighborhood, "[t]he house so drearily out of repair," "the corner house with nothing but angular rooms, the house with the blinds always down," "the house where the collector has called for one quarter of an Idea, and found nobody at home," and "[t]he showy house that was taken for life by the disappointed gentleman, and which doesn't suit him at all" (265). These confining, obscuring houses hide Society's flaws as they mirror the machinations of a government keen on pretending to do "something" without accomplishing anything. Merdle himself "was mostly to be found against walls and behind doors," "hid[ing] his hands" as if guilty of some crime and desiring to disappear (266). Indeed, when Merdle's pyramid scheme comes to light, it is hardly a surprise to the reader who has seen him skulking away from all notice. Merdle's suicide is the ultimate form of How Not to Do It—that is, how not to take responsibility for the economic situation he has in part created and its dire fallout.

Being prey to this fraudulent and dysfunctional system is not the only way in which characters like Clenham and Dorrit are "imprisoned"; there is, of course, the two men's literal imprisonment for debt in the Marshalsea. Although at the time Dickens was writing, the prison was already "extinct," as he writes in the Preface to *Little Dorrit*, the place where it stood is "very little altered if at all," and those who come to look upon the space "will stand among the crowding ghosts of many miserable years" (6). These ghosts were part of the prison's landscape before it was closed, however, since William himself is only a shell of his former self, as he tells his daughter Amy (245). And, according to Dickens, it is the "place" itself that "got free," rather than the prisoners (6).

Despite his reflection on his gentlemanly status before his imprisonment, William succeeds in convincing himself of the dignity of his situation and the positive effects of being imprisoned to the extent that he
publicly pities his brother "for not being under lock and key," a state
that another imprisoned debtor likens to "freedom" (78, 242). Yet, of
course, there are moments when this grand lie exposes itself to William,
and these are the moments when his delicate psychological balance is
traumatically disrupted. When the turnkey's son John Chivery asks for
Amy's hand in marriage, for example, William is conscious of what he
owes to the Chiverys and that he is "unfortunately dependent on these
men for something, every hour in the day" (244). He is also conscious
of "that touch of shame," so important to repress to keep the facade of
his dignity—the "shame," that is, of his daughter's birth in the prison
and his low status as prisoner (244). This is the constant battle that
causes William to "shr[i]nk before his own knowledge of his meaning"
(244). Dickens calls William's condition "jail-rot": "the impurity of his
prison worn into the grain of his soul," a "degenerate state" (246–47).
So much of William's psychological state rests on metaphors of imprisonment because it is obviously his imprisonment that has created the
dichotomous personality that we see in the novel. When he learns he
is finally free, his first act is to point at the wall that has both sym-
bolized his imprisonment and literally been the physical barrier to his
freedom. "It is down. Gone!" Clenham replies to his unspoken question (440). The Marshalsea's prisoners experienced some freedom of
movement within the prison: they could wander to their own rooms,
walk to the pump in the courtyard for water, or stop into the "Tap" for
ale, if they had money. Nevertheless, the turnkey's watchtower, the narrow entryway to the prison through the main lodge, the spikes on the
high walls, and the enormous iron gate—locked every night—barred
prisoners from leaving and visitors and family from coming in, except
when the gate was opened by the turnkey (906–11). Aside from their
literal imprisonment in the Marshalsea, debtors were also reminded
that their freedom was contingent on class: members of the gentry and
the upper classes were not imprisoned there. The debtors' prison was
solely reserved for those of the middle class and lower classes.

Although a statused individual in the prison, William recognizes the
falsity of his position and the tenuousness of his dignity in the outside
world. To be free is to not only no longer be "choking for want of air"
but also to experience new kinds of imprisonment: that experienced in the
landscape of the city, abroad in relations with foreigners, and in the social
landscape of both places (444). Dorrit's downfall comes not because he
is free, but because he consistently reveals free life in the city and in the
outside world to be the kind of imprisonment no one actively discusses.
He fails to see himself as truly free and exposes a social hierarchy without
the promise of true social mobility. In fact, when the Marshalsea itself is

demolished, much of it still remains: Dickens writes that one may go into Marshalsea Place and "find [one's] feet on the very paving stones of the extinct Marshalsea jail; will see its narrow yard to the right and to the left," and will even "look upon the rooms in which the debtors lived" (6). Many of the decrepit buildings of the prison—considered unfit for housing prisoners any longer—were renovated slightly and became tenant housing. The place where the prison stood marks one of the many palimpsests in the city of London: a haunted space that refuses its own erasure. Although the Barnacles and Stiltstalkings rigorously champion imperial expansion and the "free" capitalist market, these ghostly spaces reveal the vacuousness of their actual policies and procedures. These spaces also reveal the absence of political and economic efficiency and its effect on the general population. The debtor, writes Avrom Fleishman in his Hegelian reading of the novel, is "the servant of his creditors"; "this servitude is exacted from him in the form not of work, but of literal bondage" (1974, 579–80). "For the prisoner," Fleishman continues, "is nothing but a slave without work: he has lost his power to do what he wills, to be a member of the free community" (580). Even outside the prison, the prisoner finds himself prey to the economic laws that sent him there in the first place.

Accordingly, "Melancholy" London also figures in the novel as a space of imprisonment and oppression (Dickens 1998, 43). Perhaps this is why William finds he is reminded of his prison throughout his travels outside its walls. We encounter the novel's London on a Sunday and, as the narrator tells us, "Everything was bolted and barred that could by possibility furnish relief to an overworked people"; "Melancholy streets in a perennial garb of soot steeped the souls of the people who were condemned to look at them out of windows, in dire despondency" (43). But this is not simply a working-class problem: more generally, "[m]iles of close wells and pits of houses, where the inhabitants gasped for air, stretched far away towards every point of the compass" (44). Of course, Arthur's mother's, Mrs. Clenham's, house is an example of this urban imprisonment, but even the Barnacle residence to which Arthur goes when he wants "to know, you know" is in "a hideous little street of dead wall, stables, and dunghills," a neighborhood of "fearful little coops" advertised as "aristocratic" (124–25). If the working-class residents of Bleeding Heart Yard are "bled" for their rents by Pancks and the landlord Casby, then the middle-class and wealthy residents of other parts of London are "bled" by their desire to be or seem part of upper-class society. As Parker writes, "one's 'place' in the world is revealed not to be a substantial given but a structural illusion that collapses under the weight of desire" (Parker 2014, 132). In *Little Dorrit*, the spaces of the city itself are part of a "structural illusion"—not because the edifices of the city are not real, but rather because they mirror the tenuousness and fragility of wealth and class. Mrs. Clenham's decaying and dilapidated house literally collapses on its inhabitants, revealing the falsity of class and power seemingly built in space, or the alignment of what Henri Lefebvre (1991) calls "lived" space and "perceived" space.

Although Mrs. Clenham's invalid condition is the result of "rigid silence" through many years, and her house's "condition" is the reflection of that secrecy and silence, the characters who people the novel and the neighborhoods in which they live reveal the effects of modern industrial capitalism at work (Dickens 1998, 827). As Mary Poovey argues in her book *Making a Social Body*,

> [M]odern industrial capitalism was characterized by a new organization of space and bodies in space. The formation of the culture attendant upon modern capitalism therefore entailed the naturalization of these spatial arrangements as well as the mystification of the "framework of power" inherent in—and enforced by—the new organization of space.
>
> (1995, 25)

The Marshalsea, Circumlocution Office, and Mr. Merdle are symptoms of this framework of power. Yet, Mrs. Clenham, too, demonstrates the ways in which religion formed part of the capitalist superstructure, enforcing strict hierarchies and submission and, in her family's case, "wholesome repression, punishment, and fear" (Dickens 1998, 807). Arthur's father's upbringing was also one of "severe restraint": "besides the discipline his spirit had undergone, he had lived in a starved house, where rioting and gaiety were unknown, and where every day was a day of toil and trial like the last" (808). As a result of their childhoods and Mr. Clenham Sr.'s indiscretion, Arthur is brought up under the same restraint, so "that the child [Arthur] might work out his release [from sin] in bondage and hardship" (824). When Mrs. Clenham's house collapses, killing the assassin Rigaud/Blandois, she drops:

> upon the stones; and she never from that hour moved so much as a finger again, or had the power to speak one word. For upwards of three years she reclined in her wheeled chair, looking attentively at those about her, and appearing to understand what they said; but, the rigid silence she had so long held was evermore enforced upon her, and, except that she could move her eyes and faintly express a negative and affirmative with her head, she lived and died a statue.
>
> (827)

Dickens suggests that Mrs. Clenham's secret is what forces her to live as a statue (a decidedly problematic reading of her disability), but her austere lifestyle and exacting adherence to severe social codes also leaves her imprisoned, a source of oppression for the other characters, like her son; Jeremiah Flintwinch, her business partner; and Affery, her maid.

Society itself is, in fact, one of the oppressing demons of the novel. William Dorrit, when free from the Marshalsea, still feels acutely when the "family dignity was struck at," and "[h]is life was made an agony by the number of fine scalpels that he felt to be incessantly engaged in dissecting his dignity" (483). According to Parker, William's personal truth lies "not in a closed vault," as in Arthur's case, "but within [his] own consciousness" (2014, 136). "Mr. Dorrit's story is that of the collapse of a subjective partition set up within himself, dividing his gentility from knowledge of the reality of the debtors' prison" (136). This means that being imprisoned in the Marshalsea actually protects William from slights—real or perceived—against his dignity because he is able to craft a particular identity that shelters him from all conscious knowledge of his real condition. Once in the city—a city that replicates, but also distorts, his imprisoned state—he can no longer maintain the fantasy. In fact, being wealthy actually dismantles his primary fantasy of inherited gentility. In other words, William can neither sustain his prison fantasy of imagined gentility outside the Marshalsea, nor can he create a viable new fantasy of real gentility *because* his notion of self is predicated on who he has been for twenty-five years. As Klaudia Hiu Yen Lee demonstrates,

> London in Dickens's novels is often portrayed as a vast, impenetrable mystery. It is particularly pertinent in *Little Dorrit*, as the wider cityscape often becomes an externalization of the protagonists' innermost feelings, which in turn helps shape their identity and memory.
> (2013, 10)

While Dorrit moves from one private, exclusive space to another, he also becomes a public figure through wealth in a society with rules quite different from that which he has left behind.

This capital "S" Society is one that mimes its own values for itself. Like Mrs. Merdle's ample and admirable bosom—the perfect stage for Mr. Merdle's wealth in the form of jewels—many of its rules are merely based on show without substance. When Henry Gowan's mother finally "allows" her son to marry the wealthier, but untitled, daughter of Arthur Clenham's traveling companion, Mr. Meagles, she must "apply" to Mrs. Merdle for Society's approval. Punctuated by the screaming of her pet parrot as she "parrots" Society's values, Mrs. Merdle "thought in the depths of her capacious bosom that this was a sufficiently good catch" (Dickens 1998, 416). For she was one

> who really knew her friend Society pretty well, and who knew what Society's mothers were, and what Society's daughters were, and what

Society's matrimonial market was, and how prices ruled in it, and what scheming and counter-scheming took place for the high buyers, and what bargaining and huckstering went on.

(416)

"Knowing, however, what was expected of her, and perceiving the exact nature of the fiction to be nursed, she took it delicately in her arms, and put her required contribution of gloss upon it" (416). This "fiction" was that Mrs. Gowan "was highly to be commended, that she was much to be sympathised with, that she had taken the highest of parts, and had come out of the furnace refined" (416). Yet, of course, Mrs. Gowan, sees "through her own threadbare blind perfectly" and is completely aware that "Mrs Merdle saw through it perfectly," while being certain that "Society would see through it perfectly" and maintain the "form" in its own interests (416). The necessity of fictions like these in the world of *Little Dorrit* is a requirement for power to maintain itself. Should someone like Mrs. Gowan admit that her son's marriage is a financial necessity without any real benefit to his bride, the ruse of Barnacle power would be at an end (Mrs. Gowan is a Barnacle by marriage; she was born a Stiltstalking). The precarious power of a title or a family name is made more precarious in a capitalist economy. This is the reason the "circumlocuting" government of the novel ties up wealth, opportunity, and social mobility: without titles, money is power; without money, the Barnacles stand to lose their stronghold on the country to people like William Dorrit.

Having maintained one fiction of gentility throughout his twenty-five years in prison, Dorrit experiences the difficulty of making his new wealth and its attendant false history cohere with his former life. If London is another kind of prison for William—a prison where he must hide his history—then continental Europe is perhaps where he should find more freedom because of his relative anonymity in that social circle. But, of course, Europe to the wealthy of London is only an exchange of one setting for another. In Italy he encounters all the faces he will encounter in London society, and his sojourn once again acts to remind him of his own foreignness. Mr. Dorrit's apartment in Venice, for example, shows some of the same characteristics of London's cityscape:

It was quite a walk [to Dorrit's apartment], by mysterious staircases and corridors . . . hoodwinked by a narrow side street with a low gloomy bridge in it, and dungeon-like opposite tenements, their walls besmeared with a thousand downward stains and streaks, as if every crazy aperture in them had been weeping tears of rust into the Adriatic for centuries.

(496)

At the heart of *Little Dorrit* lies a central tension between home and what lies outside it. But since William's home is a prison— literally—everything else seems doubly oppressive because he attempts to recreate the Marshalsea and his status during imprisonment in the outside world. Social mobility in his case is precarious because he has no *psychological* mobility as does, for example, his daughter Fanny, who marries the wealthy Edmund Sparkler (Mr. Merdle's stepson, who not-so-coincidentally accepts a foreign post in the Circumlocution Office). From the very outset of *Little Dorrit*, the reader is thrown into the dichotomy of "Sun and Shadow," the title of the first chapter of the first book—Dickens's terms in this novel for the heightened sensibility and exposure that come with perceived freedom and the darkness and secrecy that come with imprisonment and its aftermath. The novel begins with the glaring—or "staring," as Dickens calls it—sun beating down on the international traders of Marseilles (15). The one spot the sun cannot touch, however, is "a villainous prison" where two men lay in the "refuse of reflected light" among the "unseen vermin" (16). The two prisoners, Cavalleto and Rigaud, who will have much to do with the resolution of the great mystery at the heart of the novel, are, respectively, an Italian smuggler and a French assassin. Thus, the space of the novel is preliminarily delineated as blinding or shadowed, exposed or secreted away, and domestic or foreign. Throughout the novel, these not-so-neat categories shift and overwhelm each other, so that William Dorrit's eventual psychological breakdown encompasses both the sunlight of freedom and the shadow of imprisonment's oppression. William's breakdown also demonstrates his improper place within the system of How Not to Do It: his escape from the confines of bureaucratic law marks him as foreign to the system Dickens illuminates.

Similarly, Flora Finching, protagonist Arthur Clenham's former lover, is trapped by her "oddness" and superfluity in a system whose management enforces participation in its economic schemes. Flora conflates her thwarted love for Clenham with his being forced to work at the family business in China. Required to return to her father's home after she is widowed as a young bride, Flora is an "excess" member of society: unmarried and with no prospects, she turns to food and drink—gustatory excess—to relieve her anxiety. Upon meeting Clenham again, she is obsessed with the fact that "being in China so long and being in business and naturally desirous to settle and extend your connection nothing was more likely than that you should propose to a Chinese lady" with "long and narrow" eyes and "feet screwed back in infancy" (167). Flora cannot imagine Clenham marrying a foreign woman for any reason other than business, and in fact, it seems most "natural" to her that he would want to marry for this reason. Flora's anxiety over her size, age, and marital prospects repeatedly manifests itself as racialized discourse about

Chinese women: "oh do tell me something about the Chinese ladies," she asks Clenham, "whether their eyes are really so long and narrow always putting me in mind of mother-of-pearl fish at cards" (167). In fact, she worries that Clenham himself may have become somehow "infected" by Chinese culture, since he must be so "familiar with the Chinese customs and language which I am persuaded you speak like a Native if not better" (167). Similar to the women she denigrates, however, her "value" in British society has everything to do with her "exchange" value in the British marriage market.[8]

Almost twenty years before Dickens published the novel, but about fifteen years after the time period in which *Little Dorrit* is set, Hong Kong became a colony of Great Britain (1841). Demand for goods remained the main drive in imperial expansion. Despite—or perhaps because of— the fact that Hong Kong was a British colony, British relations with China in the nineteenth century were tendentious at best. The Opium Wars, first (1839–1842) and second (1856–1860), a conflict over the British East India Company smuggling opium from India into China and subsequent Chinese destruction of chests of opium, resulted in Britain retaliating because they said British property had been damaged. Before this, China had the largest economy in the world; afterward, China's GDP was depleted by half. These wars established treaty ports and made Britain China's main trade partner. Thus, relations with the Chinese had everything to do with imperial power and the ethnocentric notions that informed that power. Flora demonstrates her fear that she may not be "marriageable" any longer by intricately tying together Clenham's business, the global economy, and their sexual past as a couple with racist ideology. Flora realizes that she may be as "foreign" a body to Clenham as Chinese women are to her.

William Dorrit finds disease and dis-ease in his foreign surroundings. He can only attain peace through a forgetting—an abandonment—of space. As he travels through the new space of continental Europe, "Mr Dorrit, in his snug corner, fell to castle-building as he rode along [in his carriage to Paris]" (664). By "castle-building" Dickens means the construction of an imaginary home—as someone would do when imagining the floor plans of a future abode—and the construction of a safe space apart from the incomprehensible social milieu in which Dorrit finds himself. After he acquires his wealth, William often,

> ha[s] a very large castle in hand. All day long he was running towers up, taking towers down, adding a wing here, putting on a battlement there, looking to the walls, strengthening the defences, giving ornamental touches to the interior.
>
> (664)

Along the literal road on which he travels, he is building further defenses to secure the "castle" he has acquired. As he sees the foreign road and buildings around him crumble, he builds his tower higher:

> Not a fortified town that they passed in all their journey was as strong, not a Cathedral summit was as high, as Mr. Dorrit's castle. . . . Mr. Dorrit and his matchless castle were disembarked among the dirty white houses and dirtier felons of Civita Vecchia, and thence scrambled on to Rome as they could, through the filth that festered on the way.
>
> (665)

The reality that Dorrit cannot, or does not want to, see outside the window of his carriage is an omen of death and destruction, a reflection of the fictitiousness of his castle and its fortitude. Before his death, Dorrit retreats—not into the walls of the castle he has built—but back into the Marshalsea and then finally into his own body, his own wasted frame. At one of Mrs. Merdle's parties, he announces that he will receive tributes as the Father of the Marshalsea. When he is carried to his quarters, he "knew of nothing beyond the Marshalsea," that "narrow" "London prison" (679). But, finally,

> Quietly, quietly, all the lines of the plan of the great Castle melted one after another. Quietly, quietly, the ruled and cross-ruled countenance on which they were traced, became fair and blank. Quietly, quietly, the reflected marks of the prison bars and of the zig-zag iron on the wall-top, faded away. Quietly, quietly, the face subsided into a far younger likeness of her [Amy's] own than she had ever seen under the grey hair, and sank to rest.
>
> (680–81)

Dorrit is ultimately free, but only at the cost of his life. The interminable tangle of all bureaucratic governments also constrains the individual and forecloses his ability to escape—the economic system; the "free" market; and, for Dorrit and Clenham, the economic prison of the Marshalsea. As Clenham says to Amy when he is in the prison for his own debt, the Marshalsea is a "tainted place," from whence he can hardly escape the "sensation of being stifled," much like William himself (787, 794).

   Throughout the descriptions of the Marshalsea, the Circumlocution Office, and their connection to each other (and the Office's connection to the vagaries of the market), references to the foreign, barbarism, and savagery repeat. The narrator says of Russia, the country where Daniel Doyce finds the success he cannot find in England, that it is "a certain barbaric Power with valuable possessions on the map of the world"

(702). In this comparison, Dickens is highlighting the problems of competing empires. Russia has "valuable possessions" that may increase its wealth and power. "This Power, being a barbaric one," the narrator continues,

> had no idea of stowing away a great national object in a Circumlocution Office, as strong wine is hidden from the light in a cellar, until its fire and youth are gone, and the laborers who worked in the vineyard and pressed the grapes are dust.
>
> (702)

The tone here is reminiscent of Dickens's writings on "The Noble Savage," who is "cruel, false, thievish, murderous; addicted more or less to grease, entrails, and beastly customs; a wild animal with the questionable gift of boasting; a conceited, tiresome, bloodthirsty, monotonous humbug" (1853, 337). Yet, this "savage" and his customs show themselves even in so-called civilized beings: "It is my opinion," writes Dickens, "that if we retained in us anything of the noble savage, we could not get rid of it too soon. But the fact is clearly otherwise" (339). Similarly, those who "worship" at the "altar" of Merdle "prostrated themselves before him, more degradedly and less excusably than the darkest savage creeps out of his hole in the ground to propitiate, in some log or reptile, the Deity of his benighted soul" (Dickens 1998, 581). Savagery comes easily to all humans, even those who claim to be civilized, but the great mission of society is to advance civilization. In comparing England to Russia—its enemy in the Crimean War—on the basis of commerce and invention, Dickens is also making an imperial comparison. For the "great Empire" cannot be of those barbaric powers that conquer only. The Circumlocution Office makes its "troublesome convicts" (567)—and by extension the nation—specimens who, like the African, "[are] not yet awakened to a proper sense of [their] degradation" (Dickens 1848, 69). In these writings, whiteness is codified or reified vis-à-vis Blackness, otherness, Africanness, and "savagery." As in Flora's anxieties over Arthur's sexual relationships with Chinese women, the temptation for or power over foreign markets is dangerous for British prowess.

For those of the Circumlocution Office, however, a lack of accountability is the whole science of governing. When visiting Clenham in prison, Ferdinand Barnacle (Barnacle Junior) hopes that the Office has had nothing to do with Clenham's downfall. He shrugs at the connection between the Circumlocution Office and the many unfortunate men it has ruined: "We don't want to do it; but if men will be gravelled, why—we can't help (Dickens 1998, 769). When Clenham replies that he was taken with the same fervor for investment in Merdle as everyone else in the country, Ferdinand replies, "Pardon me, but I really think you have no idea how the human bees will swarm to the beating of any old tin kettle; in that fact lies the complete manual of governing them" (771). The Office is "nothing but forms" (769). Like the shadowy figures pacing the prison courtyard; like the indigent families of Bleeding Heart Yard, who "was all hard up there," but "couldn't say how it was"; and even like Clenham himself, the product of a "grim home" in a neighborhood rife with "oppressive secrets," the men and women of *Little Dorrit*'s London are bound to an economic system that stifles all joy and creativity through its reliance on mystery and pure form(ality) (157, 567). Clenham thinks that even the dead in the church-vaults were "hoarded and secreted," "not yet at rest from doing harm," as they had "hoarded and secreted" in their living lives (567). In Dickens's novel, as we see here, physical space; institutional space; and foreign, domestic, and colonial economies, are tightly bound in an inextricable relationship that appears to be the product of chance and yet is solely the product of the institutional policy of How Not to Do It and its consistent replication across space and time.

Mr. Meagles, "who never by any accident acquired any knowledge whatever of the language of any country into which he travelled," and "address[ed] individuals of all nations in idiomatic English, with a perfect conviction that they were bound to understand it somehow," in many ways espouses the systems and philosophies Dickens criticizes in his novel (37). For the England and Englishness of which Dickens writes is one that expects Englishness wherever it goes, without any interruption or disruption from those "incoherent races" that do not understand its customs (855). Yet, most of the characters we meet in *Little Dorrit* (along with the shadowy foreign figures haunting its pages) are members of these "races": the poor of Bleeding Heart; the "prison child" Amy; the forever-ten-year-old disabled friend of Amy, Maggy; the disillusioned and wandering Clenham; and, of course, William himself. If "place" in the institutional jargon of the novel means "home," "location," and "status," then William is "A wreck. A ruin. Mouldering away, before our eyes" after he leaves the Marshalsea because he has confounded all three (391, 673). For William Dorrit, "the truth of subjectivity requires a detour through otherness," a detour "obstruct[ed]" by "the epistemological rupture of capitalist crisis" (Parker 2014, 132). Dorrit's "other" is actually himself as a wealthy man, but he cannot recognize this, having constructed the fantasy of his own gentility before he had any money on which to base it. Thus, the colonial hierarchies of wealth and status, domesticity and foreignness, work against Dorrit, leaving "his poor maimed spirit, only remembering the place where it had broken its wings" and, "cancel[ing] the dream through which it had since groped, . . . knew of nothing beyond the Marshalsea." (Dickens 1998, 679).

At the time of writing *Little Dorrit*, Dickens wrote a letter to W. C. Macready lamenting, "I do reluctantly believe that the English people are habitually consenting parties to the miserable imbecility into which we have fallen, *and never will help themselves out of it*. Who is to do it, if anybody is, God knows" (as quoted in Yeazell 1991, 37; emphasis in original). Dickens's fatalism on this account mirrors the bleakness with which he treats the institutional aspects of his novel, but it also demonstrates one of the central dichotomies of *Little Dorrit* upon which I have been trying to elaborate: not doing "it" has become an English characteristic, one that "infects" citizens at home and abroad. In fact, what William Dorrit represents more than anything are the vicissitudes of capitalist life that shake up the natural order of active citizenship at home and in foreign and colonial spaces. For Ruth Yeazell, this has to do with gendered work in the novel. But, I argue, it also has to do with tensions between bureaucratic politics at home and in places where the British have attempted to translate those politics abroad. As Yeazell points out, "*Little Dorrit* suggests that what is troubling about men's work is not merely that it conflicts with a dream of genteel leisure, but that it is inevitably implicated in a system of mutual theft and violence" (39). That "mutual theft and violence" is primarily monetary, but as we see in William's case, also psychological. Imprisonment, in other words, is a type of violence perpetuated against the "incoherent" masses with recourse only to a bureaucratic system designed to keep them in their place. Additionally, *Little Dorrit* is an important example of the ways in which the empire and perceptions of foreignness could substitute for ideas about domestic life and government. Dickens's use of the foreign as a metaphor or shorthand for the mysteries of capitalism demonstrates that this novel, as is the case with many other British novels of the period, had already begun to see the colonial and metropolitan economy as closely entwined—so closely, in fact, that the power inherent in the creation of imperial markets could be easily obscured and defended, as Dickens himself did on many occasions.

Notes

1. For more about temporality, perception, power, and visuality, see Elaine Tierney, " 'Dirty Rotten Sheds': Exploring the Ephemeral City in Early Modern London," *Eighteenth-Century Studies* 50, no. 2 (2017): 231–52 and Jayda Coons, " 'Spectral Realities': *Little Dorrit*, Stereoscopy, and Non-mimetic Realism," *Nineteenth-Century Contexts* 42, no. 1 (2020): 17–31.
2. See Elaine Hadley, "Nobody, Somebody, and Everybody," *Victorian Studies* 59, no. 1 (Autumn 2016): 65–86.
3. See Sajni Mukherji, "Telescopic Philanthropy: Attitudes to Charity and the Empire in Charles Dickens," *Economic and Political Weekly* 16, no. 42/43 (October 17–24, 1981): PE9—PE18; Lillian Nayder, "Class Consciousness and the Indian Mutiny in Dickens's 'The Perils of Certain English Prisoners,' " *Studies in English Literature, 1500–1900* 32, no. 4 (Autumn 1992): 689–705; and Alex Tickell, "*The Perils of Certain English Prisoners*: Charles Dickens, Wilkie Collins, and the Limits of Colonial Government," *Nineteenth-Century Literature* 67, no. 4 (March 1, 2013): 457–489.

4. See Hannah Arendt, *The Origins of Totalitarianism* (New York: Harvest, 1976).
5. Ruth Yeazell writes in her article, "Do It or Dorrit" that rather than not conducting business correctly, "How Not to Do It" means finding ways not to conduct business or run the country at all, phrased differently, "how to *not* do it." Yeazell, "Do It or Dorrit," *NOVEL* 25, no. 1 (Autumn 1991): 35.
6. See Elaine Freedgood, *The Ideas in Things: Fugitive Meaning in the Victorian Novel* (Chicago: University of Chicago Press, 2006).
7. Ben Parker sees this as part of the "structural blindspot" inherent in capitalist crisis. Parker, "Recognition or Reification?: Capitalist Crisis and Subjectivity in *Little Dorrit*," *New Literary History* 45, no. 1 (Winter 2014): 135.
8. See Yeazell, "Do It or Dorrit" for a reading of sexuality and gender in *Little Dorrit*.

References

Arendt, Hannah. (1951) 1976. *The Origins of Totalitarianism*. New York, NY: Harvest.

Church, R. A. 1971. "The British Leather Industry and Foreign Competition, 1870–1914." *The Economic History Review* 24 (4): 543–70. https://doi.org/10.2307/2648914.

Coons, Jayda. 2020. "'Spectral Realities': Little Dorrit, Stereoscopy, and Non-Mimetic Realism." *Nineteenth-Century Contexts* 42 (1): 17–31. https://doi.org/10.1080/08905495.2019.1686935.

Dick, Alexander J. 2012. "On the Financial Crisis, 1825–26." BRANCH: Britain, Representation and Nineteenth-Century History. 2012. www.branchcollective.org/?ps_articles=alexander-j-dick-on-the-financial-crisis-1825-26.

Dickens, Charles. 1848. "Review of The Narrative of the Expedition Sent by Her Majesty's Government to the River Niger in 1841, under the Command of Captain H. D. Trotter, R. N." *The Examiner*, August, 531–33.

———. 1853. "The Noble Savage." *Household Words* 1 (40): 337–39.

———. (1860) 1900. *The Uncommercial Traveller*. New York, NY: Doubleday.

———. (1857) 1998. *Little Dorrit*. Edited by Stephen Wall and Helen Small. New York, NY: Penguin Press.

Fleishman, Avrom. 1974. "Master and Servant in Little Dorrit." *Studies in English Literature, 1500–1900* 14 (4): 575–86. https://doi.org/10.2307/449755.

Freedgood, Elaine. 2006. *The Ideas in Things: Fugitive Meaning in the Victorian Novel*. Chicago, IL: University of Chicago Press.

Hadley, Elaine. 2016. "Nobody, Somebody, and Everybody." *Victorian Studies* 59 (1): 65–86. https://doi.org/10.2979/victorianstudies.59.1.03.

Lee, Klaudia Hiu Yen. 2013. "Cross-Cultural Adaptation of Dickensian Spatiality: The Case of Little Dorrit." *English: Journal of the English Association* 62 (236): 6–21. https://doi.org/10.1093/english/eft002.

Lefebvre, Henri. (1974) 1991. *The Production of Space*. Translated by Donald Nicholson-Smith. Malden, MA: Wiley-Blackwell.

Moore, Grace. 2009. "Turkish Robbers, Lumps of Delight, and the Detritus of Empire: The East Revisited in Dickens's Late Novels." *Critical Survey* 21 (1): 74–87. https://doi.org/10.3167/cs.2009.210106.

Mukherji, Sajni. 1981. "Telescopic Philanthropy: Attitudes to Charity and the Empire in Charles Dickens." *Economic and Political Weekly* 16 (42/43): 9–18.

Nayder, Lillian. 1992. "Class Consciousness and the Indian Mutiny in Dickens's 'The Perils of Certain English Prisoners.'" *Studies in English Literature, 1500–1900* 32 (4): 689–705. https://doi.org/10.2307/450966.

Parker, Ben. 2014. "Recognition or Reification? Capitalist Crisis and Subjectivity in Little Dorrit." *New Literary History* 45 (1): 131–51. https://doi.org/10.1353/nlh.2014.0004.

Poovey, Mary. 1995. *Making a Social Body: British Cultural Formation, 1830–1864*. Chicago, IL: University of Chicago Press.

Rosenthal, Jesse. 2017. "The Untrusted Medium: Open Networks, Secret Writing, and Little Dorrit." *Victorian Studies* 59 (2): 288–313. https://doi.org/10.2979/victorianstudies.59.2.04.

Tickell, Alex. 2013. "The Perils of Certain English Prisoners: Charles Dickens, Wilkie Collins, and the Limits of Colonial Government." *Nineteenth-Century Literature* 67 (4): 457–89. https://doi.org/10.1525/ncl.2013.67.4.457.

Tierney, Elaine. 2017. "'Dirty Rotten Sheds': Exploring the Ephemeral City in Early Modern London." *Eighteenth-Century Studies* 50 (2): 231–52. https://doi.org/10.1353/ecs.2017.0005.

Yeazell, Ruth Bernard. 1991. "Do It or Dorrit." *NOVEL: A Forum on Fiction* 25 (1): 33–49. https://doi.org/10.2307/1345660.

3   "For God's Sake, Women, Go Out and Play"

Nomadic Space in the Work of Ethel Carnie Holdsworth

Patricia E. Johnson

The work of Ethel Carnie Holdsworth has, in recent years, received new-found and much deserved attention from critics and scholars. Writing between 1907 and 1935, Carnie Holdsworth is recognized as the first British working-class woman novelist, with a publishing record that includes ten novels (one of which was made into a silent film), a novella, three books of poetry, four books of original fairy tales, and numerous short stories and editorials. She worked in a factory for almost a decade, having started half-time work at age eleven. In addition, she had a vigorous political career, supporting unionism and women's suffrage, campaigning for international socialism, and, in 1922, co-founding England's first anti-fascist organization (Smalley 2006). While her political career addressed many areas of working-class life, her writing focuses on the lives of working-class women.

Given her impressive achievements, it is surprising that Carnie Holdsworth's work has been so often overlooked. The first discussion of her comes in Edmund and Ruth Frow's overview of her life and work in H. Gustav Klaus's *The Rise of Socialist Fiction, 1880–1914* (1987). Then, in *Class Fictions: Shame and Resistance in the British Working-Class Novel, 1890–1945* (1994), Pamela Fox analyzed several of her novels in conjunction with Ellen Wilkinson's better-known *Clash* (1929). Only in the last ten years has Carnie Holdsworth's work received sustained attention, including studies by Roger Smalley (2006) and Nicola Wilson (2015) alongside the republication of several novels and her collected poetry. How did such an important, trailblazing writer fall out of sight? Certain answers are clear. As noted in other essays in this collection, working-class women writers experienced far more marginalization than their male counterparts, their voices often ignored or, worse, erased from history. One reason that little attention is paid to the novels of a writer like Carnie Holdsworth is that they do not conform to the plot of working-class protest that the male novelists established. With the exception of her 1925 novel, *This Slavery*, set in a factory town during a strike, Carnie Holdsworth fits this pattern. Also, as Fox argues, many of her novels focus on the marriage plot, which critics of working-class writing have traditionally rejected as

DOI: 10.4324/9781003119425-4

escapist fantasy. A contributing factor may be that, while her early novels were often published with the note that they were by Ethel Carnie, "an ex-mill girl," her later novels appeared under her married name, Ethel Carnie Holdsworth, or even Ethel Holdsworth, and the trajectory of her career was lost or ignored. Another reason for her long obscurity is that, unlike Ellen Wilkinson who became a Labour cabinet minister, Carnie Holdsworth did not fit easily into any political movement and remained, despite her successes, part of the working class. In 1924, she described her political independence: "I do not belong to any anarchist group or any other group. I belong to the folk" ("Editorial", 52). Despite such claims, her politics and values aligned with radical positions and social justice.

Carnie Holdsworth's oeuvre is challenging to interpret because she shifts from genre to genre (from poetry to fairytales to fiction), even in her novels (from bildungsroman to Gothic melodrama and from social protest to mystery). Her heroines are often equally restless; they are constantly on the move, leaving the city for the country and back again, switching jobs at will, and hitting the road when they suspect their relationships are turning sour. In this regard, Carnie Holdsworth's narratives offer a marked distinction from class-based story lines that often center on sites of industry or fixed, imprisoning communities. While most of her heroines end up married, many of the marriages are deeply flawed. Because of this, Fox and Wilson focus their interpretations, respectively, on her use of the marriage plot and the image of the home. The focus of this essay, by contrast, is on moments that occur away from the spaces that working-class women are typically identified with, such as home, factory, and neighborhood, instead showing them outside in nature.

Two novels that bookend her career, her first novel, *Miss Nobody* (1913), and her penultimate novel, *Barbara Dennison* (1929), contain passages that describe their heroines' experiences on the road or off-road in nature. These moments, described in detail and at considerable length, take place in the interstices of the plot. The novels' plots, in fact, can be summarized without mentioning them at all. The argument of this essay is that these unplotted, seemingly extraneous moments are vitally important to Carnie Holdsworth's vision of life for working-class women. They become, in fact, the spaces where she and her heroines are free to imagine a future for themselves, a future that does not subject them to the needs of others. In nature, her heroines define their lives for themselves, resisting the definitions and demands of the upper classes and working-class men. The upper classes wanted working-class women to be obedient domestic servants or conforming wives and mothers; working-class men depended on women's unpaid and paid labor, as well as their political support, for their claim to be heads of respectable, successful households. Given these powerful factors—economic, political, psychological—Carnie Holdsworth looks far afield for spaces that are free from such pressures.

Only outside of working-class homes, streets, and neighborhoods can her heroines not only escape entrapment, but discover the free, fluid, natural spaces necessary to reimagine themselves and their lives.

Nature in Carnie Holdsworth's Writing

Nature emerges as an important theme in Carnie Holdsworth's writing from her first book-length publication, *Rhymes from the Factory*. In the preface, she states, "I think it is no exaggeration to say all my poems came into my head at the mill" (1908, vii). But, despite this, the rhymes do not describe factory work, although they repeatedly call attention to the workers' impoverished lives and surroundings. What the poems represent, especially the poems on nature, is an escape from factory work and poverty. "Night," for example, "brings to the weary millions in crowded city tenements/Dreams of the lovely emerald vale, with its silvery singing streamlet." Another poem "Resurrection" declares, "Nature designs that all things should be glad," although this source of joy is usually unavailable to workers. As Smalley states, "Few of her poems lack a reverent reference to nature" (2006, 100), and he sees in her work a pantheistic belief in its spiritual power similar to that of the British Romantic poets.

Thus, Carnie Holdsworth continues the Romantic/Victorian tradition of nature poetry, but she also changes it by inflecting it with class and gender consciousness: for her, nature is a space of freedom and renewal particularly needed by the working class, especially working-class women. When she briefly held the post of editor of *The Woman Worker* (1909–1910), she published a number of editorials that address overlooked aspects of working-class life. In the 1909 editorial, "Our Right to Play," she urges,

> For God's sake, women, go out and play.
> Instead of staring round to see what wants polishing or rubbing, go out into the open and draw the breath of the moors or the hills into your lungs. Get some of the starshine and sunlight into your souls, and do not forget that you are something more than a dish washer—that you are more necessary to the human race than politicians—or anything.
> Remember you belong to the aristocracy of labour—the long pedigree of toil, and the birthright which Nature gives to everyone had entitled you to an estate higher than that of princes.
>
> (342)

As this command demonstrates, Carnie Holdsworth's viewpoint and voice are unique, speaking directly to working-class women with words that are squarely based on her sense of their entrapment. Her viewpoint is her own, not indebted to the labor or women's suffrage movements. She speaks from a position outside the political structures of her time and outside of typical working-class cultural assumptions. It should come as no surprise that she lost her position with *The Woman Worker* after seven months, apparently removed by the owner, socialist Robert Blatchford, because her editorials were too radical.

While the central plots of Carnie Holdsworth's novels focus on their working-class heroines in relation to work and marriage, there is a repeated pattern of the heroines walking in nature. A number of her fictions are set in rural England (*Helen of Four Gates*, *General Belinda*, *All on Her Own*) where this might be expected, but even the city-bred and factory heroines roam. *Miss Nobody* and *Barbara Dennison* develop the meanings of these spaces in detail, presenting them as more than escapes from toil or even necessary spiritual refreshment. They become, in fact, alternative spaces for life. In *Miss Nobody*, Carrie Brown visits the primitive hiding place of a poor worker and talks to a tramp on the road, considering these examples as a way, not of just temporarily escaping the oppressions of her life, but as permanent alternatives. By the time of *Barbara Dennison*, who regularly spends the day climbing in the wild space of Ridgely Fells, nature transforms consciousness. Drawing on Deleuze and Guattari's theory of nomadism to unpack the meanings of these experiences, I will argue that nomadic space allows these characters access to a non-hierarchical space of becoming that is always in motion, always connecting, allowing them to see and define themselves outside the delimiting structures of society.

Historical Context

No discussion of Carnie Holdsworth's work can take place without an understanding of the unique position of working-class women in British culture in the first decades of the twentieth century. That position was, first of all, a development of nineteenth-century domestic ideology. Throughout the nineteenth century, factory girls who exercised the freedom to walk together in the streets and to dress as they pleased were portrayed as oversexed and masculine by Parliamentary commissioners and middle-class observers (Rose 1992). British working-class men were also interested in keeping their women in their place and protested against factory work for women by marching in the streets carrying washing tubs to demonstrate that, when women worked in factories, the natural order of things was reversed, with men reduced to doing housework. The labor and union movements, which could have supported women's rights to safe, well-paid work and social freedom, focused their energies on achieving suffrage for men and the male household wage (Clark 1995). Concerns about women's wages were dismissed as distractions from the central problem of the male wage, and issues that specifically concerned working-class women, such as sexual harassment in the workplace, were largely ignored. The most extreme example of control and policing of working-class women came from the late nineteenth-century Contagious Diseases Acts. These acts legislated that suspicious women on the streets could be forcibly seized as suspected prostitutes, subjected to examination for venereal disease, and then confined to lock hospitals. This provides startling evidence of how harsh the surveillance, control, and punishment of working-class women's behavior could be.

The twentieth century might seem to be the dawning of a new age of freedom for British working-class women, but control of their lives continued by other, more subtle means. As part of its effort to guarantee working-class men their place as head of house, working-class culture enforced its own version of domestic ideology. As F. M. L. Thompson (1988) argues in *The Rise of Respectable Society*, by the end of the nineteenth century, respectability was a primary measure by which working-class men were able to secure their goals. This meant increased policing of women's behavior, even more than their own. Women, of course, could share in the success that respectability represented, but it trapped them more fully than their husbands.

Elizabeth Roberts's *A Woman's Place: An Oral History of Working-Class Women, 1890–1940*, provides a detailed picture of how circumscribed women's lives were during this time period. The "street" a woman lived on, represented by her neighbors, was controlling and censorious, keeping tabs on both sexual behavior and domestic work. Surveillance and gossip gave each woman a "character"; as one woman put it, "'she was a nice lass or she wasn't'" (1984, 193). Much of this surveillance was provided by working-class women themselves. They judged their neighbors by how clean their front doorsteps were, by how often they washed their curtains, and by how often they visited outside their own house. Another of Roberts's informants described how a housewife was expected to clean "the front doorstep and four flags to the right": "You used to stand at the top of the street and look down and the next row of flags from the door was yellow or white all the way down" (193). These demands meant working-class wives were in an "unceasing battle to keep [their homes] clean" (131–32), a battle made all the more difficult by the pollution and lack of running water in factory towns. Roberts sums up the impact of this almost all-encompassing system:

> The rules were unwritten, but understood by all. Those who broke them were punished by self-appointed judges and juries. . . . [T]he system interfered with and influenced many aspects of life which would now be regarded as matters of individual choice and decision, and it produced a very conforming and conformist class of people.
> (192)

Working-class husbands enforced additional rules, often order-ing their wives to stay in the house, even when it came to socializing with neighbors. While they could find male companionship in the fac-tory and pub, they expected their homes to be quiet, private, and free from casual visitors (196). In an illustrative story, Roberts quotes a Mrs. Pearce from Preston who described what happened when she heard a noise in the street and looked out the window to see what it was: her husband responded, " 'Sit down!' . . . My husband would never allow me to have anybody in. They might come for change for the gas, or something like that, but I never had a neighbor in" (196). A woman interviewed by health advocate Margery Spring-Rice describes a similar entrapment:

> My life for many years consisted of being penned in a kitchen 9 feet square, every fourteen months a baby, as I had five babies in five years at first, until what with the struggle to live and no leisure I used to feel I was just a machine. . . . It is the old idea we should always be at home.
>
> (94)

It is against this background of social control that Carnie Holdsworth's images of space on the road and off-road in nature—as opposed to the censorious space of the "street" and the entrapping space of the home—stand out as a longing for freedom.

Theoretical Approaches to Carnie Holdsworth's Use of Space

As a way of highlighting the radical implications of Carnie Holdsworth's use of outdoor space, this essay draws on Deleuze and Guattari's theory of nomadic space in *A Thousand Plateaus* and its elaboration by feminist Rosi Braidotti. Trapped by systemic cultural and personal exploitation and under almost constant surveillance, Carnie Holdsworth's working-class heroines follow roads in search of culturally unmapped spaces. Off-road moments in Carnie Holdsworth's novels are a part of her con-tinuing search for alternative spaces in which working-class women can unshackle themselves from the bonds of class, gender, and British cultural traditions and define their lives for themselves.

Deleuze and Guattari provide an image of the nomad that resonates with Carnie Holdsworth's restless heroines. This conceptualization of the nomad and nomadicism is grounded in the principle that space functions as the upshot of behavior and actions. Seeking to escape state surveillance and hierarchy, Deleuze and Guattari's nomads leave "striated space," with its rigid state-defined divisions and regulations, to seek "smooth space" that is unmapped and uncontrolled. This smooth nomadic space also provides lateral connections that are non-linear, non-hierarchical, and anti-centric (1987, 381). It is limiting, however, to think of Deleuze and Guattari's theories as about strictly physical movement and literal nomadism. In *Nomadic Subjects*, Rosi Braidotti argues that, while nomadism can be a physical experience, it can also be the development of a "kind of critical consciousness" (1994, 5) that takes an individual beyond the confines of her classed and gendered cultural position. Ultimately, "Nomadic consciousness is a form of political resistance to hegemonic and exclusionary views of subjectivity" (23). This is the nomadism that Carnie Holdsworth's characters pursue.

Miss Nobody (1913)

Carnie Holdsworth's first novel, *Miss Nobody*, features a fascinating heroine. Pamela Fox points out that Carrie Brown "has a distinctly New Womanish air" and reminds an onlooker of the suffragettes (1994, 154). She is also unapologetically working class. As the title *Miss Nobody* indicates, Carrie Brown is one of "the masses," a young woman who was raised in a foundling home, worked as a servant, and is, as the novel opens, the sole proprietor of a Manchester oyster shop. She is twenty-six years old, with blue eyes, frizzed yellow hair, and a missing front tooth. Aside from considering herself "of the folk," she is nothing like her creator, having no literary interests except for escapist romances and so little knowledge of politics that she does not know what socialism is. What she does have is boundless energy and curiosity. *Miss Nobody* charts Carrie's adventures in an almost picaresque fashion. During the course of the novel, Carrie leaves Manchester for a marriage of convenience with farmer Robert Gibson and leaves him after several months to return to Manchester where she works, first, in a flax factory, and then, in a Christmas card factory. After organizing a strike, she is blacklisted by Manchester factories. At the novel's end, she returns to her husband and the farm.

My reading of *Miss Nobody* approaches the novel through a spatial lens. Because of her attraction to silver fork romances, one might assume that Carrie's life is about finding a romantic partner. But reframing the novel as a search for an alternative space allows a different narrative to emerge. At some point in the novel, Carrie will hold most of the positions open to working-class women and find them lacking. Her most hated job was her first one as a servant. Her opening work in the oyster shop allows her freedom from oversight—she is the proprietor—but she labors in a small, hot kitchen and stands behind a counter, dealing with drunk patrons. She accepts Robert's offer of marriage, which, despite her romance novels, is a practical decision: she reasons, "It was the best offer she had ever had, or that she would ever have, in all probability"

(2013, 37). In fact, she is much more romantic about the space the farm offers. She loves the wide view of the blue sky:

> She saw fields of waving meadow grass, infinite spaces of tender, blue sky bending down to them. The sky fascinated Carrie. It looked so different here in the country from the narrow, hand's-breadth between the grey houses as she viewed it in slack moments from the door of the oyster-shop.
>
> (10)

Carrie wants to "drink all that blue, soothing colour into her tired soul" (10). Her view of nature is a Romantic one, intensified by her working-class life.

When she finds the farm entrapping, she leaves, but factory jobs mean 10 hours a day in ill-lit, shabby rooms. While she enjoys the fellowship of the other factory women in both the flax factory and the Christmas card shop, there are harsh supervisors. The overseer in the Christmas card factory keeps such a close watch on the women that she is nick-named "the Eye" (142) who "[w]atches you like a cat watches a mouse" (139). Every space that Carrie occupies offers only different degrees and forms of imprisonment. This parallels Deleuze and Guattari's "striated space," state-regulated, rigidly hierarchical, and surveilled by overseers who punish those who step out of bounds.

During the course of her life, at significant moments when Carrie finds herself trapped or at a crossroad, her movements, on and off-road, are described in great detail, and it is in these moments that she catches a glimpse of deterritorialized space and its potential to alter the self. This reflects Deleuze and Guattari's "smooth space," one that offers fluid freedom outside of state surveillance and control. In this sense, the individual is defined less by the confines of the space itself and more through motion and orientations in flux. Notably, the reader first sees Carrie in literal motion, taking a train trip from Manchester to Greenmeads, the small country town where her married sister lives. There, playing with her sister's children, she rolls down a lovely green hill. At this moment she meets her future husband, Robert Gibson, who tells her that she is trespassing on his land. When he tracks her down to her oyster shop in Manchester, Carrie expects him to deliver her a summons for trespass; instead, he makes a practical offer of marriage. This contrast provides the shape of Carrie's choices: arrest for trespass or what turns out to be another kind of legal confinement.

Once settled on Gibson's farm, Carrie tries to make her marriage work. She and Robert, while not romantically attached, get along well and could make a success of their bargain, but Robert's possessive sister Sarah's resentment makes life unbearable. She oversees and criticizes Carrie's every movement. Along with the other censorious women of

Greenmeads, she makes it clear that Carrie is an outsider, an unwelcome interloper. In their culminating confrontation, Sarah accuses Carrie of marrying for money while Carrie counters that, despite its blue skies, the farm has turned out to be "a prison": "I consider it next door to Holloway, where they puts Suffragettes, except the winders are bigger and there's no forcible feeding—an' you do the cooking for the jailers" (77). The forceful, political language of Carrie's description makes it clear that she is rebelling against her society's denial of women's freedom. Carrie had left the city for security and because she liked to look at the countryside's blue sky, but life there makes her feel imprisoned and under constant surveillance.

At this turning point in her life, Carrie has a significant off-road experience, involving another outsider in Greenmeads, a "queer" man named Peter Moss who has eyes "wondering as a child's whose reason is just awakening" (11). Peter lives with his older sister who takes in laundry to supplement her husband's income, but Peter does most of the work. Every few weeks, however, he disappears, leaving the village to wonder where he has gone. After her confrontation with Sarah, Carrie leaves the house, as she often does, to wander on the moor over "brown bog-patches where local tradition had it that witches had once built the midnight fire to boil the evil potion" (82). In contrast to her strong feeling of oppression and imprisonment at the farm, "the wild moor . . . gave her a savage joy" (81). This space, uncultivated by her culture, allows Carrie a momentary freedom.

Then, as a storm breaks, she stumbles upon the primitive hideout where Peter Moss escapes his sister's demands. Carrie observes the alternative space he has constructed for himself. Like a bird, he has gathered the bits and pieces the environment affords him: what is left of an abandoned house, a "slab of stone" for a table, and "a bed of ling and moss" (84). As Carrie shelters from the storm with him, Peter hesitantly describes the beauties of his retreat in language that is "a rude poetry" (86). In this unmapped spot, outside of social control, Peter finds treasures such as "the silver moon," where no one can come and "[t]ake it and squander it, and lend it and buy things with it" (85). For a while, Peter can live as the birds do, outside of society's regulated economy, in smooth space.

As they meet in this primitive space, Carrie and Peter establish the nomadic non-hierarchical relationship that Deleuze and Guattari describe. Despite their obvious differences, Carrie and Peter have much in common. Both are outsiders to the village community and viewed with suspicion by it. Both resist their enslavement to the capitalist system that measures their existence in monetary terms. Most importantly, both derive intense pleasure from being outside their culture's boundaries in the natural world. Carrie's "savage joy" on the moors is matched by Peter's "fierce, deep joy" at seeing the stars through the gaps in the roof of his shelter (86). To Carrie, Gibson's comfortable farmhouse is a prison while Peter sees his shelter as "[b]etter nor a pallis" (84). Peter has found a place like the one Carrie searches for, outside the systemic control of their society.

Carrie's last-described encounter on the road comes at another significant crossroad. After she is blacklisted in Manchester, in a chapter titled "The Long, White Road," Carrie decides to return to Greenmeads, hoping her sister will find her cleaning jobs. "The Long, White Road" describes her failed attempt to walk to Greenmeads because she cannot afford the train fare. This is Carrie's most literally nomadic moment in the novel, unattached, at this point, to Britain's social or economic structure. Here she pursues Deleuze and Guattari's "lines of flight" (1987, 381) and considers what it would be like to stay on the road permanently as a perennially dynamic entity. She notices that people look at her strangely when they see her and realizes they think she is a tramp: "Why, everybody who was on the road who had no work was a tramp! That was all it meant, that despised word—people for whom there was no work and no place were tramps" (Carnie Holdsworth 2013, 147). Now, having fallen off society's hierarchical scale, Carrie questions what it costs to be placed on it, thinking perhaps it is "better to be a tramp than a flax-mill girl, struggling along on a wretched ten shillings a week" (147). The tramp had a freedom the flax-mill girl would never know: "a tramp would always have the wide, clear sky over his head, the earth beneath his feet, and no eye, mean and watchful, like that at the end of the table, upon him" (147). For the moment, Carrie pictures literal nomadic life as a concrete good, a smooth space that would allow an access to nature and freedom from surveillance that working-class women never know.

Then, almost in answer to her thoughts, a tramp joins her on the road and the two are immediately connected by their experience of having nothing. The tramp confirms Carrie's thoughts about the life of a tramp; he is "unafraid," "jovial," with "memories of strange things he has seen" in his eyes (148). The tramp tells Carrie that "[l]ast week my second old woman died" and invites her to join him (148). Implicitly, he is offering companionship without marriage, but it comes at a cost: they must exist on the margins or outside society's boundaries. Carrie is attracted to the idea, but, thinking it over, she refuses because she recognizes, "no, her heart was not big enough, brave enough. She loved a corner and things of her own," and she fears being old without a fireside to rest at (148). Here Carrie confronts her desire for a nest of her own and the ultimate cost of life on the road: lack of safety and an early death. As the tramp tells her, "Bless you, . . . we never get old. We die young, afore the bloom is gone. . . . A short life, and a merry 'un" (150). Peter, too, finally commits suicide in his hiding place. Carrie learns that living physically as a nomad is too costly. Again, the shape of Carrie's choice is dire: imprisonment in society's system or an early death outside it.

Courtesy of several deus ex machina, including a murder trial and an inheritance, *Miss Nobody* ends with Carrie happily reunited with her husband. The overarching pattern of the novel, however, is movement, followed by stasis, and then movement again, revealing its working-class heroine's search for an alternative space of freedom. In *A Thousand Plateaus*, Deleuze and Guattari describe how the nomad "distributes himself in a smooth space" and is taken up with "immobility and speed, catatonia and rush" (1987, 381). As they argue, the nomad is always moving and becoming, rather than focused on being or existing in sedentary states. In consonance with this, *Miss Nobody*'s ending is not a conventional celebration of Carrie and Robert's restored marriage but a widening out to other lives and other paths. Its concluding words expand Carrie's incomplete quest to "the masses" she represents, imagining their lives as a continual searching down a long road: "But up and down the lamplit roads Youth wandered, and Hope and Love, . . . dreaming star hued dreams. Are not our dreams the lamps on a rainy road?" (Carnie Holdsworth 2013, 229). At moments, Carrie had tried to find a literal escape from the striated system that contains her life; now other, newer wanderers will continue her quest.

Barbara Dennison (1929)

Sixteen years after *Miss Nobody*, Carnie Holdsworth published her penultimate novel, *Barbara Dennison*. The interim between the beginning of her career as a novelist and what would turn out to be near its end was a momentous one. Wider historical events that had a direct impact on Carnie Holdsworth included WWI, the Russian Revolution, the passage of women's suffrage, and the rise of fascism. Personally, she had married, and, along with her husband, opposed the war. Then her husband was conscripted and wrongly listed as dead. When he returned home from a prisoner of war camp, they edited the anti-fascist newspaper, *The Clear Light*, together. But although they shared two daughters as well as political sympathies, Arthur Holdsworth's mental problems led his wife to separate from him in 1928 (Smalley 2006). Carnie Holdsworth had always believed that marriage was unsatisfactory as a goal for working-class women, and *Barbara Dennison* charts her complete disillusionment with the institution.

But, along with that disillusionment, her heroine Barbara finds the imaginative "smooth space" and critical consciousness that allow her a freedom of thought undiscovered by Carrie. Like Carrie, Barbara Dennison is a working-class heroine whose search for a meaningful life is played out in spatial terms. Barbara constantly moves between two charged spaces, her marital home in London and a wild region called

Ridgely Fells outside the country village where she was raised. Unlike Carrie, Barbara's off-road experiences transform her consciousness and lead her to a different view of life. The novel also reveals the shifts that have taken place in working-class women's lives in the 1920s. Now the forces that delimit them have changed: factory work and looming poverty are replaced with consumerism and the pressures of "respectability."

When Barbara's father, a sailor, dies, her disreputable mother gives her to a childless couple from the village of Rimton in Northern England. Although Dan and Sarah are poor people—Dan is a wagoner who sells provisions—they also foster another child, Dave Reid, and manage to give both Barbara and Dave a good education. Barbara's work as a teacher is cut short, however, when she marries Critchie Dennison, a clerk in London's Goffey's Emporium. The novel traces the dissolution of Barbara's marriage, along with Dave's growing realization that, although raised like brother and sister, he and Barbara are "mates," bound together by their nomadic hikes to the unmapped space of Ridgely Fells. But, as with *Miss Nobody*, to read this plot only in relation to marriage and personal relationships, leaves out a significant dimension. In *Barbara Dennison*, Ridgely Fells represents, in fact, the most significant dimension, more important to Barbara than her marriage to Critchie or her relationship to Dave. It has the power to liberate Barbara, giving her a space for freedom and the ability to create a critical consciousness separate from her culture's demands.

Barbara Dennison opens with Critchie's and Barbara's first wedding anniversary in their newly furnished London home and quickly reveals the cracks that will destroy their marriage. Critchie values possessions and is so focused on climbing up the class hierarchy by achieving a junior partnership at Goffer's that he has forgotten their first wedding anniversary. Barbara values the almond tree outside and is delighted to hear a man singing in the street as he walks by their door. Critchie sees Barbara as his possession too, and his main objective on their anniversary is to instruct her to value possessions as he does.

The central means by which their conflicting viewpoints are revealed is the description of the house that Critchie has provided for Barbara. Their bedroom is filled with objects: an eiderdown blanket, a dressing table with a Venetian jar on it, Barbara's silver slippers with Cuban heels. As he watches her wake up, Critchie thinks that "[n]o woman has a more comfortable home" (Carnie Holdsworth 1929, 15). He itemizes what he has paid for its furnishings: a "satin-wood wardrobe" for eighteen-eighteen and a porcelain screen for "[s]even, six and eleven" (16). His home contains the "best the Emporium could give for money" (25).

As Barbara wakes up, it is clear that she is indifferent to, even embarrassed by, the glossy new objects her husband has surrounded her with. When she hurriedly dresses and rips her stockings, Critchie complains that they are "the best the Emporium had in stock, double-heeled, best woven—" and instructs her, "I want you to have beautiful things, Barbara. But you might take care of them" (18). This includes maintaining herself, by powdering her shiny nose and not laughing in a way that Critchie complains will give her wrinkles. Even in this first scene, though still behaving like honeymooners, their irritation with each other begins to surface. Critchie and Barbara will never have an open confrontation about these issues, only less and less to say to one another. This first conversation establishes their completely opposed value systems and views of the world.

In the eyes of her home community of Rimton, Barbara has made an impressive marriage and achieved, not only a home, but one filled with the latest consumer objects. In her study, *Home in British Working-Class Fiction*, Nicola Wilson argues convincingly that Carnie Holdsworth's novels present home for working-class women as "a gilded cage" (2015, 74). None of her previous novels, however, had presented a more newly gilded one than *Barbara Dennison* or made so clear that the woman's sole purpose in such a home is to keep the gilding well shined. At the novel's opening, Barbara has achieved the highest goal her culture offers to working-class women.

But, while the novel opens with a description of the gilded cage Critchie has provided for Barbara, an alternative space is also described. Barbara is asleep as the novel begins and dreaming she is hiking, off-road, in her life's most significant space, Ridgely Fells:

> She was dreaming, and in the dreaming followed a clear, brown stream which frothed and murmured and tumbled over a pebbly bed where trout floundered up and out of sun-lustred pools which reflected a dawn sky; trout, with crimson spots, flashing the water in crystal spray.
>
> (1929, 13–14)

Always changing, always in a state of becoming, this utopian space provides Barbara with the most intense experiences. But it is more than just a Romantic memory; it creates her sense of consciousness and the meaning of her life.

The novel follows Barbara, Critchie, and Dave as they consider their relationship to one another, as Barbara and Dave travel back and forth from London to Rimton, and as Critchie begins an affair with a woman who shares his desires for consumerism and upward mobility. Interspersed with these plot developments, Barbara and Dave return again and again, both in reality and in thought, to the unmapped space of Ridgely Fells. The Fells is a place outside society, unmonitored, primitive, and free. Barbara and Dave's hikes offer them an immersive escape into nature and the transgressive experiences that such activities can provide. They hike for hours, leap banks, walk through "wet rushes," and climb "almost on hands and knees" (42). Eventually, they return home with feet of ice and Barbara's skirt "a dishcloth for wetness" to their foster mother's, Sarah's, disgust. And their reward for this effort is, perhaps, to witness a sunrise, "a rapid change of colours which had been something to remember for a lifetime" (42). They experience the Fells moment by moment, never with a clear endpoint or destination. It is a space of immanence that offers them what the life of their culture devalues and excludes. In some ways, it is a literalization of Deleuze and Guattari's definition of a plateau: "a continuous self-vibrating region of intensities whose development avoids any orientation toward a culmination point or external end" (1987, 20).

The culminating confrontations in *Barbara Dennison* occur, not between Barbara and her husband over their failed marriage, but between Barbara, Dave, and their foster mother, Sarah, because their walks on Ridgely Fells are offensive to working-class respectability. Here, the ways in which respectability limits, not just freedom of movement, but freedom of thought are made explicit. When Barbara separates from Critchie and returns to her home village, she and Dave decide to spend a day climbing the Fells. Sarah speaks for the village, condemning their desire, a married woman and an unmarried man, to spend time together in this free space. Dave speaks for their defiance of village respectability: "Don't see why we should sit in on a day like this is going to be just to suit Rimton. If it doesn't like it, it can lump it" (Carnie Holdsworth 1929, 205).

After their climb, it is no accident that Sarah holds Barbara responsible. That is Sarah's judgment: "[S]he was a nice lass or she wasn't" (Roberts 1984, 193), and further, she sees her behavior as inherited from her unrespectable mother: " 'Tha's got him to do this, hussy,' she accused, white to the lips. 'I know thee. I've waited for this coming along. I know thee. Tha'rt like thy mother. It's in't blood' " (266). This accusation emphasizes the costs of working-class respectability and women's particular burden in maintaining it. A good lass will live indoors; a bad one ventures, however momentarily, outside her assigned place and is blamed and punished for it. This last confrontation underlines that respectability is the central force that forbids Barbara and Dave from traveling in their nomadic space and entraps them in conformist thinking. Dave sums up the destructive force of working-class respectability in a bitter diatribe:

"You good people," he said with white heat, "you good people— blind, respectable, calling everything wrong because it upsets your ideas, not allowing of any circumstances altering anything, suspicious, watching for wrong, driving people to wrong as a refuge from your narrow minded opinions—I wonder if the God who made you counts the numbers your ultra-respectability has decided to say—that for respectability if it is a hindrance to the human happiness which is wrong in humans but right in all his lesser creatures."

(268)

The ways of nature discovered on Ridgely Fells are moral. The working class, unexposed to free thought, is entrapped by an extreme "ultra-respectability" to which Dave and Barbara must adhere or be ostracized. Only in their hikes on Ridgely Fells can they momentarily be "disrespectable, happy and moral" (271).

In the alternative space of Ridgely Fells, Barbara and David are able to imagine a different morality and lives of freedom. Outside that space, however, they remain within their culture, although increasingly alienated from it. In contrast to Carrie Brown in *Miss Nobody*, the novel does not allow Barbara Dennison to resolve her conflicts in a literal sense. Instead, it concludes by suspending her in time. When she returns to London because Goffey's has declared bankruptcy and Critchie has lost his job, she learns he has died of a heart attack. The novel's last words are Barbara's response to this news: "Thank God!" (288). The future is unmapped, but Barbara's consciousness is freed from the traps of consumerism and respectability.

Ethel Carnie Holdsworth and the Geography of Working-Class Women's Lives

Outdoor spaces allow Carnie Holdsworth's working-class heroines to seek out freedoms their culture denies them. Using a spatial framework and drawing on Deleuze and Guattari's concept of nomadism as elaborated by Rosi Braidotti, this essay moves attention away from the spaces that are normally associated with working-class women—factory, home, and neighborhood—to open, natural spaces that are seldom connected with them. In *Miss Nobody* Carrie Brown seeks open skies and longs for a literal nomadism that will free her from society's striated spaces that are governed by inflexible laws and guarded by jealous overseers. Barbara Dennison finds a nomadism of consciousness that suggests a natural way of living, outside the conformism of working-class respectability. As such, it is possible to see how space and position intertwine in texts committed to social class. As a British working-class novelist, Carnie Holdsworth helped establish this important connection identifiable in subsequent class-conscious writing. In these moments, Carnie Holdsworth continues to implore working-class women to "For God's sake, . . . go out and play" (1909, 342).

Ethel Carnie Holdsworth understood the ways in which British culture entrapped working-class women from personal experience. While early-twentieth-century British culture decided that working-class women should be kept in the home and forced them, first, with threats of imprisonment and poverty and then with the lures of consumerism and respectability, Carnie Holdsworth demonstrates her ongoing resistance to such confinement. The home may be a more attractive prison than the factory, but it remains a prison, nonetheless. Only in their nomadic walks can working-class heroines like Carrie Brown and Barbara Dennison discover alternative spaces that allow them to breathe free and to imagine a life different from the one their culture and class has assigned them.

References

Braidotti, Rosi. 1994. *Nomadic Subjects: Embodiment and Sexual Difference in Contemporary Feminist Theory*. New York, NY: Columbia University Press.

Carnie Holdsworth, Ethel. (1907) 1908. *Rhymes from the Factory*. 2nd edition. Blackburn, UK: R. Denham and Co.

———. 1909. "Our Right to Play." *The Woman Worker*, April: 342.

———. (1913) 2013. *Miss Nobody*, edited by Nicola Wilson. Edinburgh, UK: Kennedy & Boyd.

———. 1924. "Editorial." *Freedom*, October, 52.

———. 1929. *Barbara Dennison*. London: Stanley Paul & Co.

Clark, Anna. 1995. *The Struggle for the Breeches: Gender and the Making of the British Working Class*. Berkeley, CA: University of California Press.

Deleuze, Gilles, and Félix Guattari. (1980) 1987. *A Thousand Plateaus: Capitalism and Schizophrenia*. Translated by Brian Massumi. Minneapolis, MN: University of Minnesota Press.

Fox, Pamela. 1994. *Class Fictions: Shame and Resistance in the British Working-Class Novel, 1890–1945*. Durham, NC: Duke University Press.

Frow, Edmund, and Ruth Frow. 1987. "Ethel Carnie: Writer, Feminist, and Socialist." In *The Rise of Socialist Fiction, 1880–1914*, edited by H. Gustav Klaus, 251–60. New York, NY: St. Martin's Press.

Roberts, Elizabeth. 1984. *A Woman's Place: An Oral History of Working-Class Women, 1890–1940*. Oxford, UK: Basil Blackwell.

Rose, Sonya O. 1992. *Limited Livelihoods: Gender and Class in Nineteenth-Century England*. Berkeley, CA: University of California Press.

Smalley, Roger. 2006. "The Life and Work of Ethel Carnie Holdsworth, with Particular Reference to the Period 1907 to 1931." PhD Dissertation, Preston, UK: University of Central Lancashire.

Thompson, F. M. L. 1988. *The Rise of Respectable Society: A Social History of Victorian Britain, 1830–1900*. Cambridge, MA: Harvard University Press.

Wilson, Nicola. (2015) 2016. *Home in British Working-Class Fiction*. London: Routledge.

4 "Class Lives"

Spatial Awareness and Political Consciousness in British Mining Novels of the 1930s

Nick Hubble

In November 1930, the unemployed Durham miner and novelist Harold Heslop attended the Second Plenum of the International Union of Revolutionary Writers in Kharkov in the Soviet Union. He began his own address to the delegates by apologizing for the backward condition of proletarian art in Britain before going on to proclaim his belief "that during the coming period, we, in Britain, will be able to express on the artistic arena the political struggle of the workers in a manner that will effectively hasten the attainment of our socialist goal" (as quoted in Croft and Heslop 1994, 22). After this conference, Heslop went on to witness the ongoing construction of the dam across the Dnieper. In his posthumously published autobiography, *Out of the Old Earth*, Heslop adopts a critical stance and likens the scene to that of the "Pharaohs building their pyramids" (1994, 225), but in his 1935 novel, *Last Cage Down*, the memories of his Soviet visit inform the oration of the communist, Joe Frost, who holds a packed miners' hall spellbound with his inspirational account of how ordinary men and women were

> damming back the Dnieper of the ages, raising the river to drown an obstruction which had prevented the growth of the country, mounting a steel and concrete collar over the illimitable power of water to create electricity in abundance, for Donbas, for collective farms, for grain elevators, for every conceivable thing.
>
> (1984, 80)

In 1935, the unemployed Rhondda miner and communist, Lewis Jones, attended the Seventh World Congress of the Comintern in Moscow, where he witnessed Georgi Dimitrov's speech setting out the national, popular, and historical emphases of the new Popular Front strategy, which helped inform *Cwmardy*, the novel he would begin writing later that year (Taylor 2018, 178). Elinor Taylor argues that Jones was reluctant to be credited as the individual author of *Cwmardy*, seeing it as

DOI: 10.4324/9781003119425-5

a cooperative endeavor that expressed the collective values of the mining community he came from:

> Lawrence & Wishart's advert for *Cwmardy* in the *Daily Worker* certainly sold it on the terms Jones proposes here: the advert sought to convince readers that the novel showed the way forward to a "creation of a new literature, written of the people and by the people—for the people of Britain."
>
> (179)

These two cultural moments from the 1930s indicate the extent of both the spatial horizon of miner novelists, which stretched from their local pithead all the way across the vast expanses of the Soviet Union, and their political ambition, which sought nothing less than to reconfigure Britain into a socialist society, in which the solidarity, support networks, and laboring prowess of mining communities would come to characterize the country as a whole.

In this chapter, I analyze texts by Heslop, Jones, and the unemployed Nottinghamshire miner, Walter Brierley, in order to explore their mining novels within the context of the expansion of British proletarian and working-class writing in the 1930s—a phenomenon that, according to Christopher Hilliard, contested the common conception that writing was an elitist pursuit and paved the way to active mass cultural participation in the "wide-ranging examination and revaluation of the everyday in literature and the arts" that characterized post-war Britain (2006, 287). In particular, my aim is to show how the spatial awareness and political consciousness of these mining novels contributed a specific set of values to the wider structure of feeling identified by Hilliard. However, before examining the novels of Heslop and Jones in detail, I first discuss how this culturally transformative understanding of "proletarian literature"—which, in 1930s Britain, became a general term applied to books written about the working class from a working-class perspective, rather than a signifier of 1920s proletcult (Hubble 2017, 1–9)—was also the culmination both of a longer history of working-class writing that had grown in significance across the nineteenth century and of the concurrent development of a working-class consciousness.

In David Bell's study of the novels of Heslop and Jones, *Ardent Propaganda: Miners' Novels and Class Conflict 1929–1939*, he examines various modes of nineteenth-century writing about the working class. While this was often reform-minded, it tended to be "from the perspective of the established social order" (1995, 38). The growth of trade unionism and socialism toward the end of the century, especially from the radical 1880s onward, supported the development of more radical fiction; a trend culminating in Robert Tressell's *The Ragged Trousered Philanthropists* (1914). As Bell notes:

> This novel represented the climax of a development in nineteenth-century working-class fiction which had progressed from an enumeration of the trials and tribulations of working-class life in an industrial environment, through the depiction of a conflict of capital and labour, including its most extreme manifestation in strikes and lock outs, to the propagandism of socialism. This fiction forms part of the growing perception of the working class as a class, and anticipates the themes and forms of working-class fiction appearing in the 1930s.
>
> (44)

At the same time, the developing genre of working-class autobiography also played a significant role in self-identification and class consciousness, as it supported within writers the "capacity to grasp imaginatively the complexity of the life-long interaction between the self and the outside world" (Vincent 1982, 6). Bell comments that "with its emphasis on lived experience and details of personal history the autobiography offered a ready link to fictional writing, as is evident in the fictive autobiographies and *Bildungsromane* of the 1930s" (Bell 1995, 45–46). This is a point Bell comes back to in his discussion of how the fictions of both Jones and Heslop build on and out of "lived experience" and so intertwine "the conventions of the fictional autobiography with those of the *Bildungsroman*" (89; see also, 117n). The idea of a hybrid form of these two genres—an autobiographical bildungsroman—is encapsulated by Max Saunders's revival and rethinking of the Edwardian concept of "autobiografiction" as a category that exceeds autobiographical fiction by allowing writers to transform themselves performatively and represent a different understanding of selfhood:

> Autobiografiction can include material that writers may prefer not to own in their own person; but rather than suggesting that their fiction gives them away, either consciously or unconsciously, they are claiming that the fictional permits a *fuller* autobiography. This is partly a matter of its being able to include the shameful as well as the honourable, and thus assemble a more complete, more human, picture.
>
> (Saunders 2010, 205)

As Pamela Fox (1994) has argued, drawing on the work of Helen Merrell Lynd (1958), shame is a powerful force in working-class fiction because it functions as a revelatory experience leading to both self-consciousness and an understanding of the norm-based nature of societies. A recurrent feature of the representation of working-class women in working-class fiction has been to show how emancipation and agency follow from the rejection of the idea of "respectability" often internalized within working-class culture. Thus, for example, Sally Hardcastle of Walter Greenwood's *Love on the Dole*, explicitly rejects the moral and social norms of her community by entering into a relationship with the book-maker Sam Grundy:

> Yaaa, who cares what folk say? There's none Ah know as wouldn't swap places wi' me if they'd chance. Y'd have me wed, wouldn'y y'? Then tell me where's feller around here as can afford it? . . . Ah'm not respectable.
>
> (1969, 246)

As Fox concludes, such a process of revelation through shame enables the acquisition of a "self of one's 'own' that conflates individualist and collective consciousness" (1994, 203). Fox selects three fictional characters as "particularly striking examples of this hybrid consciousness" (204): Frank Owen in Tressell's *The Ragged Trousered Philantrophists*, Hester Martin in Ethel Carney Holdsworth's *This Slavery* (1925), and Jack Cook in Brierley's *Means-Test Man* (1935). All three of these books (and *Love on the Dole*) not only explore the need for a transformational shift in class consciousness but also explicitly link this shift to an explicit critique of traditional gender relations. As we shall see, Jones's *Cwmardy* and *We Live* (1939), with their hybrid protagonist, Len Roberts, contains at least some similar features and therefore may be added to this list. However, Heslop's protagonists, such as *The Gate of a Strange Field*'s Joe Tarrant and *Last Cage Down*'s Jim Cameron, seem superficially to be more straightforward male workers, invested in what Eric Hobsbawm has characterized as the "common style of proletarian life," dominant among the British working class from the 1880s to the 1950s, built around trade unionism, co-op membership, football, fish and chips, and family (1978, 281). Unlike Greenwood, Heslop rarely includes any representation of internal female consciousness, and therefore, it is difficult to situate his books alongside works such as D. H. Lawrence's *Lady Chatterley's Lover*, Lewis Grassic Gibbon's *A Scots Quair*, and John Sommerfield's *May Day*, which may be considered to express a form of proletarian modernism (Hubble 2017). Nevertheless, Heslop does target patriarchal attitudes within the working class both directly, especially in terms of older miners or trade union leaders with traditional ideas expecting to be obeyed without question, and indirectly, through dry, sardonic commentary. His protagonists do undergo shifts in attitude and perspective, although these are mostly long term and due to an accretion of factors rather than the result of major epiphanic moments. This gradual transformation, which is also a constitutive element of Jones's fiction, may be related to the particular experiences of miners and mining communities.

Heslop's autobiography suggests two main types of spatial awareness that arise from the experience of being a miner. One is governed by life in the mine and revolves around such concerns as the miners' need to walk in single file so as not to "blind" each other with their lamps. Heslop learned this lesson at the age of thirteen on his first day working underground when his father told him off for walking alongside him:

> This was my initiation into the most important rite of the men of the mine, the keeping in single file when travelling. Nowhere was it so rigorously forced as in the coal mines. A miner was not in ease when confronted by a stranger's light. I have known men stumble as if gone suddenly weak when confronted by a light coming towards them, a light so far along the tunnel as to shine like a dull star.
>
> (1994, 99)

While this aversion to light is due to the condition of nystagmus, which particularly afflicted miners, the need to keep in line—although it should be noted that these lines are not always straight because of the risks of explosions underground—also embodies a social and cultural imperative to stay on the same track as the man in front and not go against the flow. This need to work in complete concert is also reinforced by the various engineering constraints that Heslop discusses, although there are some spaces for partial deviation such as the refuge holes alongside tracks for miners to jump into out of the way of any passing train of coal tubs. These, however, are not without their dangers as Butch Reynolds finds to his cost in *The Earth Beneath*, when the train derails opposite his refuge and brings down the roof on top of him (1946, 288). It is generally the case in Heslop's novels that any deviance from the conventional wisdom on safe mining practice results in disaster and the need to rescue men from underground, which may or may not be successful.

Alongside this well-developed linear sense of space, which is gendered masculine, Heslop also reveals an understanding of life as a succession through ever-widening concentric rings surrounding the domestic center of the working-class kitchen, which is implicitly a more feminine gendering of space. The progression he describes in *Out of the Old Earth* takes him in a series of steps from kitchen to backyard and on to the street, then school and the mine, and on to an awareness of the Durham minefield as a whole. This latter awareness was heightened by election as his miner's lodge delegate to the Durham Miners' Association, requiring regular attendance at the headquarters in Durham. The association decided to fund four two-year scholarships at the Central Labour College in London, one of which Heslop won after going through two rounds of competitive examinations. At the college in London, Heslop met Jones, who had followed a very similar outward trajectory through the rites of passage of a young miner and then up the meritocratic ladder enabled by the mining union. As we have seen, this outward trajectory of the two would only reach its outer limit with trips to the Soviet Union.

Leaving aside for the moment the political trajectories involved, it is illuminating to consider how these two mining-community spatial sensibilities—the linear and the concentric—interact to create a distinctive perspective in mining novels. This perspective is not dependent on the novel focusing on mining as its principal subject as is demonstrated by Brierley's *Means-Test Man*, which includes no pit scenes or even much reference to a wider community, but focuses intently on a week in the life of unemployed miner Jack Cook and his wife Jane as they struggle to make ends meet and handle the psychological pressure generated by the forthcoming monthly visit of the titular means-test man, who will assess if Jack's unemployment benefit should be reduced. Without access to the linear space of the pit, Jack has to replicate it in the layout of his garden:

> The vegetable path ran alongside the house and stretched downwards with the roadside hedge as a boundary for a matter of twenty yards, the path from the yard to the coal-shed cut it from the flower garden. A pea row and a kidney-bean row stretched from hedge to path, cutting the garden into sections of which the first, that nearest the house, was set with early potatoes, the next, the largest section, held the main crop; the other, between the bean row and the bottom boundary hedge, was cut up into seed beds, carrot, parsnips, beet, lettuce, radish, all orderly and flourishing.
>
> (2011, 10–11)

However, at this point in July when nothing is yet ready for harvest, all Jack can do is walk along the various lines reflecting on the fact that keeping the garden had been such a chore while he was working in the pit but now he cannot wait for the early potatoes to be ready so that he could stay in the garden for whole mornings or whole afternoons. Earlier in the spring he had managed to stretch out preparing the soil and planting the seeds for days on end, but when his wife came out to call him in for tea, "she would say, as his quick alert gaze swept the newly-turned soil, 'You haven't done a great deal to-day'" (11). Here, a difference of perspective is established from the beginning of the novel. In contrast to Jack's compulsion to keep to his lines, Jane is caught within the concentric circles emanating from the kitchen, which include the need to go shopping on Saturday evening, when the meat is sold off cheap.

If Jack was working, large sections of their lives would be separate, and these two sets of perspective would not come into constant conflict. As it is, a simmering tension develops between the two as they find themselves constantly within each other's space. It is not that Jack does not help out around the house. He tidies, scrubs, blackleads, and makes beds, despite being aware that if any of the surrounding miners saw him doing these things, "he would have become a woman" in their eyes (23). However, he bridles at her checking that he has completed tasks satisfactorily and considers her desires to be materialistic. The combined psychological and domestic focus of the novel enables it to show in detail the consciousness-raising revelatory experience of shame, identified by Fox as key to working-class fiction. Fox is correct to point out that this experience is represented differently for Jack and Jane in the novel, so that his acquisition of self-consciousness and agency is much more fully realized than hers:

> The shame that Jack Cook expresses is fully privileged by the text, intended to "expose" the immorality of the ruling, rather than the working class. It is Jane Cook who becomes the explicit agent of a much more problematic shame. . . . [The] text directly employs a working-class woman to voice its anxiety about class, and ultimately gender, difference, so that such anxiety can be directly critiqued and ostensibly contained.
>
> (1994, 137)

However, reading *Means-Test Man* in the twenty-first century, it is impossible to construe the text as somehow containing or constraining Jane Cook's desire and agency. On the one hand, the need for a change in both class and gender relations has an imperative urgency that is unmissable but, on the other hand, that change is already clearly in motion. The novel is "charting an ongoing shift in gender relations," and "life will not simply revert to its former course when work is restored" to Jack (Hubble 2017, 105–6). At a formal level, the reconciliation of interests between Jack and Jane is symbolically represented at the novel's end by showing both modes of spatial awareness—linear and concentric—in play simultaneously as Jane smiles and "for the first time [meets] her husband's gaze" and the viewpoint switches to that of their son turning "head over heels, while the faces of his parents moved into greater seriousness." (Brierley 2011, 281–82)

When this linear versus concentric analysis is applied to mining novels, such as those of Heslop and Jones, which are more overtly concerned with the working conditions and labor relations of the pit and the wider social consequences that follow from these, it complicates what can otherwise seem to be the straightforward politics of these books. For example, Bell develops his analysis of the autobiographical bildungsroman, outlined above, to outline what he calls the "apprenticeship model," which

> consists of two types of exemplary narrative: positive and negative. This study demonstrates that by applying the analytical model of a

positive apprenticeship to [Jones's] *Cwmardy*, the narrative structures of the novel limit potential for interpretation to the doctrinal
assumptions underlying the text. The reader is expected to identify
with the class-conscious insights gained by the hero. [Heslop's] *The
Gate of a Strange Field*, in contrast, acts as a cautionary tale, illustrating the consequences of embracing a false doctrine.

(1995, "Abstract")

Read purely according to a linear spatial perspective, *Cwmardy* is, as
Bell notes, "an uncomplicated novel, being supported by the Left as an
example of the proletarian novel, or rejected by the Right as political
propaganda" (113). Len's boyhood initiation into the life of the miner
involves him following his father, as Heslop describes himself doing in
Out of the Old Earth, through a sequence of tunnels, learning to duck
into holes to avoid the train, and gradually becoming aware of the
other constraints of life underground (Jones 1978a, 105–28). A linear
progression through a series of events and developments—accidents,
strikes, mechanization, and pay negotiations—politicizes Len and leads
to him taking a leading role in the union affirming the analysis that
"the syntagmatic progression and the actantial structure of the novel
are designed to demonstrate that developments in the South Wales coalfield between 1900 and 1920 conformed to a 1930s Communist view
of that society" (Bell 1995, 113). At the same time, though, the novel
also features the movement through a succession of ever-widening
concentric rings out from the working-class kitchen, which is such a
feature of Heslop's autobiography. For example, there are extensive
scenes featuring a young Len and his various relationships with his
sister, who dies tragically, and his fellow school pupil, Mary, who will
eventually become his wife. The groundwork laid in these early chapters allows the novel and its sequel, *We Live*, to chart the wider social
network of the South Wales coalfield and pay particular attention to
gender relationships. Bell argues that such passages, describing home
life and leisure activities, were common to all mining novels and func-
tioned largely "to reinforce the message of the novel and to give it an
authenticity based on a perceivable link with reality" (112). However,
there is rather too much of such material to assign it to the status of
mere reality effect.

Some of the gender analysis in *Cwmardy* is clearly a transcription of
1930s communist thinking, such as Len's realization that "The boys in
work talk of girls as the owners talk of us. The owners make us slaves
in the pit and our men make their women slaves in the house" (Jones
1978a, 202). Yet, such commentary is always integrated both socially
and emotionally with what is happening in the novel as a whole. For
example, Len makes the above statement during the course of an awk-
ward but emotional conversation with Mary, which is the first occasion

he has been alone with her as an adult, and such discussions will be extended throughout the novel and its sequel. As Charles Ferrall and Dougal McNeill note in their analysis of Jones's novels in *Writing the 1926 General Strike: Literature, Culture and Politics*, "the 'proletarian novel' becomes the 'gendered proletarian novel'" and the idea of "Communism is transfigured by re-imagined gender possibilities" (2015, 169). Not only will Len, after their marriage, take responsibility for much of the housework when Mary becomes elected to the County Council as a communist representative, but we also see him "learn a new sexuality in recognition of Mary's autonomy" (170).

Len is the opposite of the typical worker hero, portrayed as physically weak and introduced in the novel as "a queer lad for his age" (Jones 1978a, 14). Furthermore, he, like Jones, is Welsh, and the novels include a sprinkling of Welsh language and cultural traditions throughout: "the 'we' of Jones's novels is not simply a working-class 'we' but also the 'we' of 'Welshness'" (Hubble 2021, 49). It is the combination of the masculine linear "positive apprenticeship," identified by Bell, which consists of progressing through the rites of passage of entry into the mine and the union, with movement through a series of femininized concentric circles of emotional ties, sexuality, and love—here connected to a Welshness that is non-normative by comparison to the dominance of English values within Britain—that enables the transformative alignment of individual and collective consciousness that animates the novels. This does not just represent a transformation of the gender relations between one couple, as in Brierley's *Means-Test Man*, but a more profound transformation of an entire community in such a manner that individual working-class lives gain agency within that collective. In particular, as Taylor points out, "the close-knit, defensive culture [of the Valleys' communities] transforms into a powerful anti-fascist front through the emerging recognition of the identity of its interests with European communities threatened by fascism" (2018, 181). This is shown by the trajectory from the opening pages of *Cwmardy*, in which Len's father shows him the site of an historical battle between the English and the Welsh, to the closing pages of *We Live*, when Mary learns of the death of Len fighting against Franco for the International Brigades in Spain. His last words to her, in a letter she receives after his death, sum up the logic of the intersecting linear and concentric perspective of the novels: "Sleep happy in the knowledge that our lives have been class lives, and our love something buried so deep in the Party that it can never die" (Jones 1978b, 332).

If *Cwmardy* is more than a novel of "positive apprenticeship," is Heslop's *The Gate of a Strange Field* more than a negative version of the "apprenticeship model" from which, as Bell argues, the reader is expected to learn from the mistakes made by the hero? The short answer is yes because, as with *Cwmardy*, the many scenes of home and leisure life are not included as signifiers of verisimilitude but are integral to both the plot and the symbolic resolution of the novel:

> *The Gate of a Strange Field* is a *Bildungsroman* in which we see Joe Tarrant's progression from school to pit and on to full-time union representative but it is also an intense record of the changing relations between the sexes in the context of women's emancipation enabled by better employment opportunities and the gaining of the vote. A large part of Joe's coming-of-age story is concerned with his relationship to Molly, a "likely lass" of his own age.
>
> (Hubble 2021, 27)

Over the course of the novel, Joe separates from Molly as his rise through the union ranks rewards him with power and leisure opportunities beyond the reach of the miner he once was. Heslop's attitude to Joe is overtly sardonic, so Bell is correct to argue that the reader is not expected to approve of his actions in the way that they would approve Len Roberts's actions. From a linear perspective, the lowest point of Joe's life is reached during the General Strike when he has been dispatched to London as a representative of the miners' union. Rather than being at the heart of political deliberations at the moment when the strike collapses, he is in fact in bed with a sex worker. However, there is a twist in the story, which is not only that this sex worker is his estranged wife Molly but also that she has clearly been more successful than he has in liberating herself from the moral constraints of internalized working-class "respectability" that still hold sway among the communities of the Durham coalfield. Therefore, it seems much more likely that, rather than a "negative apprenticeship" designed to teach readers by example, the novel is intended as a criticism of the limits of the dominant structure of feeling within the mining community, which is taken as being led by the trade unions. To this end, Heslop includes a number of sardonic observations on the shortcomings of the linear consciousness of his fellow members of the "Northern proletariat" (1929, 78), and it is these—rather than Joe's actions—which are the real negative lesson of the text:

> The average miner does not possess a logical mind. He cannot reason beyond his paynote. He is a blind, consistent struggler, willingly giving his fate into the hands of those who seem to shine more brilliantly than the rest. In due season they were certain to give their trust to Joe. He had but to glitter before them. He had to show them that he "was sufficient of a realist" and so forth—those obvious things beloved of the Independent Labour Party—and the rest would come.
>
> (115)

The Gate of a Strange Field is not able to effect a transformative resolution either between the central couple, as in *Means-Test Man*, or politically for the community as a whole, as in *Cwmardy* and *We Live*. The novel may be read, rather, as an imaginative working through of various options that in some way liberate Heslop himself by making him more self-aware. In this sense I would argue, following the discussion earlier in this chapter, that the book might be termed a "proletarian autobiografiction." In *Out of the Old Earth*, Heslop confesses to feeling absolutely depressed when he had to return to the mines after a brief spell as a private in the Fifth Reserve Cavalry Regiment in the final stages of the WWI: "I felt that utter forlorness that follows after the shearing of individual freedom, as I became a piece, a part of a pawn, in the majestic purpose of the capitalist mode of production" (Heslop 1994, 145). In the face of this forlorness, he remembers an earlier urge to write. Although he does not discuss this in the same terms of shame theorized by Lynd and Fox, this is implied by his recollection of his first ever attempt at a novel, which ended with the "spectacular suicide of the heroine by throwing herself from the topmost tower of Durham Cathedral" (146). Certainly, both Molly and Joe experience shame in *The Gate of a Strange Field*, as do Martha and Russell, the main protagonists of his next (non-mining) novel, *Journey Beyond*, who respectively turn to sex work and attempt suicide before undergoing a revelation about capitalist society: "I suppose we're all for ourselves in this world?" (Heslop 1930, 252). The implication of *Out of the Old Earth* is that Heslop found writing about his own experiences fictionally, from both male and female perspectives and with a certain melodramatic relish, to be a means of revelation leading to an altered consciousness of himself and his position in society.

Therefore, it is not surprising that a similarly contemplative, imaginative structure to that of *The Gate of a Strange Field* can be found in Heslop's next mining novel, *Last Cage Down*. Jim Cameron, the secretary of the miner's lodge, is a heroically masculine worker who has mastered the linear space of the mines. He instinctively knows "when to kirve, when to knick, when to smash down the 'caunch'" and thereby how to "make the coal leap voluntarily from its fastness with a shriek of joy" (Heslop 1984, 3). His daily routine follows an orderly progression from pit to lodge and onto the Red Lion, before heading up to the hillside for his regular tryst after closing time with Betty the barmaid. Jim's father had died when one of the seams in the mine collapsed and when he learns that Tate, the manager newly in charge of the mine, intends to reopen that seam and use modern machine methods along its entire face, he immediately calls a strike to try and stop this. Joe Frost, a communist miner, whom we know to be level-headed and progressive because he is married and listens to classical music on the radio, tells Jim to set up soup kitchens and arrange support for the strike beforehand. Jim ignores this and leads the strike, which then fails. In his subsequent frustration, Jim threatens to kill Tate, which leads to him being sent to prison for nine months. He loses his job, he gets voted out of the secretaryship of the lodge, and his mother is evicted from the house they had shared. Soon after his return from jail, the newly opened seam does collapse killing his brother. Thereupon, he realizes he was wrong to call the strike without taking Frost's advice. But this—despite some heroic worker scenes and passages about the wonders of the land over the sea ruled by the workers—hardly amounts to the didactic communist tract it is sometimes portrayed as.

In any case, the novel does not end here but with a further explosion in the mine, in which Frost and Tate the manager are trapped, and Cameron saves them both. Therefore, it is not even clear at the end whether the modern communist values of Frost are endorsed by the novel. Critics such as Andy Croft and John Connor have discussed the novel as advocating a sectarian "Third Period" politics (Croft and Heslop 1984, x–xii; Connor 2019, 325–26), but Frost's identification of the threat of fascism as marking out "a new phase of the struggle" (Heslop 1984, 300) suggests rather an anticipation of the Popular Front position that had not yet been declared while he was writing or even something closer to the revolutionary stance that was being advocated by the Independent Labour Party at this time (Hubble 2021, 26, 39–40). However, the only real change that has actually taken place by the end of the novel is that Jim is prepared to help a woman, Betty, whom he is now going to marry, to tidy away the dishes for the first time in his life, suggesting at least the beginning of the shift in gender relations that is more fully realized between Jack and Jane Cook in *Means-Test Man*. What has happened over the course of the novel is that Jim has learned to overcome his narrow adherence to the masculine, linear spatial sensibility of the pit, which Heslop appears to link in Jim's case to an oedipal fixation with his mother, and come to accept the equal relevance of a more expansive, concentric spatial awareness. In some ways this awareness is externally imposed upon him by his prison sentence, which takes him away from the pit village, and then the fact that he has to stay with his mother out in the countryside on his return. It is precisely the shame that these events cause him that enables Jim to gain what we have seen Fox describe as a "self of one's 'own' that conflates individualist and collective consciousness" (1994, 204).

Perhaps it is not surprising that mining novels of the 1930s exhibited the kinds of transformation in class consciousness analyzed in this chapter. They were written in a period when the mining unions and the culture of mining communities were, generally speaking, in decline following the three-month lockout in 1921 and then the catastrophic failure of the General Strike in 1926. The capitulation of the strike after nine days did not so much mark the failure of the organized working class in Britain to achieve a Soviet-style revolution as the swan song of a masculine style of trade union politics dating from the 1880s. The purpose of the strike had been to prevent a mine owners' lockout designed to lower wage rates, and after the other unions returned to work, the miners stayed out alone in an ultimately doomed attempt to prevent this outcome. At the time, this looked like the last stand of a culture and one might expect novels written in the immediate aftermath, such as Heslop's *The Gate of a Strange Field*, to contain some element of nostalgic lament for a lost golden age, but this is not the case at all. In fact, the four novels by Jones and Heslop discussed in detail here heavily criticize the established mining and trade union culture and are oriented instead toward a future in which aspects of that traditional culture, especially the gender relationships, have been radically changed.

All these texts may be read as proletarian autobiografictions that reveal self-knowledge and open up new intersubjective possibilities through the generation of a hybrid individualist-collective consciousness. On this reading, the fact that none were republished after the WWII until the late 1970s is not due to the fact that the post-war settlement alleviated the grievances that had motivated these novels but because they actually constitute resistance to the socially conservative aspects of that settlement, which entrenched traditional culture. Heslop is typically sardonic in the attitude to Labourism he displays in his autobiography:

> The year 1919 was a year of intense proletarian dreaming. . . . Despite the overwhelming victory of Lloyd George and his coalition, the proletarian world of men did not cease to dream. The most outrageous fantasy was the Sankey Commission. . . . How we gloated over the possibility of the mines becoming nationalised. How we dreamed. How we stretched out our hands towards the towering pit head gearing to take it, and all it signified, into our own dear keeping. Poor, soft, deluded people that we were.
>
> (1994, 146)

Because of this understanding, his work was always already resistant to the post-1945 British Welfare State, which by his logic was also a form of "proletarian dreaming." Jones died in early 1939—*We Live* was published posthumously—and so never lived to see that the promise of a transformed culture inherent to the "class lives" of the mining communities in the South Wales Valleys was never realized. In the absence of the advent of such a transformed utopian future, it was left to Heslop to provide an epitaph to the linear spatial consciousness of the male mining culture:

> It was into this shadow-existence that I was to become a man, and to behave after the manner of men who had begotten me. I was not trapped. I was immured, as were all my contemporaries, in a mining

world that we could not and would not change, but whose destiny it
was to pass away.

(52)

As a conclusion, though, this is too bleak because the culture of mining
communities, as recorded by these writers and others, has had a long-
lasting and beneficial effect on British society. More generous epitaphs
have been written to mining culture, including Heslop's last published
novel, *The Earth Beneath*, which appeared in December 1946, only
weeks before the mines were nationalized on January 1, 1947, but had
been started ten years earlier, shortly after the publication of *Last Cage
Down*. This novel is set entirely within the nineteenth century and follows
John Akers and his brothers as, following eviction from their farm in the
Yorkshire Dales at the end of the 1830s, they walk to the "New Land" of
the Durham coalfield. Interestingly, although the novel encompasses the
founding of the Durham Miner's Association, and John does, after strong
initial resistance, eventually join the union, the family's involvement with
religion and the chapel plays much more importance to the plot than
politics. John's son, George, eventually comes to a Tolstoian acceptance
of his role in life, although unlike his father he does share the caring
duties for his children with his wife. The novel is very much a celebration
of the nineteenth-century working-class mining culture and of Heslop's
own family, on whose history it is partly based. However, the difference
between the acceptance of George's son, Billie, of his lot as a miner and
that of Heslop himself quoted above is telling:

> Billie Akers did not understand the forces which were moulding his
> own life. He never appreciated the situation in which he had been
> placed. He was of pure working-class stock. He was anxious to suc-
> ceed. He wanted to become a miner, a great miner, to succeed as a
> technician where his grandfather had succeeded as a labourer. His
> desire to climb into the place held by his relative [the manager of
> the colliery] was not determined by his desire to be a servant of the
> shareholders of the company but because he wished to become an
> accomplished engineer of the underworld.
>
> (1946, 311)

What survives in this post-war mining novel, that is lamented in Heslop's
later autobiography, is a sense of possibility of the working class building
something new for themselves.

There is another way of thinking about the space occupied by
these mining novels and that is related to the material conditions of
their production. In *The English Novel from Dickens to Lawrence*,
Raymond Williams pointedly comments that not only did the three
supposedly "great autodidacts" of English Literature—George Eliot,

Thomas Hardy, and D. H. Lawrence—receive levels of formal education that by their contemporary standards were high, but also a higher
level of education "absolutely, than those of four out of five people in
mid-twentieth-century Britain" (1987, 95). The same may also be said of
Heslop and Jones, who both spent two years studying full time in London at the Central Labour College in the mid-1920s. It should also be
noted that Brierley studied part time at the University of Nottingham for
four years. None of these writers were simply celebrating their communities or writing from some (imaginary) purist position of working-class
authenticity. What they were able to do, however—as Eliot, Hardy, and
Lawrence (also a mining-area novelist) had done before—was to relate
their education, understood in Williams's terms as "the substance of a
developed intelligence," to "the actual lives of a continuing majority of
our people: people who are not, by any formula, objects of record or
study or concern, but who are specifically, literally, our own families"
(96). Therefore, these writers—Walter Brierley, Harold Heslop, and
Lewis Jones—should be considered the true successors of that literary
tradition that Williams was writing about. Novels like these illustrate not
only the meaning in ordinary working lives but show how the forms of
everyday understanding and perception, which are available to everyone,
may be combined to create new transformational forms of consciousness
and agency.

References

Bell, David. 1995. *Ardent Propaganda: Miners' Novels and Class Conflict 1929–
1939.* Umeå, SE: Umeå Studies in the Humanities.
Brierley, Walter. (1935) 2011. *Means-Test Man.* Nottingham, UK: Spokesman.
Connor, John. 2019. "Anglo-Soviet Relations in the Long 1930s." In *A History
of 1930s British Literature,* edited by Benjamin Kohlmann and Matthew Taun-
ton, 317–30. Cambridge, UK: Cambridge University Press.
Croft, Andy, and Harold Heslop. 1984. "Introduction." In *Last Cage Down,*
vii–xiii. London: Lawrence & Wishart.
———. 1994. "Who Was Harry Heslop?" In *Out of the Old Earth,* 7–38. New-
castle, UK: Bloodaxe.
Ferrall, Charles, and Dougal McNeil. 2015. *Writing the 1926 General Strike:
Literature, Culture, Politics.* Cambridge, UK: Cambridge University Press.
Fox, Pamela. 1994. *Class Fictions: Shame and Resistance in the British Working-
Class Novel, 1890–1945.* Durham, NC: Duke University Press.
Greenwood, Walter. 1969. *Love on the Dole.* Harmondsworth, UK: Penguin.
Heslop, Harold. 1929. *The Gate of a Strange Field.* London: Brentano.
———. 1930. *Journey Beyond.* London: Harold Shaylor.
———. 1946. *The Earth Beneath.* London: Boardman.
———. (1935) 1984. *Last Cage Down.* London: Lawrence & Wishart.
———. 1994. *Out of the Old Earth.* Newcastle, UK: Bloodaxe.
Hilliard, Christopher. 2006. *To Exercise Our Talents: The Democratisation of
Writing in Britain.* Cambridge, MA: Harvard University Press.

Hobsbawm, Eric. 1978. "The Forward March of Labour Halted?" *Marxism Today*, September, 279–86.

Hubble, Nick. 2017. *The Proletarian Answer to the Modernist Question*. Edinburgh, UK: Edinburgh University Press.

———. 2021. "'You're Not in the Market at Shielding, Joe': Beyond the Myth of the 'Thirties'." In *The 1930s: A Decade of Modern British Fiction*, edited by Nick Hubble, Luke Seaber, and Elinor Taylor, 17–57. London: Bloomsbury.

Jones, Lewis. (1937) 1978a. *Cwmardy*. London: Lawrence & Wishart.

———. (1939) 1978b. *We Live*. London: Lawrence & Wishart.

Lynd, Helen Merrell. 1958. *On Shame and the Search for Identity*. London: Routledge and Kegan Paul.

Saunders, Max. 2010. *Self-Impression: Life-Writing, Autobiografiction, and the Forms of Modern Literature*. Oxford, UK: Oxford University Press.

Taylor, Elinor. (2017) 2018. *The Popular Front Novel in Britain, 1934–1940*. Leiden, NL: Brill.

Vincent, David. 1982. *Bread, Knowledge & Freedom: A Study of Nineteenth-Century Working Class Autobiography*. London and New York: Methuen.

Williams, Raymond. (1970) 1987. *The English Novel from Dickens to Lawrence*. London: The Hogarth Press.

5 Remembering the Future

A Modernized London in *Proud City* and *The End of the Affair*

Elizabeth Floyd

When imagining the future of London, Frank Pick, the managing direc-tor of the London Transit from 1933 to 1940, insisted that it "cannot be an accident, like in the past. . . . [I]t must now be planned, designed, and organised" (Hatherley 2016, 82). While Pick's ideas for London were never fully realized, the post-1945 years were a fortuitous opportunity for Clement Attlee's Labour government to redesign London in utopian terms, correcting for the perceived architectural mistakes of the past in which public architecture and housing were viewed as ugly, monstrous, and overcrowded. Recognizing the need for a new all-encompassing plan following the destruction of the Blitz, government officials set forth to rebuild London as a city that would showcase a new Britain, free from the so-called squalor of the nineteenth century and the ruins of war. As with any project to reimagine a space that encompasses competing histo-ries and narratives, the task of rebuilding London was a highly fraught political project. Progressives envisioned the reconstruction as a physical means to address issues of inequality and social injustice through careful design and planning. Alternatively, conservatives viewed any attempt to modernize Britain as forsaking the past and British culture, which trans-lated into a rejection of traditionalism and the "glory" of the empire. Instead, they regarded rebuilding as an opportunity to reassert tradi-tional British values and culture through design and planning. Yet what emerged was a plan for reconstruction that upheld both perspectives: it would be an urban utopian fantasy that both celebrated the past and realized a completely modernized society. Unique in its position as the locus of the British Empire, the new London would be cosmopolitan, while clearly influenced by British traditions and values. It could be mod-ern and traditional; local and global; quaint and urban. It could be the site where the past was celebrated and the future embraced.

In this essay, I discuss how the post-1945 rebuilding of London became a project for Attlee's government to level class difference, while simulta-neously celebrating the city's past and promoting a modernized metropo-lis. By analyzing the government propaganda film, *Proud City: A Plan For London* (1946), directed by Ralph Keene, I argue that rebuilding was

DOI: 10.4324/9781003119425-6

not only a means to reinvigorate London, but a form of paternalism that sought to elevate the poor and working classes to a middle-class standing through the creation of modernized and thus more aesthetically pleasing housing and public spaces. *Proud City* elicits its middle-class viewers' support for the proposed rebuilding project's modernization by claiming the new project will promote decency, order, and dignity. Yet, despite *Proud City*'s unilateral call for systematic design and urban planning that would erase past architectural sins and social ills, the film acknowledges the insecurity of the middle class, their fear for the future, and how these concerns would be addressed in urban structures. These same spatial anxieties can be seen in Graham Greene's novel, *The End of the Affair*, in which the novel's middle-aged protagonist, Maurice Bendrix, clings to older architecture and its ruins as a physical representation of his own middle-class subjectivity. I argue that Bendrix rejects the potential for new urban spaces as promoted in *Proud City* and, in doing so, refuses the new subjectivities created in the space of a modern, post-imperial Britain. By comparing the realist propaganda film to a novel of the same period, I follow Bertrand Westphal's call that "fiction is in the real; it contributes to a fleshing out of the real, which contributes to anchoring the esthetic of representation in the ensemble of perceived contemporary society" (2016, 4). Although *The End of the Affair* relies on fictional perspectives, it illuminates alternate attitudes held toward rebuilding, particularly by middle-class men, that refute the positive, modernizing future promoted in *Proud City* and fundamentally illustrates how the same spaces can reinforce conservative views. By juxtaposing the film and the novel, the middle class's contradictory views as to the purpose and function of rebuilding are exposed and emphasize the lack of consensus or a unified class identity.

While there was a general recognition that rebuilding was needed that began with the earlier pre-WWII clearances of Victorian slums, the bombsites and ruins signified a collective history that was imperative to modern British experience; to cover over the ruins would enact a form of cultural erasure. As Susan Grayzel (2012) has noted, the air raids and bombings during WWI shattered the distinctly gendered spaces of war as the home front and the domestic were equally militarized, rewriting the relationship between space and war as those gendered boundaries disappeared.[1] To move past and imagine a future outside of the British historical past became a form of cognitive dissonance, particularly for British men who were tied to the prior notions of masculinity and class, or "decency." As Praseeda Gopinath argues, the decent man is an evolution of the Orwellian pre-war gentleman, who replicates the public-school English masculinity and "emerges to stand for the new nation when the hegemonic ideal of the onward-looking detached gentleman alters and devolves to fit the post-war nation" (2013, 8). Crucial to this perpetuation of the post-war decent man are the physical sites to which he can reaffirm his subjectivity, whether it is in the ruins of older architecture or new sites that reiterate those same middle-class values and imperial social hierarchies. This reaffirms Michel de Certeau's concept in which society, and thus individuals, use "perspective vision and prospective vision" to constitute "a twofold projection of an opaque past and uncertain future onto a surface that can be dealt with" (1984, 93–94). While the decent man views himself an individual in the space of the city, he needs physical sites to ground the more elusive and abstract values of British social class and reinforce his misguided belief in the ahistoric universality of pre-war social structures.

Rebuilding the ruins would generate new meanings and subjectivities rather than propagate a static cultural experience or reaffirm the disappearing British imperial past and thus the decent man's subjectivity. Ruins are "both a frozen moment of destruction made permanent . . . yet they also act as a way of understanding a greater swathe of linear time previously hidden or buried" (Mellor 2011, 6). To cover over these ruins then becomes a cultural "forgetting" of both the recent past of the war and a rejection of British history. Although the ruins signify destruction, they possess the familiar known of a tangible London of before and during WWII and continue a pre-1945 national identity unlike the newly built urban spaces. Ruins are dependent on the static use of space and a stable national discourse, which as Henri Lefebvre describes, occurs when the state binds itself to space and uses the material structures to reinforce certain values (2010, 224). Individuals use space to ensure a narrative that is relevant to their own present, regardless of historic accuracy, and create imagined communities through the urban landscape.[2] This continued gesture of enfolding past, present, and future by individuals in the space of the city together demonstrates London's centrality for British classed subjectivity in the second half of the twentieth century, whether through the official channels of the state or through individual experience.

While Owen Hatherley critiques contemporary perspectives on architecture, particularly those associated with "retrochic" aestheticization,[3] he points to an important personal connection that individuals have with architecture and design because it offers a "haptic experience of the past" (2016, 6). The same haptic experience occurred with the bombed ruins of London, creating a romanticized narrative of "what once was" and allowing individuals to feel a tangible connection to a pre-war Britain. While the haptic experience transcends class, the emotional connection to architecture and the post-war project of rebuilding is crucial for understanding how the aesthetic stylizations are often replicated and fetishized by the middle class, even if they do not necessarily inhabit those spaces. Before WWII, the middle class defined their subjectivity through what Ian Baucom refers to as the *lieux de memoire* encoded as "British," whether it was the individual country house or the cricket field (1999, 37).[4] As those sites were directly tied to the older imperial project, they could no longer be the material placeholders for Britishness in an era of a declining empire. What made London central to the formation of post-war British subjectivity was that it was only site that could connect an older imperial Britain to a progressive and modern future while maintaining a romanticized past. Through the space of the city, the British nation could be redefined as one all-encompassing *lieu de memoire* that enfolds both conservative and progressive ideologies. The city is the ideal site of modern nation building because it is where the state could "regulate and organize a disintegrating national space at the heart of a consolidating worldwide space" and restructure individuals' perception of their national subjectivity (Lefebvre 2010, 225). As Kristin Ross discusses in her work on post-war France, architectural and social "modernization promises a perfect reconciliation of past and future in an endless present" and acts as a mechanism to level class difference through urban planning and social programs (1995, 11). Ross argues that this utopian premise operates not by dismantling class hierarchies, but by the state's attempt to make all individuals part of a new, modern middle class through its use of modern urban design.

With hindsight, it is always apparent that the inherent struggle for the state to create a cohesive nation space leads to the state's inability to manage the chaos that arises from the attempt to create a single cohesive idea of national space, let alone the formation of cohesive national subjectivities.[5] Yet, for the post-war Labour government, their ideas to create a city that represented all visions of modernity seemed less of a utopian vision and more as something that could become a concrete reality. Produced by the Ministry of Information and featuring the chief architects of the rebuilding scheme, Sir Patrick Abercrombie and J. H. Forshaw, *Proud City: A Plan for London* (Keene 1946) offers a glimmering narrative that promotes this vision of a fully modernized London. At twenty-four minutes in length and presented in the style and tone of a realist documentary, the film's message and content are deceptively simple as it presents the new urban plans for London and various government officials' philosophies on rebuilding. In these initial designs, the city is streamlined, aesthetically pleasing in its use of modern architecture, particularly Scandinavian modernism, and devoid of debris and rubble. The architects try to sell the project to the audience by answering questions and assuage any fears rather than focus on the aesthetics of the designs. To further persuade viewers, the film emphasizes British national pride and rallies wartime patriotism, which is evoked in the narrator's introductory lines: "London—the greatest city the world has known." With this opening, viewers are encouraged to remember London as the superlative city of the world, regardless of any recent devastation. Of course, this emotionally laden declaration can only warm the cockles of any brow-beaten Londoner, faced with years of bombings, austerity, and fear. Equally important, there is no mention of empire in the film despite this national pride;

instead, any reference to history or British patriotism is always grounded in the city itself through references to Christopher Wren's architecture and the pastoral spaces that once surrounded the city.

What makes *Proud City* unique as post-war propaganda is its complete reliance on the city space for the formation of new modern, national subjectivity, rather than wartime patriotism, which relied on "the British people" and cultural tropes. The focus on urban space allows the film to simultaneously ignore the imperial legacy and promote British history. While the film celebrates famous icons like the Tower of London and St. Paul's Cathedral as intrinsic to the city's landscape and aesthetic appeal, it also critiques earlier versions of London as being "unplanned" and "unruly." The film argues that this wanton development led to the creation of slums and the promotion of rampant industrialization over the needs of the people. At one point, the narrator calls for a new form of industrialization that is planned and regulated by the state to ameliorate these historic issues. Throughout, *Proud City* continually insists that official state-run city planning is what will create an equitable city in which poverty, pollution, and disorder are remedied. Richard Hornsey has argued that the new plans for London were an attempt to create one long *durée* outside of the history of industrialism, which would then result in a new stable and self-sufficient social order and the creation of a new morality of everyday life that resided in civic participation and social responsibility (2010, 52). While Abercrombie and Forshaw's plans for London were never fully realized, they demonstrate the kind of unabashed enthusiasm for the potentiality of London and how the Labour government hoped to revive the British people through the creation of a modern, sanitized city (Wilson 1992).[6] For example, the film focuses on Abercrombie and Forshaw's designs for the London neighborhood, Stepney, which had previously been the focus of another widely disseminated film, *Housing Problems* (1935), directed by Edgar Anstey and Arthur Elton and produced by John Grierson and the Realist Film Unit for the British Commercial Gas Association, that depicted the poverty and dereliction of social housing. *Proud City* reveals that London's issues have not changed despite the eleven years that have passed since the filming of *Housing Problems*. In fact, the same slums and impoverished areas not only continue to exist and replicate the poor living conditions of the pre-war era, they have the added damage and destruction of the Blitz. Stepney becomes a metonym for London's largely unchanged urban spaces and archaic architecture, in which the slums, ruins, and rubble are all-encompassing and merge to become permanently ingrained within the material landscape. According to the logic of *Proud City*, this physical stasis needs to be altered and rebuilt using post-war modern urban planning, which advocates an architecture for the common good rather than emphasizing a specific architectural style.

To convince a potentially dismissive middle-class audience who might reject social programs and improved housing for the working classes, *Proud City* uses the physical continuity of pre- and post-war London to suggest that the city can be both a beacon of a great past, while offering a new, and thus better, space for all its inhabitants.[7] As the film opens, the camera pans over iconic London landmarks like Big Ben, Parliament, the Tower of London, and Tower Bridge. After the narrator lauds the monuments as aesthetic gems, the film pans images of 1920s' nightclubs and theaters. To keep its viewers from nostalgizing though, the film quickly jumps from the images from the Roaring Twenties to footage of firefights and the bombed streets where the theaters once stood. Once the sound of bombing and sirens fades, the narrator gently suggests that people have always asked questions about social inequities, and a woman's voice asks, "Well was the old London all that it should have been?" This question disrupts whatever lingering romanticization for a past London remains and provokes the viewer to consider that this glamorized past was never reality for most. The inclusion of this question makes it clear that *Proud City* is specifically directed toward the middle class, who must be reminded or convinced of the benefits of social welfare and the need for better social programs to create a more "orderly" society. Like *Housing Problem*, which included interviews and direct, face-on shots of the inhabitants of Stepney, *Proud City* uses voice-overs of working- and middle-class individuals over footage of 1940s' working- and middle-class life to portray a sense of class consensus and reinforce commonalities. This new society, according to the film, must factor in all aspects of everyday life for all sectors of class: work, traffic, health, living conditions, and most importantly, the use of space.

To assert an empirical tone and emphasize the rigor of the plans, Abercrombie and Forshaw discuss their use of surveys of the population and measurements of city spaces (Sandercock 2003).[8] Combining empiricism with nostalgia further underscores the rhetorical goals of the film: consensus for rebuilding and modernization that results in a classless Britain. This can be seen when Abercrombie and Forshaw discuss the results of their work in the film:

> One very important thing we discovered when we made our survey is that the spirit of the old village communities has somehow survived. . . . [T]he old local artists are still there. It's that loyalty, neighborliness, which holds a group of people together because they have the same interests and pleasures and because they share their troubles and triumphs.

What Abercrombie and Forshaw emphasize is that even within the bounds of scientific study, a nostalgia for an imagined Britain appears, one that is grounded in the past village of London to which all residents can trace their origins, however fanciful this vision is. In this portrait of London, what determines the spaces of the city are the inhabitants themselves, who are united through their shared experiences and imagined past. As Mark Tewdwr-Jones argues, it is these filmic representations of the urban environment that "grants a perspective for the interpretation and representation of places, allows for reflection, and deepens audiences' impressions of subjective experience, while at the same time providing a good spatial sense of environmental change and development" (2013, 88). While the narrative of *Proud City* conflates subjective experiences, it also wants to create shared commonalities between Londoners to rally political support.

Despite the attempt at communal consensus, the film's tone is paternalistic, particularly for a twenty-first-century audience, in its suggestion of one correct vision for what London should be: one that erases the disordered, unruly spaces, which act as the visual reminders of working-class life and as thirdspaces.[9] In fact, the pedagogical nature of the film was commented on by the Background Films Viewing Committee (BFVC) in 1946 in the *Monthly Film Bulletin* as something useful for "Youth Clubs and senior forms in schools, if given in conjunction with a short talk and explanatory material" (72). As the BFVC notes in their broader assessment of the film's content, the "creation of communities is an essential part of the plan, which, it is stressed, is not a cut-and-dried blueprint but an idea, and it rests with Londoners to make it reality" (1946, 72). The film acts as both a vehicle to reinforce localism within the cosmopolis and to instruct its viewers of the appropriate attitude toward redevelopment and elicit universal support for rebuilding. The use of the "common Londoner" motif is something that channels an immediate emotional response from the post-war viewer, relying both on wartime rhetoric and notions of the everyman (Hornsey 2010, 43). What the BFVC review also implies is that however much the planners believe in their utopian vision, Londoners, not official planners, are the final arbitrators. Interestingly, Abercrombie did not necessarily view his role as a planner as authoritarian, and he became a public figure and civic spokesperson, easily recognizable by most Londoners, in multiple films, including the documentary feature, *The Way We Live* (1946) (Lewi 2014, 271).

To appease more conservative-minded citizens, the rhetoric of the film continually returns to references of traditional British architectural aesthetics rather than discuss the modernist aesthetics of the new buildings. The answer to fixing the "ugliness" of the city is to create a plan that makes everything about the city "good" like the "dignified works of Christopher Wren." Cutting between Georgian row houses to Victorian slums, the film draws the corollary between these two urban worlds and suggests that all of London can be replaced and beautified with better architecture and living conditions. Originally shown at London's the Academy, an art house cinema on Oxford Street in Westminster, the film catered to an audience who was interested in aesthetics more broadly. In his 1945 review for *The Spectator*, Alexander Shaw wrote,

> I would not have thought it possible to have shot new views of London but Ralph Keene and Peter Hennessy have managed to do it in the two-reeler *Proud City*. In a series of beautifully composed and photographed shots they show us a strange and almost magic capital city.
>
> (460)

Although somewhat clumsy in its heavy-handedness, the emphasis of the aesthetically "good" and "bad" in the film is an effective propaganda tool, as it reminds the viewers that they know what is good for themselves and that the government is not imposing this project without approval. The way to make the city "good," then, is to make urban spaces reflect the British values of dignity and order and the corresponding aesthetics of neat row houses, well-maintained streets, and controlled industrial spaces. Equally important for Abercrombie and Forshaw, the answer does not reside in the suburbs, which are just as much a part of the unruly and "untidy sprawl" of housing parks and factories from the ugly Victorian past.

Crucial to the film's critique of London is the lack of open spaces and the need to create more green spaces, particularly in working-class neighborhoods like Stepney and Poplar, which also is reminiscent of the earlier interwar garden city and later post-war new towns like Harlow, which combined Scandinavian modernism with green spaces. In *Proud City*, the focus on greenery and spaces like Hampstead Heath are continual reminders of a British identity that is premised upon a romantic English countryside and the simplicity of an agrarian past. Tied into the idea of green spaces is also the idea of making "life pleasanter" but also to offer a "healthier" city, particularly for children, who need "light and air." These statements channel earlier liberal discourses on the health of the working class and the paternalistic remedies proffered. Yet the film also considers modern solutions and, unlike garden cities and new towns, locates the greenery and the site of modernity within the bounds of existing urban space, rather than removed to the suburbs or undeveloped countryside. Part of the traffic plan contains a cleaning up of the rail system with reductions in smoke and noise, furthering the idea of a London that will return to an idyllic town that was not only healthier, but less visibly industrialized. By integrating nature and industry as a harmonious entity, Abercrombie and Forshaw view modern urbanity as something that incorporates both conservative and progressive fantasies of place. Hornsey reads Abercrombie's plans for these new interclass neighborhoods as foundational units that allowed the city planner "to endow his London with the nostalgic qualities of pre-industrial village life, while also effecting a sly scalar confusion . . . that figured the neighborhood as the microcosm of the integrated nation at the heart of welfare-state ideologies" (2010, 45). Toward the final scenes of the film, the narrator demands: "Will London be recreated on modern lines worthy of her long history?" For any Londoner, the only answer is an affirmative one. To answer in the negative would mean a simultaneous rejection of modernity and the past.

Toward the end of *Proud City*, Lord Leithem, head of the London County Council, responds to scripted questions from locals. Each Londoner asks a question regarding logistics, costs, and overall changes to the city, to which Leithem responds with a monologue that channels earlier wartime rhetoric to convince the audience of the imperative need to modernize:

> In a way, you know, this is London's war . . . against London's war against decay and dirt and inefficiency. . . . If we miss this chance to rebuild London, we shall have missed one of the great moments of history. We shall have shown ourselves unworthy of our victory.

He finishes his statement with the rationale for why rebuilding should occur in the first place; he says the people need "[a] London where everyone can live with a healthy and happy life, a London her citizens can be proud of." Like the earlier question challenging viewers to consider a London that is both modern and traditional, Leithem's statement echoes several national sentiments. First, he challenges the people to see rebuilding as the next front of war, one in which the dirt and despair of bad building plans is under attack. He also suggests that the dirt, decay, and inefficiency of the city are everyone's burden and shameful. However, without naming any specific social programs, Leithem's words emphasize equality as something that is analogous to freedom from an authoritarian government. His assertion that London should be a city its inhabitants can be "proud of" implies that rebuilding constitutes an individual civic duty. Equally important is that he does not include any references to imperial glory, which underscores how the empire is no longer central to the inhabitants of Britain or their national subjectivity. Of course, Leithem's references to Britain's past are inherently tied to the British Empire's colonial projects. Yet, by never directly referring to the empire, the film reveals that a new British subjectivity must distance itself from those structures if it is to be fully modern.

Proud City and the Ministry of Information's perspective is that modernization is what is integral for any kind of rebuilding for Britain. *Proud City* underscores the post-war attempt to level class difference through the creation of a homogenous, modernized city, particularly in its discussion of former social housing and how they will be replaced with aesthetically pleasing buildings. Lord Leithem's comment that an "ideology of happiness" will be found in this project applies to this new class, which seems to encompass all Londoners and is removed from the wartime past. While the film does not identify specific groups for this new homogenized middle class, it was often identified as white-collar workers of pre-war London, former colonial bureaucrats who had returned to Britain, and former working classes who suddenly had increased incomes and buying power. George Orwell (2002) describes the new middle class, whom he rails against, as being made of clerks, women, those who were on the peripheries of the city (i.e., the suburbs), and servicemen.[10] Social theorists like Arno Mayer stress the erosion of difference between laborers and the lower middle class in this period and its importance in understanding class identity. The new middle class, which Mayer ascribes to the creation of new social programs, is concentrated in cities; is neither upper nor lower class; is conscious of their social position and aspires upward; and most importantly, is fearful of sinking downward (1975, 423–24).[11] By refusing to define their audience or who this project is directly for, beyond addressing pre-war housing projects, *Proud City* assumes its audience is in fact this group that is fearful of sinking downward to their working-class origins. By offering urban planning and promoting social programs like equitable housing, transit, and access to green spaces, the film expects its audience to recognize how they themselves benefit from the same programs as "common Londoners" and thus will support them. However much a piece of propaganda, the film offers a vision for London that builds upon welfare-state ideals and channels progressive politics in the hope that Britain could somehow be different from its pre-war past.

In direct opposition to this concrete plan filled with urban solutions and the creation of a homogenous, modern London, Graham Greene's *The End of the Affair* rejects the urban planner's fantasy of a progressive, modern, and classless London. Set in London from 1942 to 1946, *The End of the Affair* describes its protagonist's attempts to reconcile the loss of his lover as he retells the story of their relationship. Many critics have read the novel as a direct commentary on Greene's relationship with his mistress and his Catholic faith rather than as a realist text that reflects a specific historic moment. Instead, it should be read as a novel that refuses to accept the modern, equitable future promoted by Attlee's Labour government and instead clings to past social ideals of Britain. Early in the novel, the narrator and protagonist, Maurice Bendrix, proclaims: "If this book of mine fails to take a straight course, it is because I am lost in a strange region: I have no map. I sometimes wonder whether anything that I am putting down here is true" (Greene 2004, 39). In wandering without a map, Bendrix's statement can be read as an existential allegory for the turmoil individuals faced during the physical and social rebuilding after the war, particularly for middle-class men like Bendrix. As Raymond Williams writes about Orwell, middle-class men of this period are "simultaneously [the] dominator and dominated," which describes their problematic feelings of limited power and aliena-tion (1971, 19). This powerlessness is further augmented by the social revisions of gender roles and domestic spaces that occurred during the war and in the immediate post-war period. *The End of the Affair*, along with many of Greene's other novels, underscores this feeling for middle-class men, who are unsure of their place in a rapidly modern-izing and changing world. These men, who follow the logic of decency and order, are unable to recognize a hopeful or even peaceful future for British society as portrayed in *Proud City*. If they acknowledge the progressive, future-oriented narratives with the modernization of Brit-ain, Greene's protagonists lose their pre-war subjectivities and become socially irrelevant.

The first-person narration uses a complex and convoluted structure based upon Bendrix's jagged and questionable memories, undermining the straightforward and happy future for the common Londoner pro-moted in *Proud City*. As Bendrix is a professional writer, he is always questioning the process of storytelling and reveals the inherent instabil-ity of his world. For example, the novel's opening recounts Bendrix's memory of a rainy day in 1946:

> A story has no beginning or end: arbitrarily one chooses that moment of experience from which to look back or from which to look ahead. I say 'one chooses' with the inaccurate pride of a professional writer who—when he has been seriously noted at all—has been praised for his technical ability, but do I in fact of my own will *choose* that black wet January night on the Common, in 1946, the sight of Henry Miles slanting across the wide river of rain, or did these images choose me?
> (2004, 1)

Bendrix's conscious choice to begin the novel with that specific rainy January night operates in several ways. First, it reveals the ongoing self-referentiality between the text, the writer, and the author, which Bendrix conflates to draw attention to his narrative and signal to the reader that this is a constructed story told by a somewhat unreliable narrator. Sec-ond, Bendrix's opening statement that "a story has no beginning or end" reflects the cyclical nature of time in the novel: narratives are always ongoing stories that are in the middle of being told that look backward rather than toward the potentiality of the future. Last, the multiple lay-ers of time in the narration suggest that Bendrix could be telling this story a few months after the final events or many years later. While the novel unfolds from this chance meeting in 1946, the narration continu-ally jumps between Bendrix's various memories from 1942 to 1946. The constant references to non-linear time and memories create a circular dialogue between past and present, especially as Bendrix narrates from some unknown and undefined future perspective, and echoes Westphal's commentary on post-1945 texts, in which the "writing reveals its labil-ity, the fragility of its spatiotemporal anchor" (2011, 20). By creating a narrative that is so tenuously grounded in Bendrix's memories of the war and its immediate aftereffects, Greene emphasizes the instability of the physical post-war world for middle-class men as they depend upon specific locations, now destroyed, to anchor their sense of identity and purpose.

The layering of time is also crucial for understanding Bendrix's nihil-ism and inability to alter his perceptions of classed subjectivity. Early in the novel, he states, "for I never lose the consciousness of time: to me the present is never here: it is always last year or next week" (Greene 2004, 40). The lack of the present signals that despite Bendrix's "consciousness of time," there is no immediate present. Even the peace of the post-war years is a kind of fiction: "And yet there *was* this peace. . . . That is how I think of these first months of war—was it a phoney peace as well as a phoney war?" (36). This shows exactly how Bendrix conflates time: the peace of 1946 is the same thing as the peace of the first months of war, or a false equivalence. He also alludes to the Phoney War, the relative "calm" months of 1939 before the Blitz began in 1940, to emphasize the intrinsic artificiality of the so-called real, further echoing a post-modern subjectivity in which no meaning can ever truly be determined or estab-lished through the social programs promoted by the welfare state.

Bendrix's notion of time as non-linear and almost atemporal operates according to the same temporal framework that occurs during a state of total war. As Bendrix indicates early in the novel, "Eternity is said not to be an extension of time but an absence of time, and sometimes it seemed to me that her abandonment touched a strange mathematical point of endlessness, a point with no width, occupying no space" (39). Bendrix's present is an eternity in which time and space are absent, and thus, there is no future, which contradicts the utopian visions of *Proud City*. Paul Saint-Amour indicates the problem of foreknowledge that occurs during total war, in which the future and present become one, which "impoverish[es] the future by afflicting it with conditions of the past—that is, the condition of being subject to knowledge and memory because [*sic*] inert" (2015, 18). This process pushes an individual to live outside of time. As Bendrix demonstrates, his insistent questioning and emphasis on the "phoney" highlight his cynicism and undercut any potential for a future that addresses social inequities. When atheist Rich-ard Smythe is miraculously cured of his disfiguring urticaria, Bendrix initially wants to ask a doctor if a "faith cure is possible," but ultimately decides it is better not to know (160). The final words of the novel end with Bendrix's thoughts on Smythe's cure:

I wrote at the start that this was a record of hate, and walking there beside Henry towards the evening glass of beer, I found the one prayer that seemed to serve the winter mood: O God, You've done enough, You've robbed me of enough, I'm too tired and old to learn to love, leave me alone for ever.

(160)

Bendrix's rejection of religious and secular faith is also a rejection of the future and the possibility of change, including that of a new Britain. Bendrix has never believed in God, but in asking to be left alone, he demonstrates his complete inability to regain any sense of hope. He cannot believe in the unknown, including the future, because there is no hope left in the world he inhabits either for himself or for others. By rejecting the possibility of a miraculous cure for Smythe, he forecloses himself to the future and change, including the rebuilding and future of the city in which he lives. In many ways this refusal of the future and constant return to the past indicates Bendrix's privilege as a middle-class man: he has the luxury of looking backward because his tangible present is not precarious. He does not have to acknowledge money, food, or other material needs; they are a constant for him despite the ongoing austerity of post-war Britain.

What materiality Bendrix does emphasize are the spaces of London, which continually conjure memories of the past and make it impossible for him to establish any kind of futurity. Rather than function as a form of fragmentation, the bomb sites and ruins physically ground Bendrix within London and connect his thoughts and experiences, offering a means of holding onto the past rather than destroying it. The bombed-out doorway of Bendrix's house acts as a bulwark for history rather than a symbol of erasure: "Then I closed the stained-glass doors behind me and made my way carefully down the steps that had been blasted in 1944 and never repaired. I had reason to remember the occasion and how the stained glass, tough and ugly and Victorian, stood up to the shock as our grandfathers themselves would have done" (2). What is significant is Bendrix's description of the Victorian stained glass that remains despite the bombing like its "tough and ugly" turn-of-the-century forbearers. For Bendrix, what is timeless are his memories and conceptualization of the past rather than the emptiness of the present and future. Baucom describes this process of ruin fetishization as a holdout for privileged classes' "restoration and redemption" and where a new, post-imperial Britain can be denied (1999, 181). While Bendrix is less explicit in his refusal, he does foreclose any alternative for middle-class British masculinity by returning to Victorian grandfathers, instead of imagining himself within the modernized London Abercrombie and Forshaw envision, further entrenching not only the post-war decent man, but older iterations of middle-class masculinity.

Whenever Bendrix feels any kind of stability, it is always in the moorings of older, pre-war British architecture: the eighteenth-century church that stands like "a toy in an island of grass—the toy could be left outside in the dark, in the dry unbreakable weather" (Greene 2004, 18); the stained Victorian glass that is continually mentioned (2, 54); the glittering shops of Oxford Street that are compared to jewels (114); and the old hotels that used to stand next to Paddington Station at Eastborne Terrace, and while half-destroyed, conjure a material richness in his memory that is absent from most of the narrative:

> [T]here was a potted fern in the hall and we were shown the best room by a manageress with blue hair: a real Edwardian room with a great gilt double bed and red velvet curtains and a full length mirror.
>
> (34)

In fact, it is because of the ruins that Bendrix can so vividly fashion the memory of the hotel: it impresses upon him what was once hidden behind the facade of the building and harkens back to Edwardian society and the *lieux de memoires* so crucial for the pre-war middle-class identity. Ruins are far from destructive symbols; they allow Bendrix to access both his own personal past and the greater British cultural history so that he can continue to live in a static and atemporal present. He denies that he is in the present, but in constantly returning to the ruins and refusing to allow for rebuilding, he denies any kind of progressive temporality and the post-war futurity that reconstructs notions of class through rebuilding. The acknowledgment of the "sturdiness" of Victorian and Edwardian architecture and objects reveals Bendrix's implicit sympathy as a decent man for a past sense of order, cultural stability, and the later conservative nostalgia located within romanticized pasts. While nostalgia is not the correct description for Bendrix's emotional state, his form of mourning for the Edwardian past equates with what Baucom identifies in later neoliberal nostalgia for the country house as a reinstatement of the "ordered and hegemonic, moral economy of England's privileged classes" (1999, 173).

Bendrix denies any teleology to preserve his own self, rather than lose it in the unknown future. Toward the end of the novel, when it is revealed that Sarah has promised to end their affair if Bendrix remains alive after the bombing of his house, she writes to him to explain why:

> You took away all my lies and self-deceptions like they clear a road of rubble for somebody to come along it, somebody of importance, and now he's come, but you cleared the way yourself. When you write you try to be exact and you taught me to want the truth, and you told me when I wasn't telling the truth.
>
> (Greene 2004, 121)

Sarah blames Bendrix for what has happened; he was the one to demand that she reveal the truth, and rather than embrace another lover, she turns to religion. What is striking in Sarah's use of metaphors is the comparison between rubble and truth. For her, it is only when the metaphysical rubble is cleared from her soul and consciousness that she can both tell the truth and find happiness. Given the novel's backdrop of 1946 London and the massive amounts of literal rubble yet to be removed from its streets, there is a striking parallel. For readers at the time of publication in 1951, it would be all too familiar an image of London, in which the gaping holes in the city were daily reminders of the Blitz. By clearing any rubble, a path is opened for the future and the unknown. Removing the rubble and building over it, either metaphysically or materially, becomes a mechanism to forget the past and embrace the future, disrupting Bendrix's temporality and rejecting the totality of total war.

Any hope Bendrix may have for the future is constantly thwarted by his obsession with the pre-war past. The foreclosure of hope does not necessarily need to be entirely dire for society though. As Saint-Amour argues, it can produce new forms of what is socially acceptable, such as celibacy and childlessness, because it allows for new forms of radicalism that do not have to rely on sexual procreation or a continued legacy (2015, 8).[12] In fact, *The End of the Affair* in many ways is a story that is about the end of an extra-marital affair that can exist in the bounds of wartime but cannot during peace. Despite the guilt that Sarah feels later, she was entirely happy to simultaneously be Bendrix's mistress and Henry's wife. This love triangle only begins to fail when Bendrix pressures her to leave Henry and marry him instead. However, the novel is not entirely pessimistic in its perceptions of domestic relationships. In a somewhat strange twist toward the end, Bendrix moves in with Henry, as Henry cannot live alone following Sarah's death. The two men live a variant form of privileged bachelordom: the husband and the lover of the dead wife. They replicate their own happy domesticity that includes separate careers, meals together, and nights at the pub without the fear of every truly being alone. In this ending, the domestic becomes a masculine space in which men can continue enacting the past rather than embrace the future and the unknown. While the text states that the relationship is purely homosocial, the two men queer coupling becomes a radical relationship precisely because it is one that is non-reproductive and one that is moored in the past.

By ending with his domestic, backward-looking "peace," Bendrix reveals that there is never a future that allows one to escape or rewrite the past, including classed subjectivity. For someone like Bendrix, time acts as a circular event that offers no respite from history, nor does it allow for the belief in a different and positive future. He wants to maintain his status as a well-received and literary, albeit unpopular, writer, because he recognizes the death sentence for a writer to be labeled "popular." He states that he "ha[s] not committed that crime—not yet, but always though I retain a little of the exclusiveness of unsuccess, the little reviews, like wise detectives, can scent it on its way" (Greene 2004, 122). While this comment emphasizes Greene's own writerly acknowledgment that it is impossible to be both a literary and popular novelist, it also reveals that the formerly up-and-coming novelist Bendrix holds no power or prestige once he becomes a popular, middle-aged author. In this moment, Bendrix still has the power of the well-regarded writer when he allures the young fan, Sylvia, but even his plans to bed her are derailed by his "duties" as a middle-class British man. He embodies the Orwellian ideals that are ascribed to the middle-class gentleman of the interwar period, which include fair play, brotherhood, decency, honesty, forthrightness, and hardiness (Gopinath 2013, 3). While these traits are further upheld and perpetuated by Orwell's "classless" stylizations of British masculinity during and after WWII, *The End of the Affair* suggests that these characteristics, even when upheld, are futureless because they represent a past world that does not work within the framework of modernized Britain.

Bendrix as a middle-aged, middle-class man is fully entrenched in the structures tied to imperial masculinity and Orwell's decent gentleman. This becomes one of his failures because it prevents him from consummating his relationship with Sylvia and robs him of desire when he engages with prostitutes. His lack of desire is quickly linked to his decency, which has nothing to do with the women with whom he is about to sleep or with any kind of conflicted feelings toward them. Instead, Bendrix's loyalty to the past and memories of Sarah rob him of physical desire. This portrait of middle-class masculinity suggests that men who uphold this older form of masculinity lose their desire, physically and psychically; fail to reproduce; and, thus, self-annihilate. In darkly comedic fashion, *The End of the Affair* interrupts the consummation of Bendrix's relationship with Sylvia through a complicated plot involving Sarah's aged mother. At Sarah's funeral, her mother insists that Bendrix have dinner with her immediately afterward and Bendrix, in his need to fulfill his domestic obligation (and thus masculine decency) goes, leaving Sylvia behind. During dinner, Sarah's mother reveals the meal is simply a pretense to borrow money, but it is too late for Bendrix to return to Sylvia, whom he never sees again.

Bendrix's focus on the past and its physical iterations underscores the cultural discussion of rebuilding post-war Britain physically and metaphorically. *The End of the Affair* was published in September 1951, which was a month before Clement Attlee's Labour government lost control of Parliament to Churchill's Conservative party. Given that the novel is set five years prior, one can read Bendrix's overall pessimism about the future as representative of the failure of Attlee's government to enact the promised change of a new and better society. The novel does not make specific political comments, but Bendrix's character is emblematic of middle-class men, who faced with changing social structures and order are ultimately pessimistic and can only envision the continuation of total war and romanticize pre-war spaces. The men's inability to adapt represents a portion of society that clings desperately to the past and fails to envision any kind of social change. While *Proud City* demonstrates the positive promotion of London's post-war modernization and how it will create an equitable future for Britain, it ultimately is dismissed by the middle class, particularly the decent men like Bendrix, because there is no place for them in this project, particularly one that attempts to level class difference. The competing narratives demonstrate the ongoing conflict between the state and the individual when prescribing the space of the nation, and as Bendrix illustrates, the middle class refuses to embrace a futurity that robs them of their past and thus social power.

Notes

1. See Susan Grayzel, *At Home and Under Fire: Air Raids and Culture in Britain from the Great War to the Blitz* (2012, 3–6).
2. Benedict Anderson (2016) and Paul Gilroy (2002) have discussed this explicitly in terms of the "imagined communities" within Britain, what constitutes "Englishness" according to various nationalist discourses, and how the space of Britain, England, and other subdivisions reinforce nationalist discourse.
3. The term "retrochic" was coined by Raphael Samuel in *Theatres of Memory* (1994) to describe the cultural phenomenon in which certain aesthetics of the past become fetishized and "steals from the past at random. This is what distinguished it from the sententiousness of 'heritage' " (Hatherley 2016, 6).
4. These iconic examples of Britishness and "sites of memory" go back to Raymond Williams's discussion of the country house in *The Country and the City* (1973) as a symbol of a lost "England" that occurs during Industrialism and can be found in the remaining "natural" and romanticized spaces of the English countryside (1985). Ian Baucom also discusses it extensively in his argument that architecture is crucial to maintaining and reappropriating the structures of the empire (1999).
5. As Lefebvre describes, state space lacks the "chaos" of private space because it appears to manage space in a homogeneous and unified fashion and thus can control and watch through surveillance. Yet this is a state fantasy because private interests and the actions of public powers "sometimes involve a collusion, sometimes a collision. This creates the paradox of space that is both homogenous and broken" (Lefebvre 2010, 227).
6. Wilson describes Abercrombie's plans as "purposeful sterility" and an asexual vision of the post-war city.
7. These two dueling positions of a modernizing social project and a return to traditional aesthetics and ideals for the space of the city uphold the "paradox" LeFebvre finds in all official narratives of space (1991).
8. Post-war planning needed to assert itself as a verifiable scientific discipline, which was done through more rigorous surveys, research, and collection of data.

9. Edward Soja has argued within cities are what he calls "thirdspace," where the potential of space and its lived practice exist outside of the prescribed and official determinations of what that space should be (2015). Through understanding it as a thirdspace, the city "takes on more dynamic qualities that derive from its role in the formation of city space and the social construction of urbanism, a constantly evolving, intentionally planned, and politically charged *contextualization* and *spatialization* of social life in its broadest sense" (8).
10. See George Orwell's 1941 essay, "The Lion and the Unicorn: Socialism and the English Genius."
11. Arno Mayer, "The Lower Middle Class as Historical Problem," *Journal of Modern History* 47, no. 3 (1975): 423–424, https://doi.org/10.1086/241338.
12. Saint-Amour states that new social forms "arise precisely when the future appears barred—radical defenses of childlessness and celibacy, for example, that took imminent war as the occasion for warding off the prospect of a politically and sexually retrograde peace" (2015, 8).

References

Anderson, Benedict. (1983) 2016. *Imagined Communities: Reflections on the Origin and Spread of Nationalism*. London: Verso.

Anstey, Edgar, and Arthur Elton. 1935. *Housing Problems*. London: British Commercial Gas Association.

Baucom, Ian. 1999. *Out of Place: Englishness, Empire, and the Locations of Identity*. Princeton, NJ: Princeton University Press.

De Certeau, Michel. (1980) 1984. *The Practice of Everyday Life*. Translated by Steven Rendall. Berkeley, CA: University of California Press.

Gilroy, Paul. (1987) 2002. *There Ain't No Black in the Union Jack: The Cultural Politics of Race and Nation*. Abingdon, UK and New York: Routledge.

Gopinath, Praseeda. 2013. *Scarecrows of Chivalry: English Masculinities After Empire*. Charlottesville, VA: University of Virginia Press.

Grayzel, Susan R. 2012. *At Home and Under Fire: Air Raids and Culture in Britain from the Great War to the Blitz*. Cambridge, UK: Cambridge University Press.

Greene, Graham. (1951) 2004. *The End of the Affair*. New York: Penguin Books.

Hatherley, Owen. 2016. *The Ministry of Nostalgia: Consuming Austerity*. London: Verso.

Hornsey, Richard. 2010. *The Spiv and the Architect: Unruly Life in Postwar London*. Minneapolis, MN: University of Minnesota Press.

Keene, Ralph. 1946. *Proud City a Plan for London*. London: Ministry of Information. Documentary.

Lefebvre, Henri. (1977) 1991. *Critique of Everyday Life*. Translated by John Moore. London: Verso.

———. (2009) 2010. "Space and the State." In *State, Space, World: Selected Essays*, edited by Neil Brenner and Stuart Elden, translated by Gerald Moore, Neil Brenner, and Stuart Elden, 223–53. Minneapolis, MN: University of Minnesota Press.

Lewi, Hannah. 2014. "Plans on Film: 'Scene Five Cut to the Professionals Smoking His Pipe'." *Fabrications: The Journal of the Society of Architectural*

Historians, Australia and New Zealand 24 (2): 268–89. https://doi.org/10.108 0/10331867.2014.961224.

Mayer, Arno. 1975. "The Lower Middle Class as Historical Problem." *The Journal of Modern History* 47 (3): 423–24. https://doi.org/10.1086%2F241338.

Mellor, Leo. 2011. *Reading the Ruins: Modernism, Bombsites and British Culture.* Cambridge, UK: Cambridge University Press.

Orwell, George. (1941) 2002. "The Lion and the Unicorn: Socialism and the English Genius." In *Essays*, 291–348. New York: Alfred A Knopf.

"Proud City." 1946. *Monthly Film Bulletin* 13 (145): 72.

Ross, Kristin. 1995. *Fast Cars, Clean Bodies: Decolonization and the Reordering of French Culture.* Cambridge, MA: MIT Press.

Saint-Amour, Paul. 2015. *Tense Future: Modernism, Total War, Encyclopedic Form.* Oxford, UK: Oxford University Press.

Samuel, Raphael. 1994. *Theatres of Memory: Past and Present in Contemporary Culture.* London, UK: Verso.

Sandercock, Leonie. 2003. *Mongrel Cities: Cosmopolis II.* London: Continuum.

Shaw, Alexander. 1945. "'Blood and Sand.' at the Dominion and New Victoria.- 'God Is My Co-Pilot.' at the Astoria.-'Palestine Problem.' at the Empire.-'Proud City.' at the Academy (Book Review).'." *The Spectator*, November 16, 1945.

Soja, Edward W. (2000) 2015. *Postmetropolis: Critical Studies of Cities and Regions.* Malden, MA: Wiley-Blackwell.

Tewdwr-Jones, Mark. 2013. "Modern Planning on Film: Re-Shaping Space, Image and Representation." *Berkeley Planning Journal* 26 (1): 86–106. https:// doi.org/10.5070/BP326118144.

Westphal, Bertrand. 2011. *Geocriticism: Real and Fictional Spaces.* Translated by Robert T. Tally Jr. Basingstoke, UK: Palgrave Macmillan.

———. 2016. "A Geocritical Approach to Geocriticism." *American Book Review* 37 (6): 4–5. https://doi.org/10.1353/abr.2016.0115.

Williams, Raymond. 1971. *George Orwell.* New York: Viking Press.

———. (1973) 1985. *The Country and the City.* London: Hogarth Press.

Wilson, Elizabeth. (1991) 1992. *The Sphinx in the City: Urban Life, the Control of Disorder, and Women.* Berkeley, CA: University of California Press.

6 "Low Tastes"

John Braine, Drinking, and Class

Ben Clarke

On September 4, 1957, just a few months after publishing *Room at the Top*, John Braine wrote to tell Richard Hoggart he "bought *The Uses of Literacy* in London on the eve of going to France, began it at Victoria, and finished it in Toulouse" (57). He thought the book "so good that it annoyed me," in part because "there was so much in it that I was saving to write about myself" (57). The statement emphasizes the parallels between Braine's work and that of Hoggart, like Braine a working-class "scholarship boy" from the West Riding of Yorkshire (Hoggart 1957, 238). Contemporary commentators recognized Hoggart's relation to the novelists and dramatists of the period, and Carl Bode even described him as the "theoretician" of the "so-called Angry Young Men" (1959, 332), but critical attention often focused on their shared frustration with what Tom Maschler called the "apathy, the complacency, the idealistic bankruptcy" of post-war England (1958, 7). This emphasis on subject matter and perspective neglects the methodological parallels between artistic works in the period and the new field of cultural studies. Hoggart and Braine not only shared an interest in changes in working-class communities but employed similar techniques to represent and analyze them. The significant parallels between their texts suggest working-class writing extends across generic boundaries and is defined partly by a concern with the significance of the everyday objects, spaces, and practices through which identities and values are negotiated. Hoggart's analytical method and comments on "working-class art" (1957, 100) in *The Uses of Literacy* provide a basis for an interpretation of Braine's texts that recognizes the complexities of his technique and the way in which it embodies a distinct working-class literary and critical sensibility. This reading intervenes in broader debates about the definition of working-class writing, which cannot be adequately understood simply in terms of style, authorial biography, or even subject matter; there is more to being a working-class writer than being born in poverty or writing about factories. The category is better seen as a project than a genre, an attempt to explore not only working-class experience but the knowledge, values, and modes of thought it produces. It employs a variety of techniques

DOI: 10.4324/9781003119425-7

but consistently involves a concern with the ways in which meaning is generated, explored, and sometimes disrupted in familiar acts, spaces, and interactions. Working-class writing is defined in part by its materialism, the recognition that shared concrete structures inform but do not in any simple sense determine individual ideas and experiences and that an understanding of working-class life consequently depends on a critical engagement with the specific, often restrictive, conditions under which it is produced.

In his introduction to the French edition of *The Uses of Literacy*, Jean-Claude Passeron argues that Hoggart's text is innovative partly because it analyzes its subject "according to the structures, if not always in words, or [*sic*] working-class consciousness and speech" (2007, 29). Hoggart insists that "working-class attitudes" are founded upon a concern with "the personal, the concrete, the local" (1957, 32), and his own text emphasizes the specific; as Collini observes, even his prose is insistently "concrete" (1999, 219). The focus on the particular is central to what Lawrence Grossberg describes as his attempt to "validate working-class culture as embodying legitimate forms of knowledge practices" (2007, 128). *The Uses of Literacy* demonstrates the value of working-class modes of analysis and their ability to extend the academic forms the book also uses and values. Its argument that "working-class art" is "essentially a 'showing' (rather than an 'exploration')" that "starts with the assumption that human life is fascinating in itself" (Hoggart 1957, 100) is founded upon this broader understanding of working-class thought. While the characterization of working-class art risks obscuring its formal experimentation and establishing a false dichotomy between "showing" and "exploration," it emphasizes its commitment to objects and acts often ignored or dismissed as trivial. There is a conspicuous parallel between this and the "vigorous realism" that Braine saw as the "only possible way for the novel," with its focus on "the surface" of things (1974, 46). Braine's advocacy of realism to the aspiring author in *Writing a Novel* is informed by practical calculations, a conviction that "[e]xperimental novels aren't accepted," but also by a belief in its artistic and intellectual possibilities. He insists that there "is nothing which you cannot say within the framework of the straightforward realistic novel" and that "[n]o person, no place, no object, no event is dull or boring or commonplace" (46). Braine argues that the "true novelist is perpetually fascinated by the life around him" (40), a description that constructs fiction as the embodiment of the cultural values Hoggart identifies, a paradigmatic working-class form. The function of the novel is to transfigure the ordinary or, more accurately, to demonstrate that no such transfiguration is necessary. Fiction challenges the failures of imagination and empathy that prevent people from recognizing that the everyday is always already fascinating and complex.

The Uses of Literacy not only analyses familiar spaces but represents them in literary terms. It incorporates detailed, sensitive descriptions of places like the public library, the "special refuge of the misfits and left-overs, of the hollow-cheeked, watery-eyed, shabby and furtively sad," where an

> eccentric absorbed in the rituals of his monomania sits between a pinched unmarried brother, kept by a married sister for the sake of his war-pension, and an aged widower from a cheap lodging or a house smelling permanently of old tea and the frying-pan.
>
> (Hoggart 1957, 60)

The two elements of the text are inseparable; the interpretation of working-class life not only depends on a recognition of its specificity, its variety, and its density, but an ability to represent and evoke these things. Hoggart's considerable descriptive talents are essential to his critical method rather than merely a way of making his arguments more attractive and suggest that the boundary between literature and cultural analysis is, or at least should be, porous. Braine's interest in *The Uses of Literacy* is founded partly on a recognition that he and Hoggart contributed in intersecting ways to a common project. Braine did not simply intend to produce a text like *The Uses of Literacy* but in fact employed some of the same techniques throughout his career. The obvious differences of style and genre that distinguish his work from that of Hoggart illustrate the diversity of working-class writing but should not obscure the parallels in their methods and concerns.

Braine's critical interest in the intricacies of the everyday can be illustrated by a detailed analysis of his representations of drinking and the places where it occurs. His first and best-known novel, *Room at the Top*, is driven and structured by alcohol from its opening page, when Joe Lampton travels toward Warley, his head still "buzzing" from the "drinks of the night before" (Braine 2013, 3), to the last when, crying and "pie-eyed," he insists to Bob and Eva that "I murdered Alice" (218). A concern with the act and sites of drinking extends across his work. Many of the most significant scenes in his novels involve the consumption of alcohol in places ranging from pubs and bars to private houses. In *The Vodi*, Dick and Tom's adult relationship is negotiated in the "lounge of Frumenty" (Braine 1978, 102) and the "Bar Parlour, tucked away in the west wing of the Blue Lion" (143); in *The Jealous God*, Vincent explores his cultural background and family partly through his experience of the Hibernian Club; and in *The Crying Game*, the transformation of Frank Batcombe's life begins in the Salisbury, "one of the few remaining Victorian pubs" in London (Braine 1968, 12). These places are not passive, homogeneous backdrops to the actions of the characters but complex, specific material spaces that generate as well as express meaning. As Hoggart argues, working-class identity is articulated in the seemingly trivial acts that constitute and express an "all-pervading culture." including the way a person "order[s] drinks or trie[s] to stand drinks" (1957, 13). In Braine's work, a wide variety of social positions and values are not only articulated but also negotiated in the rhythm, form, and sites of drinking. The performance of class, gender, and sexuality in spaces such as pubs exposes their contingencies, the fact that their identical reproduction is never assured in advance. Identities are risked as well as reinscribed in everyday practices from standing rounds to flirting, and this potentially opens a space for new exchanges and modes of self-fashioning. Public houses and bars may often be places in which divisions and inequalities are reinforced, but they can also be sites of unexpected, unpredictable, subversive interactions, locations in which boundaries blur or even collapse.

Braine's attention to the material qualities and symbolic connotations of drinks, to their social functions, and the spaces in which they are consumed is significant, not simply because it reveals the complexity of the ordinary but because, more fundamentally, it makes the ordinary visible. His writing intervenes in what Rancière calls the "distribution of the sensible," disrupting the hierarchies of significance that structure both literature and society. By incorporating what is conventionally seen as undeserving of representation into his texts, Braine not only insists on the complexity and value of everyday objects and spaces but also, by extension, the people that use them. In this sense, his texts are inherently political, even when they do not engage with parties, movements, and philosophies. As Rancière argues, politics properly describes the discourses and practices that establish "what is visible, what can be said about it, who is entitled to speak and act about it" (Rancière 2009, 121). It is not contained in formal systems and institutions but is "a way of framing, among sensory data, a specific sphere of experience" that "allows (or does not allow) some specific data to appear; which allows or does not allow some specific subjects to designate them and speak about them" (Rancière 2012, 152). Literature participates in this process insofar as it "contributes to the reframing of forms of experience" (Rancière 2009, 122). The politics of literature is consequently not determined by "the politics of its writers," by their "their personal commitment to the social and political issues and struggles of their times" (Rancière 2012, 152), but by the nature of its intervention in this process. Despite Braine's drift to the right over the course of his life, his texts are not only radical but specifically democratic, questioning divisions between "high and low subject matters" (154), and insisting on the everyday as meaningful, complex, and valuable.

The democratic method of Braine's novels does not mean that they ignore the ways in which practices such as drinking express and reinforce class hierarchies. On the contrary, his textual politics is enacted partly through his exposure of these processes, which are normally represented as insignificant matters of taste, individual preference, or convention. As Barthes insists, the "anonymous ideology" of bourgeois society, including its class structure, is reproduced, not just in its "inventive core" but in ordinary acts, spaces, and exchanges, in "our remarks about the weather, a murder trial, a touching wedding, the cooking we dream of, the garments we wear" (2000, 140). As a consequence, radical theory and practice cannot focus simply on overtly political institutions or statements. Because, as Rastko Močnik argues, ideology has an "interpellative force" only "so far as 'it goes without saying'" (1993, 144), it often functions most effectively in acts and discourses that seem to be outside politics. Exposing such practices to critical scrutiny makes them potential sites of struggle rather than reinscription. Braine's texts emphasize that the drinks characters choose, the ways in which they order them, and the spaces in which they imbibe, all assert social and economic distinctions that can potentially be contested at the moment of their reproduction. A conventional choice can serve to reinforce a specific position within class, gender, and sexual formations; choosing differently can consequently be a subversive act, exposing and disrupting expectations. The recognition that popular culture is, as Stuart Hall argues, a place where the "struggle for and against a culture of the powerful is engaged," an "arena of consent and resistance" (1981, 239), is one of the key insights of early cultural studies, extending both social analysis and political practice. In Braine's text, the idea is not only expressed in the thoughts of his characters, who recognize the way in which status and values are negotiated in ordinary spaces, interactions, and objects, but in his technique, his attention to the mundane and unremarked.

Braine's concern with the way in which drinking reproduces such divisions is visible throughout his work but is most conspicuous in his first novel, on which this chapter focuses. *Room at the Top* recognizes that the differences between the Leddersford Conservative Club where Joe drinks "double whiskies" (2013, 190) with Jack Wales and the bar of the unnamed pub where he later consumes pints of bitter surrounded by resentful "Irish navies" (209–10) are determined by broader structures of power. These structures are never simply economic but always have a financial component that not only informs the differences between spaces but the ways in which interactions are organized within them. Wealth obviously matters, and purchasing expensive drinks is a form of conspicuous consumption that signifies other forms of privilege, as Joe recognizes when he notes that the fifteen shillings Jack Wales casually spends on whisky is the same amount that "poor snivelling little Raymond" (190) stole from petty cash in an effort to "keep up with the Joneses" (186), an act that would have condemned him "to the equivalent of a life in the galleys" (190) had it been exposed. Asserting status is nonetheless more complicated than having money. A series of conventions prescribe who can legitimately buy drinks, particularly for others, and what drinks they can choose; in this, as in other spheres, working and lower-middle-class characters cannot successfully alter their position through expenditure alone. At the Civic Ball, Jack Wales rejects Joe's offer to buy a round of whiskies with the observation "No, no old boy, frightfully dear stuff this," an act Joe sees as a "grace note" in a "well-known game, its object being the humiliation of those with less money than yourself" (150). Joe can obviously buy whisky and in fact does so immediately before he joins Susan and her group; what he cannot do is exploit its function as a signifier of class privilege. The representation of Joe's offer to stand a round of drinks as presumptuous enables Wales and the Browns to control their interactions, reducing him to the passive object of a purely formal generosity. The implications of this process reach their logical conclusion in the Conservative Club, where non-members cannot order drinks, a "club rule" (190) that Jack not only informs Joe about but emphasizes by buying him a drink as he departs, a gift that cannot be reciprocated. The restriction emphasizes the difference between those who belong and those who do not, making the latter dependent on the former.

The control Jack Wales and Mr. Brown exercise over the purchase and even choice of alcohol evokes the patriarchal convention whereby men buy drinks for women, who are thereby constructed as both passive and under an obligation. In "Nowhere," a sketch of a roadhouse published in the *New Statesman and Nation* six years before *Room at the Top*, Braine argues that the "gin-and-it and Pimm's and Moussec" the women receive in the Lounge are "paid for on the back seat of the Jaguars or after yet another drink in the expensive flat" (1951, 250). What is presented as an act of generosity is exploitative, a form of power reproduced by mediating access to pleasure. At the Civic Ball and the Conservative Club, Joe is implicitly feminized, positioned within gendered stereotypes that render him dependent. In both instances, this is reinforced by a sense of physical threat; at the Civic Ball, he fantasizes about breaking Jack Wales's "white teeth" but realizes he "would have smashed mine first" (Braine 2013, 148), and at the Conservative Club, he sees Jack as someone who could have "broken my back across his knee without putting himself out of breath" (189) even before he identifies him. The juxtaposition identifies the seemingly insignificant matter of purchasing drinks with an aggressive masculinity, suggesting a domination that operates through everyday interactions rather than just being signified by them.

Joe responds to being feminized, not by challenging patriarchal structures but by asserting himself in other terms they make available; intimidated by Jack Wales, he consoles himself with the thought that he has seen much more of Susan's "firm young breasts" than the "rich oaf beside her" (148). The reaction emphasizes his tendency to identify with power rather than to contest it and to rely on a masculinity that is in practice always threatened and precarious, a source of vulnerability as much as strength. Joe's progress exposes the ways in which inequalities are reproduced in ordinary spaces and exchanges, but despite his frequently acute reading of social dynamics, he only uses this information instrumentally, to advance within existing structures. He remains trapped within broader ideological narratives that he cannot read, at least in the moment; the retrospective narrative voice achieves a limited understanding of the ways in which his investment in ideas of success meant that he missed his "chance to be a real person" (113). In contrast, Alice recognizes that renegotiating even small rituals can not only expose the broader systems they reinforce but in so doing alter the terms of individual relationships. When Joe first drinks with her at the St. Clair, Alice tells him, "I always pay for my own," a practice she "learned in Rep" (47) and which therefore emphasizes that she worked before she married. The scene contrasts with that in the theater bar, where Susan not only accepts a drink but checks its suitability, asking Joe whether he will "laugh if I have a grapefruit" (65). The moment establishes a pattern of expenditure that Joe understands in transactional terms, even when his investment does not yield the desired results; he complains to Charles that going out with Susan "[c]osts me the hell of a lot of money—flowers, chocolates, and all the rest of it—and I get nothing in return" (78). Alice's insistence on choosing and paying for her own drinks emphasizes from the outset that "*I'm* independent" (47) and establishes a basis for a more equal and fulfilling relationship with Joe. He cannot achieve this partly because he can neither recognize nor reject the patriarchal assumptions that shape his thoughts and actions, despite Alice's attempts to draw his attention to them. His "chance to be a real person" depends on extending his reading of social situations to recognize the possibility of challenging established formations rather than just maneuvering within them.

The idea of camaraderie often obscures the economic and class content of drinking, suggesting that the social consumption of alcohol is important precisely because it creates a temporary space outside normal hierarchies. These pervasive narratives argue that drink reveals an equivalence between individuals normally obscured by social and professional hierarchies, that it is, as Steven Earnshaw puts it, a "social lubricant, breaking down barriers of age, gender, race and class" (2000, 1). The claim depends on the implicit idea that both alcohol and the spaces in which it is consumed are inherently accessible, that people can participate in communities sustained by pubs and bars for the price of a pint of beer. Joe consistently recognizes that this is a fantasy. In practice, financial and ideological distinctions shape not only conspicuously stratified events such as the Civic Ball but even more informal occasions and homogeneous groups. The "Warley NALGO Men's Evening" (Braine 2013, 97),[1] held in the "Bar Parlour of the Western Hotel" (96), a venue for those who "like to drink without women but who have no taste for the saw-dust and spittoons of the tap-room" (97), reinforces the structures of the workplace it claims to suspend. Even at an entirely male event, attended by those in the same profession, the costs and rituals of drinking are used to reinscribe distinctions of status; Hoylake, Joe's immediate superior and the "richest man in the room," buys rounds "not out of kindness, but because of a protocol that wasn't, when one weighed it up, very much less rigid than diplomatic protocol" (103). As at the Civic Ball, standing drinks is used to assert social hierarchies through the control of expenditure and consumption. The process again involves restrictions as well as obligations. As Joe notes, the fact that Hoylake "had, in effect, refused a drink from me and then from the Librarian" (103) empha-sizes his position and comparative wealth, even if his motivations are less overtly aggressive than those of Jack Wales and the Browns; Hoylake takes his whisky with him when greeting the Librarian because he "was paid twice as much . . . and didn't wish to force him into buying expen-sive drinks" (100). The object is not humiliation but a comparatively subtle reiteration of distinctions that function through the ritualized dis-play of generosity.

In *Room at the Top*, distinctions in status are mapped both within and across everyday spaces. Joe Lampton's understanding of this shapes his decisions about where to drink. This is visible not only in Warley but in Dufton; he walks half an hour from his Aunt Emily's house to the Siege Gun, the "only respectable pub" in the city, where the landlord discourages "anyone entering the Best Room without a collar and tie." The Siege Gun might be "too small, too dingy, too working-class" for tastes that have been reshaped by "four months in Warley," but it still enables Joe to separate himself from the "overalled and sweaty" (77) and consequently to assert his status. He uses ideas of respectability to present social distinctions in terms of behavior, dress, and morality rather than wealth, although economic inequalities often remain visible despite his attempts to obfuscate them; the overalls Joe dislikes are not an aesthetic choice but the imposed signifiers of a specific form of labor. The respectability of the Siege Gun emphasizes the respectability of Joe himself and, by extension, his superiority to those who drink in other places. His choice is consequently part of a broader pattern of conscious self-fashioning that is repeated throughout Braine's work. In *The Crying Game*, Frank Batcombe uses the Salisbury, which is "solid and comfort-able and respectable," to situate himself in London society, establishing a distance not just from his home town of Charbury but from the margin-ality embodied in his "tiny flat in Chelsea . . . nearer the World's End than Sloan Square" (1968, 11). Like Shalott House, the Salisbury enables him to project a particular image of himself; it is, appropriately for a "theatri-cal pub" (12), a performative space. This is also true of the Hibernian Club in *The Jealous God*, which is frequented by "respectable and

responsible Catholics, mainly middle-class" (2001, 36), and so emphasizes the social solidity as well as the origins of the Dungarven family.
Vincent's brother Matthew explains that their father took him there for
his first drink because "[h]e'll not get robbed nor get a dose at the Hibs"
(35), a decision that constructs less prestigious public houses, bars, and
clubs as sites of literal contagion. In both these instances, propriety is
understood partly in gendered and sexual terms; respectable sites of
drinking are places where only respectable women go or where women
do not go at all. Frank emphasizes that the Salisbury is one of the few
pubs in London "which a woman who wasn't a whore or a Lesbian could
visit unaccompanied" (12), a statement that figures other institutions as
immoral or deviant, insisting that established hierarchies of value depend
on the regulation of the sexualized female body.

The choice of bar and pub and the ritualized practices of ordering and
consuming alcohol within them often reiterate distinctions of status, but
they can also be used to disrupt such structures and reimagine personal
relationships. Drinking produces meaning rather than just expressing differences established elsewhere, communicating what language conceals
or cannot address. Joe and Alice initially negotiate the economic and
social distance between them in the Snug of the St. Clair. The space is
at once open and intimate, an ambiguity central to the public house and
embodied in the term itself, which, as Earnshaw argues, suggests a "a
home from home available to everyone" (2000, 1). The "[d]ark" pub,
which "smells of beef and tapers," is a liminal space, on the boundary of
a "working-class area" and the "world of private swimming-pools and
poplars and the new M.G.'s" (Braine 2013, 45). It functions in opposition to the Clarence, favored by the Thespians, which Alice finds "too
clean and well-lighted" (45), and possesses an authenticity embodied in
the "Old" it serves, a "*real* beer" (46), unlike the "gassy bottled stuff
and lager" she complains she is given by middle-class men who drink
"whisky and gin" (48). Like the pleasure Alice and Joe take in "potato
crisps . . . [p]ickled onions and fat pork," their enjoyment of this specific
beer is an example of their shared "low tastes" (48), which not only
contribute to what Tracy Hargreaves calls their "shabby kinship" (2011,
115) but enable them to disrupt the gendered structures of respectability that would normally constrain their interactions. With certain exceptions such as stout, which was widely believed to have health benefits
for women due to its iron content,[2] beer was strongly associated with
working-class men. Drinking, which reinforces class and gender boundaries at the Civic Ball and "Men's Evening," provides a way for Alice and
Joe to precariously communicate across them, a process that depends on
their shared willingness to challenge the rigorous but unspoken expectations that normally dictate its sites and forms.

Alice's choice of pub and drink, as well as her insistence on paying
for her own beer, not only challenge Joe's initial vision of her as the

"Lady of the Mansion" (Braine 2013, 46) but the gendered transactions that characterize his relationship with Susan. Joe understands his expenditure on Susan as a speculative investment or, more strictly, a gamble, a "weekly shilling on the pools" (156), a wager made in the hope that he will "never count pennies again" (126); as Charles observes "Daddy's bank balance" is at least as much a factor as "lust" (79) in his desire. The inequalities Joe and Alice temporarily bridge, not through rational calculation or even conversation but in the sensual and signifying exchanges of sex, drink, and food, are the foundation of his relation to Susan; he is courting her "not as Susan, but as a Grade A. lovely, as the daughter of a factory-owner, as the means of obtaining the key to the Aladdin's cave of my ambitions" (127). Pints of "Old" cannot enable communication between them, not only because Susan is concerned that "pubs are low" (65), does not drink alcohol, and enjoys cakes "of the kind which young girls like" (68) rather than "salty things with beer" (48), but because Joe does not seek such a connection. He does not want to ignore the distance between them or share with her some space seemingly outside social and economic structures, like the Snug of the St. Clair or the cottage where he holidays with Alice. Susan is desirable precisely because she is the abstract embodiment of privilege, "the girl in the American advertisements" (31), the "princess in the fairy stories, the girl in old songs, the heroine of musical comedies" (50).

As these descriptions suggest, Susan is a cultural rather than individual fantasy; what appeals to Joe most at first sight is that she is "conventionally pretty" (31). The possession of such a generic figure requires a similar loss of individuality in Joe, who recognizes that she already has an image of him which "I'd never to depart from in the smallest detail" (127). He begins suppressing his own tastes and concerns on their first evening together, believing that "it was essential that I should appear to share Susan's interests—or rather, that they should appear to coincide" (66). His consumption of alcohol is central to this process; he orders "gin-and-lime" at the theater bar, despite the fact "the price is sheer robbery" and "I don't care for the stuff," because "it wouldn't make my breath smell" (65). The choice emphasizes the performative quality of drinking but also the ways in which it can enable an integration in established social systems that is all the more complete because it is chosen. In Warley, the consumption of alcohol helps to sustain an illusion of freedom; making decisions about its sites and forms is part of a process of self-fashioning that offers material rewards. For Joe, this is central to the town's appeal. In Dufton, he and Charles can distinguish themselves from others by choosing the Siege Gun rather than its less respectable rivals, but once in the Best Room, their options are limited; Charles complains that "I don't even have to order" because the bar staff "*automatically* issue a pint of wallop" (78). Both men leave for places where their identities are not already known; Charles takes a job in London, where he also achieves mobility through his charm rather than his profession, becoming *"entangled with . . . a delicious little Grade 5—if not 4 . . . with a daddy who is a MANAGING DIRECTOR"* (162). For Joe, at least, the cost of these decisions is the replacement of his own preferences by class expectations he accepts but never entirely internalizes. As he notes in the opening pages, these dictate even his choice of clothes; he is "forced to be a living proof of the firm's prosperity" and "daren't be ill-dressed if I want to" (9). His recognition of social codes only ensures his more complete submission to them, his ability to perform more convincingly a part he has chosen but not scripted.

Looking back, Joe realizes that he rejects rather than simply misses his "chance to be a real person" (113). His vision of himself as "one of the characters in a magazine advertisement" (170) parallels his earlier image of Susan as "the girl in the American advertisements" (31), suggesting submission to the class she embodies rather than a successful process of self-determination. The control he attempts to exercise through sexual dominance and eventually violence, most clearly expressed when he tells Susan that "I'm the one who says what is to be done" (184), cannot obscure the fact that all he gains by sacrificing his individuality is a contingent position in structures where she is secure. This is confirmed in the sequel, *Life at the Top*. George Aisgill claims that Joe, who "used to be a rebel," has become a "member of the club" (Braine 1962, 86), but Joe's position is more precarious than this suggests; as he observes, even the house he inhabits is "in Susan's name" (20). In the earlier novel, he understands his struggle for mobility and self-definition as an assertion of his masculinity; in the later text, he understands his interpellation in the social order in the same terms. He feels that living in a house he does not own "diminished my stature as a man" (20) and that working for Susan's father makes him "something less than a man" (63–64). He can only recover his identity in his leisure time by confirming his desirability, the fact that "women had wanted me" (145), a need that paradoxically emphasizes his dependency; even his remaining connection to Susan is founded on his conviction that "she desired me physically" (42). His fears of aging and the decline of his looks displace a broader recognition that he not only lacks agency but is responsible for this because, as he recognizes in *Room at the Top*, what "has happened to me is exactly what I willed to happen" (Braine 2013, 113). As Lawrence Grossberg argues, "[P] eople live their subordination actively" (1997, 8); Joe's integration is complete because he consents to it, even desires it. His active participation in his own subjugation is visible not only in his deliberate decision that "I wanted an Aston-Martin, I wanted a three-guinea linen shirt, I wanted a girl with a Riviera suntan" (Braine 2013, 24), but in the calculated acts through which he suppresses his own preferences. The cost of this is exposed in the moment in the earlier novel when, sipping his gin-and-lime, he experiences a "fierce longing to be drinking Old at the St. Clair with Alice" (65). The rejection of *"real* beer" is also a rejection of the opportunity to be a "real person" and demonstrates the way in which interpellation is reproduced through seemingly trivial material practices.

Room at the Top identifies authenticity with "the personal, the concrete, the local," the qualities Hoggart argues are central to working-class thought and culture. Individuality implies idiosyncrasy, even imperfection; the "speck of decay on one of her incisors" is part of what makes Alice attractive, especially when contrasted with Susan's "white and small and regular" teeth (70). Susan is the seemingly perfected product of an unequal society, as Joe recognizes when he represents her as an advertisement for capitalism, insisting that "if I wanted to put paid to Communism once and for all, I'd have a hundred girls like Susan ride on 'buses the length and breadth of Great Britain" (122). The statement constructs her as an idealized but exchangeable figure; other women can fulfill the same function. These contradictions are visible in her conventional good looks, which are both attractive and impersonal; when Joe first goes out with her, he feels that her body is a costume, that her "full neck and firm little breasts seemed at moments not to belong to her but to have been borrowed for the occasion like an older sister's stockings and lipstick" (69). In contrast, as Hargreaves observes, the novel repeatedly insists on Alice's "bodily imperfections" (2011, 42). When Joe first meets her, he sees her as "pale and haggard." She has "an angular fashion plate figure" but "big breasts" that "didn't seem to belong" to it (Braine 2013, 42). When inactive, she sometimes looks "plain, in fact downright ugly" (43), and her body is repeatedly represented as aging or even decaying; her fingers are "on the verge of boniness, the index finger yellow with tobacco and the nails flecked with white" (119). As Hargreaves argues, these perceived failings "rebut the physical perfections of women in advertising and mass-market publications" (2011, 115) with which Susan is identified, but they also challenge the post-war expression of status through the consumption of the goods such women advertise. The "Hamilton watch or Cannon Percale (whatever that is) Sheets or Nash Airflyte Eight" (Braine 2013, 31) are signifiers of class rather than individual tastes, at once exclusive and generic. Despite Alice's contradictory class position, she embodies the working-class values of the novel; her physical "imperfections" mean that she is distinct and concrete and consequently can be desired as an individual rather than a type. The contrast with Susan's appearance reinforces the identification of the dominant classes with the generic and anonymous.

The places where the prosperous drink confirm their lack of the specific, localized identities valued by the text and the working-class culture that shapes it. When Joe rejects even the Siege Gun on his return to Dufton at Christmas, it is because he has developed in Warley a "fixed taste for either the roadhouse or the authentic country pub," a shift that accompanies his rejection of "Aunt Emily and her family" who are "kind and good and generous" but are not "my sort of person any longer" (77). His altered preferences demonstrate a loss of human connection, complexity, and meaning. In "Nowhere," Braine condemns the roadhouse, not just because it is the site of exploitation and prejudice, of transactional sex, and conversations about "the bloody Jews," but because it "doesn't belong anywhere"; it is an "independent state founded on paper money" (1951, 250). It is a simulation of a public house for people disconnected from the social and material world by wealth and privilege, the kind of people who "sit inside their cars at beauty spots, the windows closed and everybody silent" (77). In *The Jealous God*, Vincent, who "can't bear pubs" (Braine 2001, 90), enjoys contemplating the drinkers in the bar of the Country Club, but recognizes in them a similar detachment from any specific place or culture; they "belong less to the West Riding than to London and less to London than New York and Paris and Copenhagen and West Berlin." Even their clothes are "curiously uniform—Italian cut suits for the men and sheath dresses for the girls" and are "stage properties rather than covering" (91). They are not simply copies of an original located elsewhere, in the fashionable, fetishized metropolitan centers of Continental Europe and North America, but simulacrum, a term that, as Baudrillard argues, goes beyond the notion of the "unreal" to denote an image that is "never exchanged for the real, but exchanged for itself" (2000, 6). Their presence consequently indicates the loss of place rather than just a distance from it; the Country Club, a generic institution defined by its class connotation rather than its location is, like the roadhouse, nowhere.

Consuming alcohol is a significant activity, in both senses of the word; it matters, and it produces meaning. Braine's work, and *Room at the Top* in particular, demonstrates this, exploring its part in the "human life" that Joe trades for prosperity. His detailed, sensitive accounts of drinking and the spaces where it occurs use interpretative strategies employed in early cultural studies and are grounded in the same working-class modes of thought. Braine recognizes and values the complexities of the everyday, which is both a site of struggles in which established hierarchies can be contested or reinscribed and the foundation of solidarities. Individual and collective commitments are negotiated, rather than simply reproduced, in public houses and bars, not least through material rituals and interactions. The shared experience of consuming pints of Old with "salty things" is a form of sensual communication that can extend, complicate, or even challenge what is said, strengthening existing bonds in some contexts and disrupting established hierarchies to enable new connections in others. For Braine, these exchanges depend upon working-class modes of thought and occur predominantly in working-class spaces, though they are not the exclusive preserve of working-class people; Alice is often better able to recognize and use the possibilities of a space such as the St. Clair than Joe is. In contrast, Braine's texts associate contemporary middle-class life with the generic and placeless; the road-house leaves him thinking "with nostalgia" of the

> pubs that have notices of darts and dominoes fixtures, and Christmas clubs and raffles and charabanc outings and even the tough pubs in industrial cities (a pint of swipes for ninepence, hard wooden benches, sawdust and the smell of sweat) where no stranger dare enter . . . places and people, somewhere and someones.
>
> (Braine 2013, 252)

The longing, similar to that Frank Batcombe experiences in *The Crying Game* for "any Charbury pub . . . even the dingiest and roughest one in Bradford Road where, they used to say, the gutters literally ran with blood every Saturday night" (Braine 1968, 12), is a desire for the concrete and specific, for human connection and meaning threatened by consumer capitalism. It is precisely these qualities that Joe feels himself losing when, sipping his gin-and-lime at the theater bar, he experiences a "fierce longing to be drinking Old at the St. Clair." What is slipping away as a result of his own choices is his access to the dense, particular structures of working-class life. Braine, like Hoggart, traces the ways in which these forms are reproduced in the unremarked practices of the everyday. The two men contribute, in different ways, to the same radical, democratic project, to a working-class writing that extends across generic boundaries and is defined, not by its subject matter, but its intervention in the struggle over what is visible and valued.

Notes

1. NALGO was the National and Local Government Officers' Association.
2. Richard Hoggart observes that his Aunt Lil would drink with other women but stuck to "safe" pubs and "safe, preferred drinks," including "stout—especially Mackeson's" to ensure they were not "taken for prostitutes" (Hoggart 2002, 257).

References

Barthes, Roland. (1975) 2000. "Myth Today." In *Mythologies*. London: Vintage.
Baudrillard, Jean. (1981) 2000. *Simulacra and Simulation*. Translated by Sheila Glaser. Ann Arbor, MI: University of Michigan Press.
Bode, Carl. 1959. "The Redbrick Cinderellas." *College English* 20 (7): 331–37. https://doi.org/10.2307/372651.

126   *Ben Clarke*

Braine, John. 1951. "Nowhere." *New Statesman and Nation* 42 (September): 250–52.

———. 1957. "Letter to Richard Hoggart," September 4, 1957. Richard Hoggart Papers, University of Sheffield.

———. 1962. *Life at the Top*. London: Eyre and Spottiswoode.

———. 1968. *The Crying Game*. London: Eyre and Spottiswoode.

———. 1974. *Writing a Novel*. New York: Coward, McCann and Geoghegan.

———. (1959) 1978. *The Vodi*. London: Eyre Methuen.

———. (1964) 2001. *The Jealous God*. London: House of Stratus.

———. (1957) 2013. *Room at the Top*. Kansas City, MO: Valancourt.

Collini, Stefan. 1999. "Critical Minds: Raymond Williams and Richard Hoggart." In *English Pasts: Essays in History and Culture*, 210–30. Oxford, UK: Oxford University Press.

Earnshaw, Steven. 2000. *The Pub in Literature: England's Altered State*. Manchester, UK: Manchester University Press.

Grossberg, Lawrence. 1997. "Introduction: 'Birmingham' in America?" In *Bringing It All Back Home: Essays on Cultural Studies*, 210–30. Durham, NC: Duke University Press.

———. 2007. "Rereading the Past from the Future." *International Journal of Cultural Studies* 10 (1): 125–33. https://doi.org/10.1177/1367877907073907.

Hall, Stuart. 1981. "Notes on Deconstructing 'The Popular'." In *People's History and Socialist Theory*, edited by Raphael Samuel, 227–40. London: Routledge and Kegan Paul.

Hargreaves, Tracy. 2011. "The Uses of Literacy, the 'Angry Young Men' and British New Wave." In *Richard Hoggart: Culture and Critique*, edited by Michael Bailey and Mary Eagleton, 108–22. Nottingham, UK: Critical, Cultural and Communications Press.

Hoggart, Richard. 1957. *The Uses of Literacy: Aspects of Working-Class Life with Special Reference to Publications and Entertainments*. London: Chatto and Windus.

———. 2002. "Bill and Lil." In *Between Two Worlds: Politics, Anti-Politics, and the Unpolitical*, 256–69. New Brunswick, NJ: Transaction.

Maschler, Tom. (1957) 1958. "Introduction." In *Declaration*, 7–9. New York: E.P. Dutton.

Maschler, Tom, and Lindsay Anderson. 1958. *Declaration*. London: MacGibbon and Kee.

Močnik, Rastko. 1993. "Ideology and Fantasy." In *The Althusserian Legacy*, edited by E. Ann Kaplan and Michael Sprinkler, 139–56. London: Verso.

Passeron, Jean-Claude. 2007. "Introduction to the French Edition of The Uses of Literacy." In *CCCS Selected Working Papers: Volume 2*, edited by Ann Gray, Jan Campbell, Mark Erickson, Stuart Hanson, and Helen Wood, 25–34. London: Routledge.

Rancière, Jacques. 2009. "A Few Remarks on the Method of Jacques Rancière." *Parallax* 15 (3): 114–23.

———. (2010) 2012. "The Politics of Literature." In *Dissensus: On Politics and Aesthetics*, 152–68. London: Continuum.

7   Addressing Stigma
Demonized Locales in Pat Barker's *Union Street*

Simon Lee

Although the idea of a working-class canon is up for question, novels and plays associated with British working-class women writers are often eclipsed by the work of their male counterparts. Yet it might be argued that working-class women's writing provides a more granular representation of society through an increased emphasis on the way space and class intersect with other categories of identity. Negotiations of both the domestic and the social are understandably gendered affairs, so women's perspectives add nuance to the more androcentric tropes and motifs of proletarian fiction. For example, Shelagh Delaney and Nell Dunn's mid-century writing about the intricacies of women's work illuminates shifts in gender relations in British culture while highlighting the way class was negotiated in terms of the home and institutions like the pub or the factory. Further, the increased value of such nuanced portrayals is also registered through the texts' tangible impact on society. Case in point, it is commonly understood that Dunn's 1963 text *Up the Junction* helped initiate discussions of the 1967 Abortion Rights Act while Delaney's 1958 play, *A Taste of Honey*, paved the way for new articulations of home life that subverted traditional domestic relations. Clearly, the voices of working-class women add dimension to notions of lived experience in post-war British culture. Pat Barker's early novels—*Union Street* (1982), *Blow Your House Down* (1984), and *Liza's England* (1986)—achieved much of the same effect, largely through their analysis of domestic space and working-class communities impacted by deindustrialization. Facing rejection from sexist and classist publishers who deemed her work too miserable to publish, Barker insisted on writing about the kinds of spaces that shaped the lives of British working-class women.

This chapter reads Pat Barker's *Union Street* as a microcosm of alienated working-class communities and the bonds formed between working-class women. Similar to Dunn and Delaney's narratives, environment plays a pivotal role in this feminist configuration, with Barker's text introducing characters who reject their prescribed social identity by staging acts of resistance to societal expectations. For instance, characters such as Kelly Brown and Joanne Wilson adopt oppositional stances

DOI: 10.4324/9781003119425-8

to the notion of home, but the cultural moment of Barker's work marks a shift away from the kind of representation seen in the work of Dunn and Delaney. Whereas texts like *A Taste of Honey* and *Up the Junction* illuminate gender relations, *Union Street* amplifies the abject and the visceral in a manner that speaks to the way working-class women's bodies are figured as a semiotic index of subjugation. As such, this chapter considers cultural change, from the post-war boom of working-class productivity to the period of deindustrialization that reduced once-proud communities to literal and metaphorical rubble. Focusing specifically on the way Barker negotiates comprehensions of community within precarious working-class environments, it centers on the stigmatization of space such as how certain streets in working-class regions gain negative reputations. It also looks at the way working-class communities subdivide as a consequence of the stigma experienced within traditional class confines. To that end, it considers how such divisions are developed from within as well as from outside the community. The novel argues for the sustenance of community in such states, specifically as seen through the eyes of the titular street's characters who perform acts of maternal care in spaces devoid of the kinds of work required to sustain working-class identities.

Union Street was published as the result of Angela Carter's intervention and endorsement. In an interview with the author, Rob Nixon notes how Barker struggled to find a publisher willing to take on the project, largely due to the content being deemed "too bleak and depressing" for publication (Barker 2004, 4). Barker wrote the text in the late 1970s, knowing full well that the subject matter—the lives of working-class women—would not be seen as commercially appealing. Until then, she had focused on writing "middle-class novels which weren't published and didn't deserve to be" (4). So, *Union Street* proved to be an exercise in authenticity, one in which Barker could document her own experiences as a woman living in working-class spaces. She was intimately familiar with the kinds of characters she created as well as the environments they inhabited. In her own words, she refers to the book's characters as the "voices that had not been listened to" (2), with Nixon rightly adding that she "possesse[d] a fine ear for their diction, the intonation of their wit, their blunted dreams, and their survival skills" (2). The use of manifold voices is critical to the author's work, as it simulates a sense of community in space that can no longer sustain community through labor. It also underscores her commitment to veracity through corroboration, with the various voices and characters bearing witness to one another's experiences. Barker notes that "I think my voice, more than most people realize, is rather like the voices of the women I write about" (5), adding that "the narrative voice can't afford to be too far away from the voices of the characters; otherwise it really does sound like a social worker demonstrating these people" (5). The book received mixed reviews, partly, Barker suspects, because depictions of the lives of working-class women were still relatively absent in cultural production:

> I think in this country regional, working-class voices are very, very marginalized, and there's a tendency either to not review the work or to review it in slightly different terms. So what they're asking questions about is whether it's authentic sociology, rather than looking at your themes or the way you've treated characters.
>
> (5)

The novel features seven interlinked vignettes, each telling the story of a working-class woman's life in an anonymous deindustrialized town in Northern England. Intrinsically, the titular street acts as a portrait of disenfranchised working-class women's lives, with dereliction and entrapment serving as symbolic manifestations of stasis and abandonment. Barker takes what Roger Manvell has called "Industrial Romanticism" (as quoted in Lay 2002, 22)—depictions of gritty, mechanized landscapes that juxtapose the factory against a verdant British countryside—and infuses it with something more ominous and malevolent. There is no romantic nostalgia to be found; the book is violent, graphic, and often disconcerting. And, while Barker does stress the value of community throughout, the general tone is forlorn, suggesting a reconsideration of the stiff-upper-lip mantra of "getting by." Accordingly, the text imagines stasis as a core constituent of working-class tenacity, with characters undergoing hardship, but continuing on with their day-to-day lives all the same. While discussing her most-known novel, *Regeneration*, Barker referred to her own writing as "ethical," in that it is invested in "staging the dilemmas of [a] condition" (2004, 7). Arguably, the condition plaguing *Union Street* is the rise of Thatcherism and the inevitable push to deindustrialize working-class communities, decimating their economy and their spirit in the process. In this regard, *Union Street* is a novel willing to explore the paradox of what happens to a working-class community—particularly, a working-class community of women—when the work itself is stripped away. Barker's response is that new forms of gendered class articulation are required. A number of these forms, I suggest, are established in relation to the kind of environment portrayed in the text.

John Brannigan's exhaustive study of Barker's writing contours the themes and motifs that emerge and reemerge throughout her work. He positions Barker's style as "critical realism," in which a traditional epic structure of victory is inverted to narrativize the experiences of the marginalized. For Brannigan, this constitutes a rethinking of post-war social realism to "accommodate the unrepresentable trauma of twentieth-century mass warfare or post-industrial urban dereliction" (2005a, 5).

He adds that this offers "a more complex realization of the constructed and intersubjective experience of the real" (5), in which "characters experience time as a series of historical resonances, through notions of cyclical recurrence and repetition, so that it is impossible to see the present except through images of its otherness" (5). Given Barker's training as a historian, Brannigan's assertion that her novels demonstrate "a critical understanding of modern history and society" (5) ring true, and the cyclical plotlines—a common trope in proletarian fiction used to simulate day-in-day-out drudgery—are well represented in *Union Street*. John Kirk has also discussed the persistence of certain themes in Barker's early writing—the intersectional collision of gender and social class in particular. For Kirk, Barker's representational strategies counter romantic notions of a monolithic working-class culture informed by nostalgia. He argues instead for "nostalgic memory" in which nostalgia functions less as a sentimental device and more as a "symbolic act of recovery—of neglected experience, forgotten voices, silenced groups" (1999, 605). Citing Stuart Tannock's work on nostalgia in fiction, Kirk underscores Barker's dedication to cultural memory in a manner that "can act as a rhetorical practice providing 'resources, as supports for community and identity building projects in the present'" (606).

For Roberto del Valle Alcalá, texts like *Union Street* clarify shifts in the way gendered labor is understood, specifically how depictions of women's work depart from more traditional post-war representations of labor in other class-conscious fiction. Barker's work, according to Alcalá, shows how social life is absorbed into a capitalist system, specifically how "the realm of reproduction emerges as an organic and feminized backdrop to the convulsive and hyper-masculine universe of industrial labor and conflict" (2015, 196). Critics such as Margaretta Jolly (2005) and Sarah Falcus (2007) have spoken of Barker's emphasis on female companionship, showing how the author highlights feminist insurgency within active states of oppression. More specifically, Falcus discusses Barker's focus on the way women's labor highlights bonds and relations structured upon the navigation of social codes, arguing in particular that female solidarity is never idealized in Barker's work (260). Such critics help highlight aspects of gendered labor present in Barker's texts, but *Union Street* offers additional perspectives also worthy of exploration.

For example, critics have noted Barker's dedicated engagement with space and domesticity in her early novels. In a collection of essays on Barker's work, Brannigan highlights the author's depiction of post-industrial dereliction. He argues that the emphasis placed on space and identity is one of the most salient factors that distinguish Barker's writing from other class-conscious texts of the post-war era. Somewhat reflective of Falcus's discussion of the dynamics of social relations, Brannigan concludes that *Union Street* inaugurates "a sustained attempt in Barker's work to explore the ways in which fictional narrative can represent the experiences and feelings of displaced and disrupted communities without itself displacing the voices of those communities" (2005b, 34). Lucy Gallagher (2011) also builds on the way space interacts with class and gender, specifically exploring how representations of cleanliness work to link domestic interiors to the interiority of characters themselves. For Gallagher, the novel maps not only the post-industrial space of a working-class community, but the way such spaces are subdivided in relation to social worth. Barker herself has commented on similar notions, discussing in an interview with Valerie Stivers how post-war slum clearance projects displaced not just physical communities but notions of identity pertaining to space as well: "People were moved out of the old streets for miles around, and those houses remained boarded up and empty, and the streets empty and echoing and deserted, for what seemed like quite a long time" (2018, 172). Critics like Maroula Joannou also build on these ideas, particularly how Barker's work shows a certain respect for traditional notions of working-class cultural history while simultaneously suggesting its susceptibility to sentimental idealism. The intensified function of place in Barker's texts, then, prove to be fertile grounds for critical analysis in ways that, as Joannou argues, "offer representations of working-class communities that reflect what Habermas has termed the importance of 'vital heritages' while avoiding the dangers of an impoverished traditionalism" (2004, 42). However, I would add that Barker's text also reveals a pronounced critique of the way space and environment are socially marked by stigma in a manner that prescribes certain behaviors and actions from those who occupy the space.

The Function of Stigma

In its original Greek form, stigma is understood to be a mark or a brandishing of disdain or shame. Today, though, the mark can also be understood as a trait or characteristic of a social position that deviates from a culturally determined social norm. Émile Durkheim outlined this concept in *The Rules of Sociological Method* as a way to account for anomalies in a collective and the collective's response to perceptible deviation (1982, 101). For Durkheim, deviations are indispensable in their ability to define a standard of what is and what is not deemed acceptable by a given group. Of note, though, is Durkheim's addendum that it is not the deviant act itself that matters, but the cultural response to the strength of the deviation. Although he sidesteps the term, the phenomenon described is precisely what powers the notion of social stigma: "By reacting against the slightest deviations with an energy which it [the common consciousness] elsewhere employs against those what are more weighty, it endues them with the same gravity and will brand them as criminal" (101). It is not difficult to imagine how such a concept can be extended to pathologize a wide range of social practices, and Steven Lukes, in his introduction to Durkheim's text, is right to note class conflict as one of them (21).

Erving Goffman developed this idea further by considering the impact on the individual excluded from the norm via what he refers to as a "spoiled identity." In this case, the individual demonstrates distinction that might otherwise be recognized as an asset but is transformed into a liability through stigma. This transformation, according to Goffman, happens through a divergence of an "actual" and a "virtual" social identity. A "virtual" social identity is perhaps best understood as the base-level assumption of a culture's definition of what constitutes normality—the expected attributes or behaviors of an individual pertinent to their culture. The "actual" social identity is the real identity of the individual (1963, 2). When the "actual" moves too far from the "virtual," then stigma activates. However, as with Durkheim, Goffman is interested less in the attributes of the "actual" social identity and more in the ways that the "virtual" deems the "actual" a betrayal. Types of stigma discussed include physical, mental, and social characteristics, some of which Goffman deems "discrediting" and others "discreditable," the distinction here being that the first signifies clearly, while the second is masked in some manner (4). Goffman's work deploys insensitive terminology by today's standards, but much of his analysis is perceptible in a range of social contexts such as his use of "normals" to describe what Durkheim would consider a representation of the collective conscience, one that we might associate with contemporary critiques and discourse around the topic of ableism. The gap between the "normal" and the stigmatized, Goffman argues, is bridged by "The Own," those who embrace their stigma and build community among similarly stigmatized individuals, and "The Wise," those who act as intermediary figures between the two.

It goes without saying that both Durkheim and Goffman's theorizations of stigma are applicable to the experience of social class and its various dynamics. As Garcia et al. have observed, a lower-class socioeconomic status is often stigmatized under the assumption that a middle-class socio-economic position functions as the norm or, to use Goffman's vocabulary, the "virtual" (2007, 100). Furthermore, a lower-class individual is more apt to experience a heightened awareness of their reduced state and might attempt to mask their status in order to "pass" (106). This leads to problems of assimilation but also intraclass conflict in that a lower-class individual demonstrating a desire for upward mobility is apt to be viewed as a class traitor or as one ashamed of their roots. Yet, as noted by both Durkheim and Goffman, the source of stigmatization resides not in the stigmata itself, but in the power dynamics that deem the stigmata sufficient enough to warrant a disruption of the norm. Put differently, stigma and abnormality can be understood as an assignation rather than a phenomenon produced by the marginalized. Stigmatization, then, can be understood as a dialectical process akin to what Anthony Giddens calls "structuration"—a reciprocal combination of domination and agency (1982, 197). In this regard, it is possible to see how stigma underwrites social stratification and furthers divisions within a defined group. Agency, for Giddens, is a way of understanding how stigma is enacted once naturalized through shared behavior and characteristics akin to Bourdieu's (1984) notion of "habitus." Goffman's notion of the "virtual" social identity—the presumed norm within a particular group—can be understood within the context of working-class culture through shared notions of tradition and behavior. Additionally, Durkheim's "collective consciousness" is structured upon the same supposition, with deviations from the norm perceived not just as an aberration of working-class identity, but as a potential threat to collectivity and as a threat to the notion of a coherent working-class culture. In this sense, stigma—particularly in terms of social class—is bound up in gestures of self-preservation in addition to operating as an expression of collective self-definition.

Imogen Tyler pursues such ideas in *Stigma: The Machinery of Inequality*, advocating for a more robust understanding of the way stigma is mobilized against the working class as part and parcel of neoliberal governance. In a preceding essay, Tyler, alongside Tom Slater, argued that British elites "have engaged in an intensive program of *welfare stigma production*" (2018, 727). This claim provides the basis upon which the concept can be unpacked as a set of power dynamics pertinent to social relations. Tyler calls for a more situated understanding of the way stigma is weaponized for political gain, or what she terms "stigma power" in which stigma is "always enmeshed with wider capitalist structures of expropriation, domination, discipline and social control" (2020, 17). To that end, Tyler considers how stigma works in nation building through borders and national delineations that actively stigmatize the other—a move that locates nationalism alongside Goffman's "virtual" identity. In doing so, Tyler elevates our understanding of the way stigma works by porting Goffman's original ideas into the contemporary moment in a manner that echoes discussions of biopolitics and the spatialization of social orders. Yet it can be argued that cultural production such as Barker's text also allows us to extend Goffman's concepts in similar ways, particularly in relation to Durkheim's notion of collectivity. In essence, focusing on the way stigma operates as a socially manufactured phenomenon lays the groundwork for understanding class through a spatial and spatially informed lens. Barker's text, like much class-conscious fiction, is invested in detailed studies of the way landscape and environment impact identity. In this sense, *Union Street*, like Tyler's sociological approach, offers hypothetical case studies of what stigma looks like in terms of the power dynamics associated with social stratification.

Stigma and Space

While spatial marginalization is well documented as a top-down, prescriptive factor of urban planning akin to what Mike Davis has referred to as "urban apartheid" (1990, 226), the onset of stigma linked to particular streets and naming systems is perhaps less well understood despite copious scholarship on the topic. In other words, what does it mean for a space to become stigmatized? In what ways might such spatial stigma shape behavior? What is the nature of the relationship between an occupant of a space and their own comprehension of social marginalization? One particularly concentrated body of analysis comes from the French social anthropologist, Loïc Wacquant, a figure credited for the term "territorial stigmatization." Analyzing both US and European cities, Wacquant identifies regions within already impoverished areas that he refers to as "splinters of the dualized market society that collect in the dispossessed zones of the metropolis" (2007, 73). Territorial stigmatization, the dissolution of "place," and disappearance of cultural "hinterlands," all contribute to what Wacquant terms "advanced marginality" (68). The result, he argues, is that such additional degrees of fragmentation challenge notions of solidarity and collectivity (73). In a 2020 report, Jensen et al. show how territorial stigmatization yields a range of effects in different locations, and reactions to its impact vary in similarly distinct ways. Analyzing responses from one particular marginalized region in Denmark, the researchers show how reactions to stigma cause additional splintering: "in cases where residents tended to accept the stigma of denigration of their neighborhood, attempts to symbolically wash off the stigma produced internal divisions that hampered local solidarity and collective mobilization" (2021, 8). Writing with John Howe, Wacquant argues that territorial stigma acts on the individual as "a taint of place" that is "superimposed on the already existing stigmata traditionally associated with poverty and ethnic origin or postcolonial immigrant status" (2008, 238). However, the authors claim that its effects can be challenged through forms of social mobility or articulations of cultural identity that resist such dynamics (238).

Although Wacquant's theorizing of territorial stigmatization lends itself well to delineated geographic regions, it is possible to imagine how a similar process might occur in terms of types of space associated with marginalization. For example, Annette Hastings has focused on the way that the kinds of stigma associated with council housing estates are more than just the concretization of behavioral dynamics tied to their vilification. Akin to Davis's notion of "urban apartheid," Hastings shows how territorial stigmatization is compounded by a range of factors such as social services, estate agents, and insurance companies as well as by the public's interpretation of regeneration initiatives (2004, 250). She concludes that fully understanding the way stigma forms around specific sites through a range of external actors pushes back against more prevalent pathologi-cal analyses of working-class marginality in which antisocial behavior is somehow figured as an innate characteristic (253). Simply put, full anal-ysis and comprehension of what produces stigmatization serves as the hypothetical antidote to the stigma itself. Similar research has focused on street names and the way specific names become associated with stigma. Perhaps the most prominent example of this is in the United States where streets named after Martin Luther King Jr. are frequently associated with social deprivation and racialized poverty, as well as conduct deemed marginal or disorderly. According to Mitchelson et al., this striking phe-nomenon stems not from innate characteristics but from the proliferation of unchallenged stereotypes in addition to the commemorative and refer-ential nature of street naming. The authors declare such streets as "sym-bolic texts within cities" that are "embedded in larger systems of meaning and ideology" (2007, 123). They note specifically how a generalized pub-lic resistance to renaming central thoroughfares results in King's name being attached to roads in African American and minoritized commu-nities marked by poverty and disenfranchisement (123). Consequently, a sizable number of the 777 Martin Luther King Jr. Boulevards in the United States are pathologized along racist lines rather than understood to be the result of NIMBYism impacting the development of commemo-rative landmarks. Maoz Azaryahu (1986) underscores the global practice of such phenomena, demonstrating the political nature of street naming and the ways in which the tradition has been used for ideological means. Turning to sections of East Berlin, Azaryahu shows how naming imparts assumptions about identity and behavior, reiterating Mitchelson et al.'s claim that street names act as symbolic texts. Wilbur Zelinsky hints at the way an understanding of such naming systems produces taxonomic hierarchies that help illuminate the cultural forces shaping urban devel-opment (2002, 253). In light of what is essentially burgeoning research, it seems appropriate that cultural production can also act as a source of such analysis as well.

In most cases, British working-class housing is commensurate with mass housing—often pre-WWII terraces or post-war housing estates and high-rises built hastily in response to housing crises. Mass housing, by definition, is high-density, and working-class identities, by and large, activate through their proximity to others who share similar economic and social positions. As Giddens and others have stipulated, classed iden-tities infer a degree of agency and reciprocity—the recognition and reit-eration of characteristics and practices associated with a social grouping. As such, there exists the potential to understand how marginalized spaces such as mass housing produce types of behavior that reinforce stereotypes and, ultimately, class stigma. John B. Calhoun's "Population Density and Social Pathology" (1962) argued for "defensible space" in response to the phenomenon of so-called behavioral sink, the latter of which is categorized as antisocial behavior associated with overpopulated spaces. The principle of "defensible space" refers to the inclusion of comforting elements used to construct a familiar territorial sanctuary in spaces the inhabitant deems antagonistic or oppressive. Correspondingly, Proshansky et al.'s (1983) conception of "place identity" reveals the way one's environment imparts certain values and beliefs about the world. The concept of "place identity" posits that an environment's capacity to meet basic cultural and biological needs dictates an individual's self-worth. This is buttressed by the concept of "place attachment," in which meaningful links develop between the individual and the space they inhabit based on meaningful, individual connections. That is to say that for an environment to have personal meaning, aesthetic appeal is not a necessary requirement; the concept implies that ties can be formed to beautiful and ugly spaces in equal measure. What this suggests is that when a space is marked by territorial stigmatization, there exists the possibility of certain negative behavioral attributes that can emerge in response to perceived marginalization as a source of comfort. One particular example of such behavior is the use of graffiti or vandalism to mark territory while simultaneously registering aggression toward sites marked by deprivation. This points toward the possibility of a vicious cycle in which territorial stigmatization leads to a sense of social alienation producing, in turn, actions that further exacerbate stigmatization. With this in mind, it can be understood how stigmatized space contributes to class alienation through Giddens's theory of structuration, transforming working-class marginalization into a self-fulfilling prophecy.

Barker's Spatial Awareness

Barker follows a tradition of class-conscious writing invested in representing space and place with authenticity while also using setting as a critical constituent of the text itself. Nixon, alluding to this, stresses Barker's "singular gift for immersing readers in the atmospherics and pathologies of violence—whether rape, murder, trench warfare, torture, or unremitting confinement" (2004, 3). The use of "established haunts" (2) plays a critical role in her engagement with space as a crucial character of a text. Similarly, when discussing the Craiglockhart war hospital from her 1991 novel *Regeneration*, Barker herself noted how "that building, with its long, narrow corridors, it becomes a character inevitably, and you want to use it to keep the pressure on. It's a terrible place" (as quoted in Barker 2004, 18–19). Inevitably, Barker uses a range of "terrible places" in her fiction but counters them by showing how characters can still form bonds, ad hoc communities, and dynamic survival skills. *Union Street* is no different in this regard, with the setting portrayed in a manner indicative of a number of northern industrial communities. Although the streets of the text are hardly analogous to Craiglockhart, links between "terrible" spaces of abjection and spaces stigmatized by poverty and abandonment persist. Yet Barker engages the specific nuances of such streets in detail to position them not merely as characters akin to the Craiglockhart hospital but as a symbolic representation of socio-political temporality.

Barker's depiction of the working-class street draws on a century of realist representation methods, highlighting in particular the way that place and class intersect at the site of the domestic. An initial introduction to the titular street in fourteen-year-old Kelly Brown's story marks it as distinct from the broader milieu, requiring residents to pass by the steelworks and factories that lend the street its suggestive name before descending under a railway tunnel that acts a symbolic point of traversal (1997, 24). This marked border reiterates Garcia et al.'s notion that spatial stigma is understood as a deviation from a tacit set of socio-economic and, presumably, middle-class norms. Union Street stands distinct from the other nearby regions such as "The area bordering on the park [that] was one of the wealthiest in town; the houses big, substantial Victorian houses that had preserved their air of smug assurance into a more violent and chaotic age" (51). Conversely, it is marked by relative deprivation, dereliction, and abject poverty—a space where a character like Kelly, while playing childhood games in piles of rubble, can stumble across such horrors as a deceased newborn: "a baby as red and translucent as a ruby" (62). Barker uses factory-specific pollution as an aesthetic filter, tinting the space in a manner that amplifies its dejection:

> Beyond the chemical works in the far distance the sun was setting, obscured by columns of drifting brown and yellow smoke. A brutal, bloody disc, scored by factory chimneys, it seemed to swell up until it filled half the western sky.
>
> (64)

Such images, operating as a kind of industrial sublime, echo throughout the text as poetic gestures that balance prismatic beauty with melancholia:

> Autumn sunlight filtered down, hazy with smoke and soot. The grime on the glass almost defeated it, but enough got through to gild [Jo's] face and hair. She gave herself up to it completely, lying back in her chair, her eyes screwed up against the brilliance of the light.
>
> (95)

Union Street, like many streets featured in British class-conscious writing, is characterized by a paradoxical mix of alienation and sustenance; the grit and grime of the place acts as an index of labor as well as a window into a unique kind of beauty.

Hierarchy of Stigma

Joanne Wilson's story establishes how the streets surrounding Union Street operate as a hierarchy of social position in ways that mirror Wacquant's notion of territorial stigmatization. For instance, when Joanne's husband's Wharfe Street roots are discussed, the narrator informs the reader that it "was the worst street in the town, or had been until a couple of years ago, when the people were rehoused" (73). Although the community appears small and relatively sequestered, the novel situates Union Street as one of just a handful of streets in an impoverished region in which the residents' identity and self-worth is constructed in relation to other streets nearby. The streets are described as a microcosm of social stigma, demonstrating how intraclass divisions can produce, to use Wacquant's term, "advanced marginality" within an already marginalized community: "In the hierarchy of streets it came almost as far below Union Street as Union Street came below Buchanan Street, with its bay windows and strips of garden outside the front doors" (74). While Union Street itself is plagued by problems stemming from factory closures and social abandonment, it is still considered a relative step up into "respectability." Wharfe Street, on the other hand, is rife with desperation:

> It was true. Suicide, mental illness, crime, incest had flourished there, as though inhaled with noxious fumes from the river. Those who had lived there, whether they had loved or hated the street, did not find it easy to forget.
>
> (74)

Although Union Street is stigmatized in its own way, to exist on the street is a mark of pride for those who once considered Wharfe Street their home. Iris King, for example, belies her rough, aggressive exterior by performing traditional domestic tasks as a way to keep her Wharfe Street roots at bay: "She was proud of her reputation as the cleanest woman in the street. Although she worked full time as a home help, her own doorstep was scoured every day. Fresh curtains appeared at the windows once a week, sometimes twice" (185). These actions, perhaps demonstrative of an obsessive self-consciousness, are amplified by the homogeneity of the street in that, for Iris, diminutive gestures of personal elevation serve as protection against the residual stigma of Wharfe Street. This maps onto her own personal presentation, in that we learn that "Iris, for the first time in many years, spent some money selfishly on herself. She went out and bought some bleach and dyed her hair blonde" (195). While the reader might register the classed stereotype and semiotic valence of home hair bleaching, for Iris, it is an effort to distance herself from her past through genuine attempts at beautification. This is made especially clear when the reader learns that "Iris, in these later years, was often depressed. A blackness would come over her, a blackness she linked in her mind with those early years in Wharfe Street" (195). Yet, following the other stories of trauma experienced by Union Street's women, Barker proves that even in marginalized communities, attempts are made to subdivide and self-elevate. What the text renders clear is the function of proximity, in that Wharfe Street, while more stigmatized than Union Street, is still part of the same community. This form of "territorial stigmatization" builds on Goffman's conception of social identities established through complex forms of "actual" and "virtual" states. In the case of characters such as Iris King, this is demonstrated through aspirational gestures that, by default, require the marginalization of another group in order to register as self-elevation.

Despite its impoverished state, Union Street is assumed to be a street of relative respectability. The name alone signals a degree of propriety shared by the residents, in particular those familiar with the wretched Wharfe Street. Yet, as Joanna Wilson's story makes clear, Union Street is still an impoverished working-class space, cordoned off from the more affluent, socially-elevated spaces of the upwardly-aspiring middle class. This distinction registers in the minds of the residents who struggle to envision their own future beyond the street's social and material limits. For example, Jo discusses her new boyfriend in a transactional manner, as though a relationship with him might grant access to a new tier of life. Yet, she expresses doubt over her plan's success when the time comes to meet his parents, noting how the relationship itself is based on division: "I never feel as if I can talk to him. I'm not his class" (105). When this concern is questioned, she provides a response based on spatial signifiers: "Well, they've got a furniture shop and a nice house. I don't suppose they know where Union Street is" (105). Jo's anxiety is compounded by internalized stigma about her own social class, adding "You can see why he's afraid of telling his Mam, Can't you? She's not going to be overjoyed" (105). An awareness of what it means to live and exist on Union Street is felt throughout the text in a manner that recalls the phrase "knowing one's place." For Kelly Brown, hailing from Union Street relegates her to a lower rung of the social order, registered in her mind by a sense of abandonment and disregard. When the man who inevitably rapes her comments that her name is unusual, she shrugs because "[i]t wasn't particularly unusual where she came from" (15). Furthermore, when he "looked at her so intently" (15), she responds positively because "[o]ther people—her mother, Linda, the teachers at school—merely glanced at her and then with indifference or haste, passed on" (15). Barker establishes Union Street as the baseline of this particular community in a manner that highlights intraclass divisions as well as the way social positioning operates through stigmatized space.

Community and Identity

What is also clear in Barker's text is the absence of identity-defining work. Although published in 1982, Barker wrote much of the novel in the 1970s, a period marked by a political turn away from the socialist politics of the consensus era in lieu of what would become Margaret Thatcher's neoliberal conservatism. It was during this time that industrial regions, particularly in the north and the northeast of England, witnessed a forceful restructuring of work through privatization and deindustrialization. While *Union Street* does reference operational sites of labor, it prioritizes factories now shut down and boarded up—a symbol of a reality that, for a working-class community predicated on labor, is nothing short of devastating. Barker underscores this devastation by focusing on individual stories and experiences of work, particularly the impact of job loss on identities structured around labor and pride. For example, Lisa Goddard's husband lost his job when the factory modernized and, presumably, replaced his position with machinery (113). His ensuing depression is so severe and his redundancy so prominent that his own wife barely even associates her husband with work anymore: "Now, through his eyes, she saw the blast-furnaces for the first time, bigger than the house they lived in" (120). Much of his day-to-day activity amounts to collecting dole money and sitting "in the armchair with his face in his hands" (120). This, of course, he takes out on his wife through periodic bouts of absence as well as alcohol-fueled bouts of abuse. Other characters, mostly men, pine for labor in ways that reiterate how much of their identity is bound up in their work. For George Harrison in Blonde Dinah's story, for example, retirement fuels his existential crisis. After receiving a clock as a less-than-subtle leaving gift after forty years of labor in the furnaces (221), he becomes despondent, dependent on his wife Gladys for an allowance while she, in turn, grows resentful at him for spending so much time at home. When Gladys takes on a part-time job, George feels notably demoralized, showing up to the labor exchange and pleading for any kind of work at all: "I don't care what it is. Just as long as it's work" (223). Therefore, it can be seen how *Union Street* centers on the kinds of economic and psychological crises produced in working-class communities marked by an absence of identity-defining labor, be it the kind of labor lost to conservative policies or mid-century shifts in the gendered makeup of the workforce. Indicative of Proshanksy et al.'s notion of "place identity," the environments that Barker depicts lack any meaningful resources that might help support an identity beyond one characterized by labor. The result is that alienation and melancholia dominate, and identities are formed in relation to stigmatized characteristics associated with the street itself in a manner reflecting Giddens's concept of structuration. As once-thriving industrial communities continue to perish under deindustrialization, assumptions about social behavior and working-class people continue to cement.

Barker's emphasis on the way deprivation impacts the individual psyche is suggested in the novel's opening line: "There was a square of cardboard in the window where the glass had been smashed" (1). For fourteen-year-old Kelly Brown and her older sister, the makeshift window is something to be tolerated, as Kelly is described as "doubled up under the sheet, her body jackknifed against the cold" (2). Just as the community fails to provide identity-sustaining work, the home no longer provides sanctuary against the world outside. This scene book-ends the novel's closing moments in which Alice Bell succumbs to the cold, while Kelly bears witness in a manner highlighting the novel's cyclical structure. However, the cause of the broken window is rendered ambiguous, in that Linda, her sister, situates Kelly as the culprit, noting "[t]hat wouldn't be there either if you'd watch what you're doing" (1). Although suggestive of an accident, broken windows do indeed mark the community in ways that signal behavioral problems linked to a perceived sense of abandonment and stigmatization. As Kelly approaches "the blackening school yard," the reader is alerted to the fact that the windows are covered by metal encasements—not to keep students inside where they might presumably gain from education, but because "the children threw bricks" (12). Furthermore, the community is tainted by grit and filth registered through the grimy buildings as well as through the bodies of the residents. Kelly's rapist uses this spatially encoded defilement as an opportunity to dehumanize his victim as a means by which to preemptively assuage his own guilt: "[S]he was not one child but hundreds of children, rough, noisy dirty children, the kind his mother dragged him past at bus stops" (25). By describing the "row of houses that was boarded up and waiting for demolition" as well as the boarded-up factory windows that render "the whole place as derelict" (27), Barker demonstrates how space and class unite to subjugate residents in ways that place them into danger. Following the news of the assault, the women of Union Street extend superficial condolences to Kelly and her mother, but Barker makes it clear that such events are less of an anomaly and more of an inevitability to be acknowledged but not addressed. Her mother, who "turned to housework when she was especially distressed" (58), can no longer look her own daughter in the eye, and the women of Union Street continue about their business, with Kelly inevitably following their lead: "[S]he bent her head and followed in their footsteps. She was going home" (69). Yet, Barker had previously marked "home" as permeable and, therefore, a site of potential danger, and Kelly notes that her mother's "hard exterior had cracked to reveal an inner corruption" (59), causing the girl to reject "the spurious safety of home" (59). Although Kelly learns how to sidestep "the hopeless, the abandoned, the derelict" individuals of the community

(60), Barker makes it clear that the entire region is marked by behaviors dictated by the space itself.

Resilience and Sustenance

Despite the alienation and melancholia prevalent on Union Street, Barker's characters respond with gestures of earnest resilience—which, clearly, is the novel's guiding message. This resilience is echoed in the buildings themselves that, while perhaps condemned or derelict, stand strong to resist the punishing forces of neoliberalism. Despondent over his newly reduced position in life, George Harrison pays a visit to Blonde Dinah, a sex worker. Upon seeing his dejected state, Dinah tells a story about working-class communities coming together to celebrate what they share: " 'I used to live round here, you know. Bit further. Wharfe Street.' She stood with her back to the river, looking at the row of derelict houses opposite. 'Good houses, you know. Some of 'em' " (225). When George reminds her of their pending demolition, she responds with regret but draws on her own experiences living there in a manner that suggests urbanization itself: "The cracked and seamed face lit up, her voice came out warm and spluttery between badly fitting teeth, and her hands, shaping the darkness, re-created a community, as she talked about the past, about the people she had known" (226). While the novel is indeed bleak and often upsetting, *Union Street* maintains a steady hold on notions of working-class solidarity and self-directed community in response to sites devastated by callous social and political policies as well as the ensuing stigmatization that results.

Returning once more to the community of women that form in response to Kelly Brown's rape, attempts made at care are registered as futile:

> Nobody knew how to react. They all knew and liked Kelly. You couldn't very well ignore it. And yet to come right out with it. . . . In the end they behaved as if the child had been ill.
>
> (45)

Claims were made about "punishing sexual offenders," but soon after, "the excitement died down," and "Kelly remained alone" (46). The positioning of this scene so early in the narrative suggests, at first, the futility of solidarity in a space marked by excessive trauma and neglect. Yet discussions of community persist in a manner that mirrors the perseverance of working-class solidarity against all odds. As mentioned, the assault is regarded by several of the women on Union Street as a kind of initiation into their world: "Whatever else she was, she was no longer the child they had known. Dimly, they sensed an inner transformation that paralleled the one they saw. But they did not try, or hope, to understand it. She was accepted in Union Street as her mother was not" (47). The experiences that these women share is mapped onto other areas of their life, exhibited by Lisa Goddard's time in the maternity ward: "They went together, a whole crowd of women in billowing, shapeless dressing gowns, smelling of milk and blood, walking with that curiously splay-legged, rolling gait that sailors and recently-delivered women share" (134). While Barker's text is deeply troubling in its depictions of abandoned communities, it does reinforce the notion of resilience as a mode of survival and sustenance. At times, Barker's articulation of what constitutes a community is little more than shared abuse, but the reader is reminded of the dynamic, fluid nature of community itself, even in light of this collective trauma.

While the text is characterized by struggle, the persistence of community spirit serves to counter the spirit of community lost through deindustrialization and alienation. Such a state, arguably, serves as the formation for stigmatization, in that certain attributes and behaviors are concretized relative to space. On the one hand, Barker's text implies social stasis—a state that, despite the changes underway in the built environment, produces little change in the livelihoods of the residents. In this regard, the novel captures the lived experience of a working-class community in Thatcher's Britain. On the other, the text emphasizes persistence and the stability of a working-class identity in response to social and economic breakdown. From the ad hoc community of the abused ready to welcome Kelly Brown into their fold, to the references of women's solidarity in the factory, the home, and the maternity ward, *Union Street* positions shared experience as a counter to attacks on traditional forms of working-class community. Although perhaps ineffectual as a response to economic changes underway in a manner that recalls working-class women's writing of prior decades, the text reminds the reader that the construction and upkeep of an ideological, virtual community within an oppressed space is a kind of space unto itself. To return momentarily to Goffman's conception of the "virtual" versus the "actual" social identity, it would appear that (virtual) assumptions formed about the women of Union Street based on the stigma of impoverished spaces are challenged by an "actual" identity characterized by the resilience, spirit, and reciprocity that the women demonstrate. Such constructions not only unite individuals in their struggles, but remap the territory under conditions dictated by the marginalized themselves.

References

Alcalá, Roberto Del Valle. 2015. "Crisis, Reproduction, and Resistance in Pat Barker's Union Street and Blow Your House Down." *LIT: Literature Interpretation Theory* 26 (3): 194–214. https://doi.org/10.1080/10436928.2015.106 1902.

Azaryahu, Maoz. 1986. "Street Names and Political Identity: The Case of East Berlin." *Journal of Contemporary History* 21 (4): 581–604. https://doi.org/10.1177/002200948602100405.

Barker, Pat. 1984. *Blow Your House Down*. London: Virago.

———. 1986. *Liza's England*. London: Virago.

———. 1991. *Regeneration*. New York: E.P. Dutton.

———. (1982) 1997. *Union Street*. London: Virago.

Barker, Pat. 2004. "An Interview with Pat Barker." Interview by Rob Nixon. *Contemporary Literature* 45 (1): 1–21. https://doi.org/10.1353/cli.2004.0010.

Barker, Pat. 2018. "The Art of Fiction No. 243." Interview by Valerie Stivers. *The Paris Review* 2018 (227) (Winter): 167–89.

Bourdieu, Pierre. 1984. *Distinction: A Social Critique of the Judgement of Taste*. Translated by Richard Nice. Cambridge, MA: Harvard University Press.

Brannigan, John. 2005a. *Pat Barker*. Manchester, UK: Manchester University Press.

———. 2005b. "The Small World of Kelly Brown: Home and Dereliction in Union Street." In *Critical Perspectives on Pat Barker*, edited by Sharon Monteith, Margaretta Jolly, Nahem Yousaf, and Ronald Paul, 3–13. Columbia, SC: University of South Carolina Press.

Calhoun, John B. 1962. "Population Density and Social Pathology." *Scientific American* 206 (2): 139–49.

Davis, Mike. (1990) 2006. *City of Quartz: Excavating the Future in Los Angeles*. London: Verso.

Delaney, Shelagh. 1958. *A Taste of Honey*. New York: Grove Press.

Dunn, Nell. (1963) 1988. *Up the Junction*. London: Virago Modern Classics.

Durkheim, Émile. (1895) 1982. *The Rules of Sociological Method*. Edited by Steven Lukes. Translated by W. D. Halls. New York: The Free Press.

Falcus, Sarah. 2007. "'A Complex Mixture of Fascination and Distaste': Relationships Between Women in Pat Barker's Blow Your House Down, Liza's England and Union Street." *Journal of Gender Studies* 16 (3): 249–61. https://doi.org/10.1080/09589230701562947.

Gallagher, Lucy. 2011. "'He Had Always Believed That There Were Two Sorts of Women: The Decent Ones and the Rest': The Female Body, Dirt, and Domesticity in Pat Barker's Union Street." *Contemporary Women's Writing* 5 (1): 36–51. https://doi.org/10.1093/cwwrit/vpq010.

Garcia, Stephen M., Mark Hallahan, and Robert Rosenthal. 2007. "Poor Expression: Concealing Social Class Stigma." *Basic and Applied Social Psychology* 29 (2): 99–107. https://doi.org/10.1080/01973530701330835.

Giddens, Anthony. 1982. *Profiles and Critiques in Social Theory*. Berkeley, CA: University of California Press.

Goffman, Erving. 1963. *Stigma: Notes on the Management of Spoiled Identity*. Englewood Cliffs, NJ: Prentice-Hall.

Hastings, Annette. 2004. "Stigma and Social Housing Estates: Beyond Pathological Explanations." *Journal of Housing and the Built Environment* 19 (3): 233–54.

Jensen, Sune Qvotrup, Annick Prieur, and Jakob Skjott-Larsen. 2021. "Living with Stigma: Spatial and Social Divisions in a Danish City." *International Journal of Urban and Regional Research* 45 (1): 186–96. https://doi.org/DOI:10.1111/1468-2427.12850.

Joannou, Maroula. 2004. "Pat Barker and the Languages of Region and Class." In *Contemporary British Women Writers*, edited by Emma Parker, 41–54. Essays and Studies: 57. Woodbridge, UK: Brewer, for English Association.

Jolly, Margaretta. 2005. "Toward a Masculine Maternal: Pat Barker's Bodily Fictions." In *Critical Perspectives on Pat Barker*, edited by Sharon Monteith, Margaretta Jolly, Nahem Yousaf, and Ronald Paul. Columbia, SC: University of South Carolina Press.

Kirk, John. 1999. "Recovered Perspectives: Gender, Class, and Memory in Pat Barker's Writing." *Contemporary Literature* 40 (4): 603–26. https://doi.org/10.2307/1208796.

Lay, Samantha. 2002. *British Social Realism: From Documentary to Brit Grit*. London: Wallflower Press.

Mitchelson, Matthew L., Derek H. Alderman, and E. Jeffrey Popke. 2007. "Branded: The Economic Geographies of Streets Named in Honor of Reverend Dr. Martin Luther King, Jr." *Social Science Quarterly* 88 (1): 120–45. https://doi.org/10.1111/j.1540-6237.2007.00450.x.

Proshansky, Harold M., Abbe K. Fabian, and Robert Kaminoff. 1983. "Place-Identity: Physical World Socialization of the Self." *Journal of Environmental Psychology* 3 (1): 57–83. https://doi.org/10.1016/S0272-4944(83)80021-8.

Tyler, Imogen. 2020. *Stigma: The Machinery of Inequality*. London: Zed Books.

Tyler, Imogen, and Tom Slater. 2018. "Rethinking the Sociology of Stigma." *The Sociological Review* 66 (4): 721–43. https://doi.org/10.1177/0038026118777425.

Wacquant, Loïc. 2007. "Territorial Stigmatization in the Age of Advanced Marginality." *Thesis Eleven* 91 (1): 66–77. https://doi.org/10.1177/0725513607082003.

Wacquant, Loïc, and John Howe. 2008. *Urban Outcasts: A Comparative Sociology of Advanced Marginality*. Cambridge, UK and Malden, MA: Polity.

Zelinsky, Wilbur. 2002. "Slouching Toward a Theory of Names: A Tentative Taxonomic Fix." *Names: A Journal of Onomastics* 50 (4): 243–62. https://doi.org/10.1179/nam.2002.50.4.243.

8 Ghost Towns

The Haunting, Deindustrialized Spaces of Ross Raisin's *Waterline* and Martin Amis's *Lionel Asbo*

Nick Bentley

What does it mean to talk about working-class space? How is space bound up with the idea of identity? And what happens in a post-industrial context where the traditional meanings of those spaces and the identities associated with them have been dismantled? This last question especially is the primary concern of this chapter, explored with respect to two twenty-first-century novels of very different styles and approaches: Ross Raisin's *Waterline* (2011) and Martin Amis's *Lionel Asbo: State of England* (2012). Both novels contain central characters that are representative, in differing ways, of post-industrial working-class identities symbolically rendered in the profound changes each undergoes. These changes are presented in economic terms, with respect to their family relations and kinship networks, and in their relationship with the spaces they inhabit. Although different in style, I want to argue that both novels reject a straightforward realism in their engagement with contemporary issues of class.

Before analyzing the two novels in detail, however, it is necessary to offer some theoretical reflections on the nature of space in relation to individual and collective identities associated with social class.[1] Class is, of course, a complicated concept: as Raymond Williams notes, it is "an obviously difficult word, both in its range of meanings and in its complexity in that particular meaning where it describes a social division" (1976, 60). This complexity is only increased when considered in terms of space, itself a difficult term that can include notions of area, location, region, and nation, as well as specific places. When thinking of space in terms of working-class identity, the notion of space combines both concrete, physical places with culturally constructed or imagined places that carry with them whole sets of connotations, such as the factory, the council house, or the pub. This complicated nexus of physical, culturally constructed, and imagined spaces has a long history in literary and cultural analyses of class. Traditional Western Marxist theories around class and space, for example, have often identified location as one of the superstructural components conditioned by the economic base from which identity is produced.[2] In much Marxist thought, the prevailing economic divisions

DOI: 10.4324/9781003119425-9

under capitalism carry with them an implicit sense of spatial demarcation. Space and geographical identification more broadly, however, has predominantly taken a back seat to issues of historical development. As Edward Soja argues,

> Social theorization thus came to be dominated by a narrowed and streamlined historical materialism, stripped of its more geographically sensitive variants . . . and, with a few exceptions, less attentive to the formative spatiality of social life as a template of critical insight.
>
> (1989, 31)

This privileging of temporality and historicity over spatiality began to be challenged in what came to be known as the spatial turn in cultural theory. Henri Lefebvre, for example, in *The Production of Space*, notes that "the class struggle is inscribed in space" (1974, 55). For Lefebvre, space is not (just) a corollary of economic frameworks but is also socially produced and carries with it a set of spatial imaginaries. Benedict Anderson (1983) develops this sense of space as a cultural imaginary to consider the ways in which nations, national identity, and relationships between nations (in the form of economic competition and Western imperialism) are produced through the development of the industrial revolution and are thus implicitly bound up with notions of class. Indeed, we might also think of the working class as an imagined community.[3] The focus on the production of space under industrial capitalism has also been transferred to a post-industrial context by a series of other cultural Marxist-influenced critics such as David Harvey (1973, 2006), Edward Soja (1989), and Doreen Massey (1995). Massey, for example, notes that the move to a post-industrial framework of economic and social structure in Britain since the 1960s has resulted in "a major recomposition for the working class . . ., a recomposition in which the geographical reorganization has been integral" (281). Massey's focus on the importance of geographical and spatial contexts is primarily concerned with mapping new economic and social structures that have responded to changes in industrial practices and organization. She sees space in this context as the "historical product of the combination of layers of activity" (114) that change over time with respect to an area's differing "economic activities and forms of social organisation" (115).

Where spatial concerns are considered, then, Western Marxist theories recognize that the relationship between class and space is culturally produced but tend to focus on abstracted, macro categories of space that rely on broad socio-economic infrastructures such as nations (Benedict Anderson), regions (Doreen Massey), internal city zones (Lefebvre), the specific geographies of post-modern cities (Soja, Harvey), or in the case of Raymond Williams's *The Country and the City*, the differences between the urban and the rural. As important as this body of work has been in understanding the ways in which class and spatiality have been configured, space has been broadly understood in terms of geographical abstracts without the specificity of individual cases.

It is perhaps unfair to include Williams in this list, as he, in a sense, is also part of the development of approaches to class and space that offer an alternative (although still Marxist influenced) approach that can be associated with the cultural materialist turn of the New Left in the 1950s. This movement within the left began to move away from the broader, abstracted categories of class to a focus on the specificities of lived experience.[4] In this context, Richard Hoggart's *The Uses of Literacy* (1957) is an illuminating example in its focus on the intimate relationship of working-class people to their environments and how that everyday connection to place constituted a major aspect of their identity. As he writes about the working-class home, the "neighbourhood," or even with a more critical edge on the "shiny barbarism" of the new youth cultures in the milk bars, we get the sense of the affective influence of space in the creation of collective identities and the way that cultural practices of working-class people are bound up with the notion of the places they occupy. For New Left writers like Hoggart, then, the spaces of working-class culture are not (just) an economically conditioned backdrop against which identity is formed but are crucial in the very production of those identities.

Hoggart's working-class spaces are drawn from his autobiographical experience and thus retain a certain level of authenticity; however, the spaces he identifies seem to occupy a combination of real and imagined space. The sense of working-class space developed here lends itself to a notion of the working class not (only) as a set of observable and quantifiable statistics around economic income, social organization, and cultural practices but also as a sense of an imagined community occupying both real and culturally produced spaces. In this culturally imagined landscape, those traditional markers of working-class places—the factory, the council house, the estate, the allotment, the corner shop, the pub, the dance hall—take on meanings imbued with class imaginaries and psycho-social meaning. This understanding of cultural location resonates with Gaston Bachelard's notion of a poetics of space in which individual examples can be analyzed through a "systematic psychological study of the sites of our intimate lives" (1994, 8).[5] Working-class spaces, then, can be seen as a series of overlayerings of singular spaces, preconceived cultural meanings, and traces of past histories. It is this palimpsestic model of working-class spaces that is particularly attuned to their rendering in literary fiction, which operates in a complex matrix of realistic description, aesthetic construction, cultural resonance, and historical tracing.

The Place of the Novel: The Genre Spaces of Working-Class Fiction

In order to explore literary representations of working-class space in terms of the shift from the industrial to the post-industrial, we might begin by looking at examples from the 1950s, the last decade in which industrial work practices could be said to be dominant before the gradual process of deindustrialization, and the period often cited as the last great moment of working-class fiction.[6] In Alan Sillitoe's *Saturday Night and Sunday Morning* (1958), for example, the main working-class figure Arthur Seaton moves in a rhythm between factory, home, and pub as the triangular spatial nodes of his existence. It is within this cultural environment that his identity is formed and performed, and, although Arthur questions the class system, he is eventually consumed back into a rhythm of work, rest, and entertainment that is shown to be intricately tied to his geographical area. The novel's bildungsroman form renders Arthur's potentially subversive and libidinous youthful energies as ultimately contained within a dominant model of society that is still class based, represented by his impending marriage and move to a new housing estate within a stone's throw of his parents' house. In 1950s fiction, then, individuals like Arthur Seaton (or Joe Lampton in John Braine's *Room at the Top* [1957], Arthur Machin in David Storey's *This Sporting Life* [1960], or Billy Fisher in Keith Waterhouse's *Billy Liar* [1959]) may be at tension with the social milieu in which they find themselves, but that milieu itself is not ultimately in threat of disappearance. The characters in these novels represent a psycho-cultural response to their environments, which plays out through their narrative trajectories. In all these works, there is a sense in which the working practices of groups map clearly and directly onto demarcated spaces. There is a symbiotic relationship between economic/working structures, spatial inhabitation, and an individual/collective sense of identity as manifest in descriptions of their lived experiences. This triangulation between working practices, space, and identity provides the fixed points within which the drama of working-class characters and plots play themselves out in the traditional working-class novel.[7]

Although registering changes in the socio cultural makeup of the immediate post-war period in Britain, the working-class novel that developed in the 1950s can still be described as industrial fiction. So, what happens to characters experiencing the shifts in working practices and the changing nature of spaces under post-industrialization? What happens when characters are placed in situations where one or more of the points in the triangular model of working practices, space, and identity are profoundly disrupted? Beyond its economic impact, post-industrialism can be identified as a dismantling of the affective relationship between work, space, and identity that threatens to explode the very basis on which the model has been conceived for one generation in its transition to another. If one of the points of the triangle shifts, it produces profound change in the others and the structure overall. At such moments, places lose both their real and culturally produced meanings (although traces of those meanings linger on); identities are destabilized, causing individuals and collectives to experience trauma, neurosis, and existential crisis.

Raisin's *Waterline* and Amis's *Lionel Asbo* dramatize the effects of such a profound shift in those working-class identities that were configured in the fiction of the 1950s, especially as manifested through the disruption of the meaning of space. This shift can also be noted in terms of literary form; the working-class novels of the 1950s are generally agreed to follow a tradition of literary realism, itself part of a reaction to the modernism of the early decades of the twentieth century and the interwar years.[8] The post-industrial, I will argue, has disrupted that reliance on realism as a mechanism for portraying the lived experience of working-class life. Both Raisin and Amis challenge conventional realism. For Raisin, a realistic mode is still evident, but it is disrupted through the central character's experiences of the post-industrial. Similarly, Amis continues a career interest of complicating realism in a novel that foregrounds an exaggerated hyperrealism of excessive grotesque and cartoonish behaviors. We can, then, think of the post-industrial working-class novel as an interrogation of the realist mode that has predominated its history. In what follows, I will suggest that one modal intervention that distinguishes both Raisin and Amis (in differing ways) is the gothic. This is not something new to the post-industrial period: think, for example, of the host of working-class characters that emerge from the urban shadows in Dickens's novels such as Bill Sikes and Fagin in *Oliver Twist* (1838), Magwitch in *Great Expectations* (1861), or Rogue Riderhood in *Our Mutual Friend* (1865). These novels feed on the assumption that working-class spaces are inevitably other, secluded, and potentially dangerous from the perspective of a middle-class gaze. The modern equivalents of this kind of gothicization of working-class fiction are the urban crime novel and the hypermasculine gangster movie that present working-class spaces as dangerous zones beyond civil society, for example, in films like Guy Ritchie's *Lock, Stock and Two Smoking Barrels* (1998), Steven Knight's *Peaky Blinders* series (2015), and, of course, in the long tradition of American gangster TV and film from the *Dead End Kids* series of movies in the 1930s via *The Godfather* (1972) and *Goodfellas* (1990) to *Boardwalk Empire* (2010–2014).

The gothicization of the working class can also be identified in some recent critical commentary and socio cultural analysis of space. This is hardly surprising, given that the very notion of the post-industrial suggests that we are "after" or "beyond" a living culture—a culture that continues to remind us of its passing in the form of nostalgic memories, ghostly traces of the past, and uncanny experiences of places that are no longer what they once were. Many writers have focused on the haunto-logical aspects of the post-industrial: for example, Mark Fisher's (2014) notion of the "lost futures" of contemporary urban landscapes and cultures.[9] Much of this approach highlights how the lives of past people and experience leave traces in the present. As Tim Edensor has noted in a study of the working-class spaces of Manchester:

> The haunted spaces represented here evoke the multiplicity of this temporal urban collage, highlighting the varied ways in which the past haunts the presence by its absence, is everywhere folded into the fabric of the city, and especially possesses its mundane spaces.
>
> (2008, 325)

Edensor's writing represents a form of working-class psycho-geography that extends the typical bourgeois identification of the literary palimp-sests of an area to a focus more on the industrial past and the ghostly hauntings of those previous work practices. Inevitably, those hauntings of place evoke ghostly identities of past workers. Edensor's spaces, for example, are no longer peopled by industrial workers, but they evoke their lost presence.[10] As Sherry Lee Linkon has stated, "Perhaps because it emerges out of the historical moment of loss, deindustrialized literature emphasizes a critical and productive nostalgia about industrial labor" (2017, 394). Intriguing and seductive as this kind of dwelling in the post-industrial past is, it has to be noted that contemporary (albeit often dein-dustrialized) working-class people continue to inhabit these spaces, and there is always the danger of lamenting the lost pasts (and in Fisher's terms, the lost futures) of the industrial period to the extent that the working practices and economic and social inequalities of the present are overlooked.

These contemporary inequalities are rendered in the two fictional artic-ulations of British working-class identities and spaces discussed in this chapter. While Raisin provides a largely realistic account of the decline of a working-class character from a position of collective security to one of precarious homelessness, Amis's novel offers a satirical analysis of working-class expediency and criminality set in a fictional London sink estate. The chapter argues that the contrasting approaches taken by Amis and Raisin reveal the complexities of articulating and representing contempo-rary working-class characters and environments in the textual space of literary fiction. I will argue that the novels represent two different modes of writing about working-class environments, characters, and concerns, one of which attempts to convey an accurate and authentic portrayal, while the other is concerned with the interrogation of the very process of representation and, indeed, the concept of the "working class" as a sociological and aesthetic category. If Raisin's *Waterline* tends toward the realist tradition, then Amis's *Lionel Asbo* represents a post-modern examination of the very idea of the working-class novel in the contemporary moment, while deploying characters, plot moves, and locations that intimate a gothic demonization. However, I do not want to suggest a straightforward binary model between a realist *Waterline* and a gothic *Lionel Asbo*. Indeed, the very disruptive effects of deindustrialization can be mapped onto the way both these novels complicate established genre categories: Raisin's novel is full of ghosts, while a realistic set of implications can be identified through Amis's post-modern satire of his gothic anti-hero.

Ross Raisin's *Waterline* (2011)

Ross Raisin's *Waterline* tells the story of Mick Little who, at the opening of the novel, is mourning the loss of his wife, Cathy, to mesothelioma, a disease caused by her proximity to asbestos. This asbestos has been brought into their home on Mick's overalls due to his past work in the Glasgow shipbuilding industry. With his wife dead and the shipyards closed, Mick decides to move from his home city of Glasgow to London where he takes up a series of precarious jobs before ultimately falling into alcoholism and homelessness.

Cathy's death sets in motion an existential crisis for Mick; as Arthur Rose notes, "If Cathy represented stability or normality for Mick, then her death was the end of this normality" (2018, 156).[11] However, the novel also shows how this moment of personal crisis has its origins in Mick's earlier loss of employment in the traditional shipbuilding industry. It is, then, in the combination of the public and private that the novel conveys its analysis of the history of industrial decline in Britain in the period from the Thatcherite eighties to the early twenty-first century. The damage, registered physically by Cathy and mentally by Mick, is mapped on to the general effects on the landscapes of traditional urban industrial centers in Scotland, Wales, and the north of England, an example of what Rob Nixon (2013) calls "slow violence" as applied to the effects of the processes of deindustrialization on traditional working-class communities in the industrial north.[12] In *Waterline*, the cancer Cathy contracts can be read as an example of the drawn-out injuries caused by capitalist practices. Mick's decline in mental health can also be seen as a direct effect of the changed industrial landscape. The dismantling of a collective and relatively stable working-class identity established during the industrial period is thus dramatized in Mick's psychological breakdown.

This decline is specifically registered in spatial terms as *dis*-placement, as Mick is compelled though his own traumatic experiences and the guilt he feels toward Cathy's death to leave his home in Glasgow and move to London to find work. This example of economic migrancy is shown to be attendant on aspects of deindustrialization and is also registered in

Mick's backstory as he has had previous stints in shipyards in Australia and on Tyneside. With this industry decimated, at the opening of the novel, Mick is eking out a precarious existence as a temporary taxi driver. Mick's narrative trajectory then is determined by a series of displacements as he moves from his home, to a brief period sleeping in his shed (because he cannot face the unsettling ghosts of the past he is reminded of in his house) to a hotel room in London, then to work digs at Heathrow Airport, and ultimately to the streets as he becomes homeless. This series of displacements is presented as a narrative of decline that maps personal experience on to a wider commentary on the effects of deindustrialization on the working class.

Mick's crisis (and the wider effects of deindustrialization) is presented through the novel's focus on both the cultural meanings of imagined spaces and the affective response to real places. This combination of the imaginative and the concrete resonates with Michel Foucault's (1986) concept of heterotopias: real spaces that are overlaid with symbolic significance for particular occupants and visitors to the space. Foucault identifies several types of heterotopias, one of which refers to moments of crisis and another related to deviance. The former is of particular import to Mick's situation. The places he has previously occupied carry with them layers of cultural meanings that relate to the imagined community of the working class generally. Deindustrialization is a moment of crisis for working-class identity; the very concept of what it means to be working class after all, as Raymond Williams has noted, was grounded in the industrial revolution (1976, 60–69). Once the very concept of the working class is put under pressure, then a concomitant shift is registered in the class consciousness of those previously employed in industrial labor. In Mick's case, the process sets in motion an existential crisis that ultimately drives him toward homelessness.

To trace this heterotopic crisis, it is illuminating to analyze the presentation of space in the novel. Markers of the post-industrial can be identified in terms of change in the function of space, such as gentrification and the transference of previously industrial spaces into heritage/tourist sites. One passage in the novel focuses this through an observation of the changing urban landscape in one of the novel's frequent shifts in point of view to characters who either observe Mick or are used to offer commentary on the landscapes through which he moves:

> He's heard about the crane. Turned into a visitor centre. He's seen it lit up pink and red at night a couple of times when he's been over near Clydebank. The last he knew, they were talking about putting a restaurant in the jib and making it revolve. He'd read that in the paper. It was part of a project to represent the industrial heritage of the area. A revolving pink restaurant. You've got to wonder how they dream these things up. And see the view? That's one thing for starters

they'll have to change. All very well getting the full panorama but if all you're looking at a puddled wasteland every direction—gangs of weans playing football and smoking, pigeons roosting and crapping over the rusted fabrication sheds—it isn't going to make your mozzarella parcels taste much better, is it?

(Raisin 2011, 5)

In this passage, the paradoxes of the heritage industry[13] are brought to the fore as the visitor center replaces the site of heavy industry: the productive primary industrial landscape of the past is replaced by the allure of non-productive consumption in the form of heritage tourism. As Phil O'Brien has noted of this passage, "History has been turned into spectacle as capitalism absorbs and guts it of its core" (2020, 99). This kind of shift in spatial function transforms the workers in those lost industries into exhibits, curated and recommodified in a way that is palatable to the middle-class gaze, while simultaneously excluding the workers from any profit made in their name. But the anticipated view is frustrated by the continuation of the debilitating effects of deindustrialization represented in the passage by the "puddled wasteland." This inadequate attempt to paper over lost industries is juxtaposed in the novel with images of the past in which the organic solidity of fixed working practices/space/identity nexus is recollected. This is achieved through the presentation of old photographs:

It wasn't always like this, of course. Their fathers and their grandfathers have shown them enough photographs. . . . These same streets a hundred years ago, sixty, forty even, mobbed with hundreds of workers starting out for the day shift. Tired and quiet, like this pair, getting moving. The noise of the boots on the road, the hooter about to sound up the way and signal the start of work . . . grouping up as they move on—riveters, caulkers, blacksmiths, the welders clear visible in their spotted hats and their leathers, boilermakers, platers— the whole black squad marching on up the road. And at the back, the apprentices pishing about.

(Raisin 2011, 9)

The latter paragraph reminds us of Tim Edensor's (2008) observations of the lingering spaces of a deindustrialized urban landscape, in which the buildings and spaces of that lost culture remain, but their meaning has shifted to leave an uncanny trace. The recall of a vibrant industrial past can also be seen in the description of the pub that Mick (now only occasionally) frequents, poignantly called *The Empress*, where photographs decorate the wall that combine images of working practices (in the form of famous ship launches from the Clyde), working people, and working-class entertainment (in the form of well-known footballers):

> Ships and footballers, mixed together: the Bloodhound, HMS Valiant, Davie Meiklejohn, HMS Indomitable, Willie Johnston, RMS Empress of Japan, Alan 'The Wee Society Man' Morton. Clydebuilt, each every one, crafted and revered all down the water, talked about over people's teatimes, sold off to England. Some of the players probably worked on these ships. . . . They would have served their apprenticeships on the yards, black squad, up early for a day's work, and then away for a quick shower and a bite to eat and they'd be down the training pitches.
>
> (Raisin 2011, 27)

This combination of footballers and ships, both "Clydebuilt," suggests a sense of working and cultural practices being cemented into a fixed structure of feeling, but one located in the past. The photographs of a unified and proud community look down on a deserted pub in the present, where only a few old regulars still haunt the parlor. This post-industrial pub contrasts poignantly with the description of the club in, for example, *Saturday Night and Sunday Morning*, where such spaces reveal the bacchanalian, lived cultures of a vibrant working-class industrialism: where the "bingiest glad-time of the week" is had and where on a Saturday night, "[f]loors shook and windows rattled, and leaves of aspidistras wilted in the fumes of beer and smoke" (Sillitoe 1994, 5). At Mick's pub, in post-industrial Glasgow, "there's two old boys on the faded red wall seat that goes around the parlour, pattering away together" (Raisin 2011, 26).

Mick's experience of these post-industrial spaces is bound up with his guilt at being the inadvertent cause of his wife's contraction of mesothelioma and combine to cause his to move to London. Mick's move south, however, does not constitute an escape from the post-industrial climate of Britain and serves only to exacerbate his changing identity further. After a stint of precarious employment in the kitchens of a Heathrow hotel, he ultimately finds himself homeless. The "street" (along with the workhouse), of course, is a location that hovers throughout working-class writing, as a place of threat for those who buckle under the pressures of industrial capital. Homelessness in this context equates with what Giorgio Agamben (1998) describes as "bare life," a form of human existence excluded from the benefits of public life and political representation. This bare life (or *homo sacer* as Agamben calls it following the concept in ancient Roman law) is ultimately prefigured through the observations of legitimate society, through what we might call the "middle-class gaze" of a dominant cultural point of view.[14]

Once homeless, Mick's bare life existence is registered in the way people look at him:

> Odd. Like he's there but he's in fact no there. They are looking at him, but from somewhere else, another consciousness, another world. Like being bevvied. Operating in your own space and everybody else fogging up around the edges of it.
>
> (Raisin 2011, 183)

This "somewhere else" is, of course, the space of the dominant culture, which would previously have been a complex interaction of both middle-class and working-class observation. The shift in Mick's identity thus places him in a different space, "another world," as an industrial revenant, uncannily haunting the post-industrial urban landscape. Later, when he finally finds a place in a hostel and is able to remove his clothes for the first time in a long time, this changed identity is marked on his physical body. As he looks at himself naked in a mirror, he notes:

> As if the body isn't his; it belongs to another time when nakedness was something that had to be dealt with on a daily basis, and now he doesn't own it—he's removed himself from his body like he has from everything else. The only clue that it's there the now: that it hurts.
>
> (188)

In this doubling of perspective, Mick simultaneously observes his own existence as well as recognizing how he might look from the viewpoint of the society that has deemed him redundant.

This moment in Mick's narrative represents an extremity in his existential crisis from which he gradually reassembles a form of identity adapted to his post-industrial circumstances. The novel concludes with Mick being partly rehabilitated in dominant society, first through his engagement with the people running the hostel and then in his own rented accommodation. He is eventually reunited with his son, and the final scene sees him shopping in a post-industrial superstore for a football shirt for his grandson. This large commercial space of everyday consumption is presented as a poor substitute for the productive industrial spaces of the past: a "massive warehouse-type shop floor, mobbed out with swivel rails of trackie bottoms and luminous shirts" (258). The use of the term "shop floor" here is double-edged, as it recalls a unionized, factory context from a lost industrial period, now leached of its significance of political resistance to the prevailing consumer capitalism. Ultimately, then, Mick is forced to consent to the prevailing economic forces that have swept across his industrial past. This is, however, akin to what Jeremy Gilbert (2015) has described as a "disaffected consent," one in which Mick accepts without enthusiasm or any sense of personal investment in the dominant culture to which he acquiesces.

The transition Mick goes through in the course of the novel represents an interconnected shift in all three aspects of his working-class identity—his working practices, the spaces he inhabits, and the identities that give his life meaning. *Waterline*, then, dramatizes the shift in working practices imposed by deindustrialization in the late twentieth and early twenty-first centuries, which in turn destabilizes the spaces of working-class life and the identities of those that inhabit them.

Martin Amis' *Lionel Asbo: State of England* (2012)

Lionel Asbo, like Raisin's *Waterline*, addresses the twenty-first-century effects of deindustrialization as well as the effects of that economic and political transition on the everyday experiences and lived ideologies of traditional working-class communities. In Amis's novel, however, a very different kind of post-industrial working-class is constructed, one that treads a tightrope between a state-of-the-nation critique and a mockery of what Amis perceives of the contemporary working class. In the first two sections of this chapter, we looked at the way literary fiction operates through the dramatization of characters moving against and through the social imaginaries of working-class space. This can produce positive responses that celebrate vibrant working-class cultures and structures of feeling. Alternatively, the power of these social imaginaries can often contribute to an alternative demonization of working-class people, their cultural practices, lifestyles, and environments, especially in popular media. There has been some excellent recent criticism on this subject. Imogen Tyler (2013), for example, notes how during Tony Blair's New Labour governments (1997–2010), many working-class people (under the pejorative moniker of the "chav") were routinely abjectified in popular screen and print media, while Owen Jones, in *Chavs: The Demonization of the Working Class*, argues that "Chav-bashing" is a "form of class hatred [that] has become an integral, respectable part of Modern British culture" (2011, 5). Tim Edensor has similarly noted, "A distorted reflection of contemporary working-class identity is . . . articulated by a recent imaginary of 'chavs', hen-parties, 'trailer trash' and monstrous, excessive behavior which provides the 'constitutive limit' of respectable behavior" (2008, 328). Beverley Skeggs has identified the ways in which working-class women, in particular, are often "framed by associations of contagion, pollution, danger, distaste and excess heterosexuality" in media representations of "hen-parties" in certain twenty-first-century British TV shows (2005, 966). This kind of demonization is often located in specific spaces: Lynsey Hanley, for example, in her illuminating book *Estates: An Intimate History* (2007), notes how "the shorthand for proletarian hell used by those who don't live on them is 'council estate' " (44). Tyler notes that "it was under New Labour that a powerful consensus emerged that council estates were abject border zones within the state that were not only *liminal* with regard to wider social norms and values but were also actively *antisocial* spaces" (2013, 160, emphasis in original). It is in this context that Martin Amis's *Lionel Asbo: State of England* was published in 2012.

If Raisin's novel evokes the ghostly lived spaces of a post-industrial Britain, then Amis's novel explores another space of working-class identity in the post-industrial, twenty-first century—the mediated spaces of tabloid demonization of working-class culture. One of Amis's themes throughout his career has been the shifting mores of the British class system, and he has written several novels that focus on working-class characters and environments.[15] However, Amis's hyperbolic post-modern style eschews the representational ethos of social realism that predominated in the working-class novel in the 1950s and '60s. Amis is particularly interested in the new formations of masculinity and class and in characters that respond to, negotiate, and often flounder under the experience of post-industrialism and late capitalism. Many of these characters are distinctive in their attempts (and sometimes successes) in traversing class boundaries, and much of Amis's dark humor is at the expense of the misbehavior and cultural embarrassments in which his deracinated characters find themselves. *Lionel Asbo* treads familiar ground in this context. The novel focuses on the eponymous anti-hero's move from petty criminality to celebrity nouveau-riche figure through his winning nearly £140 million on the national lottery.[16] This mixing of representational social critique and exaggerated and cartoonish figures lifted from the British tabloid media is disconcerting for a reader expecting the kind of social realism that has become the dominant form of fiction about the working class in the post-war period. As Megan Faragher notes, "The eponymous protagonist, a rabid consumer of tabloids, has become the very stereotype of working-class loutishness that tabloid culture constructs" (2018, 107). One of the problems, then, with *Lionel Asbo* is that of its mixing of genres.

Despite its shortcomings in terms of accurately depicting working-class life,[17] I want to argue that *Lionel Asbo* has revealing things to say about class in Britain and the way in which it corresponds to demarcations of space, both in a physical sense and the imagined and mediated spaces of class. The attention paid to inner-city space in the novel is focused on the fictional London suburb of Diston, where "nothing—and no one— was over sixty years old" (2012, 9) and which "received more than its fair share of car alarms, burglar alarms and fire alarms . . . a world of italics and exclamation marks" (33–34).[18] Amis's descriptions of Diston focus on the worse aspects of the tabloid depiction of such inner-city areas where a (predominantly white) working class eke out an existence based on benefit claims, low-level criminality, and yobbish violence. This is condensed into the figure of Lionel, who we are told changed his surname from Pepperdine to "Asbo" in honor of the acronym commonly given to "Anti-Social Behavior Orders."[19] In Lionel's case, the adoption of this moniker is not presented as a thoughtless act of bravado, but as a calculated declaration of resistance against the authorities; as the novel's narrative voice tells us, you could only change your name to "Asbo," "if you gave being stupid a lot of intelligent thought" (27). Lionel clearly has an inherent desire to fight against his position in society, but part of his tragedy is that his rebellious energies are not directed at the architects of his conditions of existence but fellow sufferers within his ideological milieu as manifest in his acts of criminal violence in his locale. One of the chimeric reflections of the novel is to ponder " 'you could only change your name to Asbo, "if you gave being stupid a lot of intelligent thought" ' (166). This can, of course, be read as a belittling comment on contemporary working-class people and culture (and their lack of class consciousness); or at least the aspects of it that seem, in the media, to promote a boorish hypermasculinity and individualistic hedonism. Amis frames this question as a choice, thus promoting a sense of individual response and resistance to the debilitating effects of neoliberalism on an abjectified underclass. Indeed, the thought is focalized through Des Pepperdine, Lionel's nephew, who does, in fact, use his intelligence to navigate an underfunded and creaking comprehensive education system and go on to university.

One way to read Lionel's criminality then, is as a form of resistance to the slow violence of deindustrialization, an expedient fight against the system that tries to interpellate him worthless. The contemporary effects of a period of deindustrialization are presented through the description of Diston, where mutual anger at the enforced conditions of existence is palpable. Amis wants to suggest that certain inner-city areas are at the sharp-end of a series of policies of deindustrialization in Britain over the latter quarter of the twentieth century and into the new millennium. Although the satire is often crude and insensitive, the text does draw attention to the rapid increases in inequality and poverty in Britain during this period. This manifests itself, for example, in poor education provision as depicted by "Squeers Free," the local comprehensive attended by Des and previously by Lionel: [U]nder a sky of white: the weakling headmaster, the demoralised chalkies in their rayon tracksuits"—a school that "set the standard for the most police call-outs, the least GCSE passes, and the highest truancy rates" (19).

Lionel's fortunes are changed when he wins the lottery (while in prison) thus propelling him to a very different kind of culture. Amis has described the novel, with respect to this unlikely event, as a modern fairy tale, but it is also a convenient plot device to allow him to develop a satire of Britain as two nations, simultaneously evoking his Victorian

novelistic precedents[20] and offering a critique of the one-nation conservatism expounded by right-leaning politicians in Britain (most recently in
the manipulative rhetoric of Boris Johnson).[21] After a series of debauched
escapades and another spell in prison, Lionel moves to Short Crendon,
another imagined space, this time of a privileged, home county idyll of
rural Britain. The contrast is made explicit: "In Diston, everything hated
everything else. . . . In Short Crendon, on the other hand, everything con-
templated everything else with unqualified satisfaction. As if the whole
village was leaning back, hands on hips, and lightly rocking on its heels"
(165). This spatial contrast contributes to a series of other binaries in the
novel that mark out England as an economically, culturally, and ideo-
logically divided nation: light/heavy, fragility/permanence, ephemerality/
longevity. As Lionel explains to a tabloid reporter, "See Daph, the rich
world . . . is heavy. Everything weighs. Because it's here for the duration.
It's here to stay. . . . And *my* old world, Diston as was, it's . . . it's light!
Nothing weighs an ounce! People die! It, things—fly away!" (151). This
passage represents Lionel thinking through, in terms that resonate with
his lived experience, the effects of two or more generations of deindustrialization in Britain and the impermanence that it has caused in working-
class consciousness.

Lionel's shift from one spatial imaginary to another then, represents
a shift in the working practices/space/identity model developed in the
first section of this chapter. It is the movement between rich and poor
cultural spaces that causes Lionel to suffer his own form of existential
crisis. This is noted when he first acquires his win, as he enters a new
world of wealth:

> Having hosed himself down and all that, Lionel expected to feel
> twice the price. But he had to admit he was still coming over slightly
> queer. Not himself. In fact, he was coming over very peculiar indeed.
> The air seemed glazed and two-dimensional: filmic.
>
> (94)

The sudden shift in Lionel's identity from petty criminal to wealthy
celebrity involves an existential as well as a cultural wrench. Lionel
is "queered" by this experience, suggesting that the new wealth is
doing something to his previous reliance on hypermasculine behaviors
as well as drawing attention to a new constructed, mediated quality
to his life ("filmic"). This move between two distinct socio-cultural-
economic environments not only creates a present cognitive shift but
also alters his life ahead. As he notes to Des, "[T]here's something new
in my life. A new uh, *dimension*. . . . The future!" (105). Lionel tries
to bridge the gap by bringing aspects of Diston culture to Short Crendon, where he builds a tacky mansion that he playfully titles "Wormwood Scrubs" (152). In doing so, he aims, "To go from the floating

world . . . to the heavy" (151). However, this transition proves to be too difficult to make. Later, when he is encouraged by his girlfriend, the fame-seeking "Threnody," to embrace tabloid culture and the wealth and fame it brings, he recognizes the loss of his old identity: "What's happening, Des? Me face—me face, Des, it's all distorted! From the *smiling.* I can't get it back to what it was before! . . . What's happening? Where's Lionel Asbo? Gone. I'm gone, boy, I'm gone" (181).

As already noted, this identity shift is precipitated by his sudden acquisition of wealth; however, the sense that Lionel is moving into a permanent world from one that is impermanent suggests that his previous life is grounded on precarity. In this sense, Lionel can be read as representative of a new, deindustrialized working class. In Amis's novel, the impermanence caused by deindustrialization is mapped on to Lionel's cognitive sense of self, which lurches between a series of precarious locations. He is buffeted between Diston, prison, a stay in a celebrity-frequented hotel in London, and his mansion in Short Crendon, never feeling fixed or permanent in any of them. Ultimately, he tries to get back to Diston with increasing visits to his old council flat that Des and Des's wife, Dawn, have been living in since Lionel's lottery win. His return to Diston represents a paradoxical attempt to find fixity in a culturally impermanent space. Lionel's existence, then, is always in jeopardy—framed in a series of imaginary constructed spaces; for example, when the tabloid journalists target him as a subject of derisory fascination: he "disappeared into the front page" (101). Or, when his portrait is painted to hang in "Wormwood Scrubs," he is rendered as "a Young Pioneer of early Soviet propaganda, the humped shoulder muscles, the corded forearms, the sheen of honest exertion on his open brow" (158). This image at once evokes and mocks the kind of industrial labor that Lionel has been denied. In this sense Lionel is a figure that is out of time, a masculinity perverted and warped by the unavailability of the very industrial labor that honed those constructions of masculinity. Behind the comic mockery, there is, in this sense, something of the ghost about Lionel, reminding us of Edensor's point about working-class hauntings. That Lionel is a gothic figure sits uneasily with the broader tradition of working-class writing grounded in social realism, but thinking of him in this way is fruitful—as a kind of Frankenstein's monster, returning to wreak revenge on the society that has created him.[22] Asbo is indeed "anti-social" in a wider anarchic, apolitical sense; he is a figure produced by slow violence and returning with (rapid) violence.[23]

The aggression that defines Lionel's behavior, then, is an unthinking reaction to the slow violence of deindustrialization. As with Mick Little in Raisin's novel, Lionel is responding in the only form available to him, to the rapid and fundamental changes meted out to working-class cultures and locations in post-industrial Britain. Published only a year apart, there are clear differences between Raisin's and Amis's stylistic and thematic approach. Where Raisin is keen to convey the lived experience of Mick Little as he copes with losing his wife, his job on the shipyards, and ultimately his working-class consciousness, Amis directs his satiric ire on what he feels is a debilitating hypermasculinity as an indirect response to deindustrialization. However, in their distinctive literary engagements with contemporary configurations of class, both are attempting to offer a critique of the effects of deindustrialization on working-class practices, spaces, and identities.

Notes

1. See also Simon Lee's introduction to this book, which discusses some theories and positions relevant to this chapter.
2. Marxism is not, of course, the only body of theory that addresses concerns over the relationship between social class and space, but theories developed from Marxist thinking are the most important with respect to the development of prevailing notions of the relationship between the working class and the spaces they inhabit.
3. Megan Faragher (2018) makes a similar move when discussing the way British tabloid media constructs the working class as an imagined community.
4. Indeed, Williams's concept of "structures of feeling" encapsulates the contradiction played out in much New Left writing between focusing on the macro, generalizing categories suggested by "structures," and the individual and singular experiences suggested by "feelings."
5. Bachelard is focused on the imaginative resonances associated with particular rooms in a house, but this can be extended to other spaces within what can be deemed a working-class environment of both private and public space.
6. A recent study identified 1966 as the year that saw the greatest percentage of secondary industry (manufacturing and construction) in Britain. See: www.ons.gov.uk/economy/nationalaccounts/uksectoraccounts/compendium/economicreview/april2019/longtermtrendsinukemployment1861to2018, accessed July 28, 2021.
7. The traditional working-class novel, of course, is a loose categorization that includes different kinds of fiction, but I am thinking in particular of the tradition that moves through Elizabeth Gaskell and Arthur Morrison in the nineteenth century to Lawrence, Tressell, and Greenwood in the first half of the twentieth to the angry young men novels of the 1950s and 1960s and on to writers like Pat Barker and Livi Michael; this is the tradition traced, for example, in Ian Hayward's *Working-Class Fiction from Chartism to* Trainspotting (1997). These novels can be described as industrial novels in terms of what we might call the high/middle capitalist period (as opposed to the sense of late capitalism defined by writers such as Fredric Jameson).
8. See, for example, Bergonzi (1993), Lodge (1979), and Rabinovitz (1967). It should be noted, however, that several critics have challenged this straightforward reading of the 1950s novel as a return to realisms. See, for example, Gąsiorek (1995) and Bentley (2007).
9. The main influence for the focus on hauntology is Jacques Derrida's *Specters of Marx* (1993).

10. There is perhaps an element of post-industrial tourism here—of gaining intellectual pleasure from an informed recognition of the pastness of working-class spaces—a more sophisticated form of heritage industry tourism: one that retains authenticity as the exhibits of the past have to be tracked down by the keen psycho-geographer rather than cataloged and curated in the museum.

11. Arthur Rose's (2018) article offers an excellent comparison between *Waterline* and Tahmima Anam's *The Bones of Grace*, which shows how the shipbuilding industry should be viewed in an international, post-colonial context.

12. Nixon's concept is grounded in how environmental and climate change affects the poor, especially in the global south, but it might also be applied to the debilitating health effects caused by industrial work practices in old industrial areas in Western countries.

13. The "heritage industry" is a term that has been used to describe the way popular tourist attractions and museums often sanitize and commercialize the past. See Hewison (1987).

14. I am adopting, here, Laura Mulvey's (1975) phrase, "the male gaze" and transferring her feminist concept to the context of class. See Laura Mulvey's Visual Pleasure and Narrative Cinema' *Screen* 16, no. 3 (1975): 6–18. Samantha A. Lyle (2008) also uses the notion of the "middle-class gaze" in her article on the reality TV show *Wife Swap*.

15. Characters like Terry Service in *Success* (1978), John Self in *Money: A Suicide Note* (1984), Keith Talent in *London Fields* (1989), and a host of characters in *Other People: A Mystery* (1981) and *The Information* (1995) represent boorish, hypermasculine behavior as a symptom of post-war cultural decline.

16. Amis based the narrative on Michael Carroll, a petty criminal who won the lottery in 2002, or, to be more specific, Amis bases Lionel on the sensationalist media coverage of the man the tabloids dubbed "Lotto Lout." See Gary O'Shea (2019).

17. Huw Marsh (2020) offers a perceptive critique of Amis's articulation of working-class identity in *Lionel Asbo* and other Amis novels.

18. The name "Diston" clearly amalgamates a sense of distance (presumably from Amis's projected reader) as part of a middle-class intellectual readership and "dystopia" reflecting the effectively fantastical and hyperreal feel of the descriptions.

19. "ASBO"s were introduced by Tony Blair as part of the Crime and Disorder Act 1998 and which criminalized behavior that caused harassment, alarm, or distress to other members of one's community.

20. Dickens's characters are referenced in a number of location names in the novel such as, "Blimber Road," "Carker Square," "Crimple Way," and the school, "Squeers Free." Disraeli's *Sybil, or, The Two Nations* (1845) is another of the novel's Victorian intertexts.

21. See Johnson (2019). Johnson often quotes Disraeli as one of his ideological touchstones; see Mornington (2020). This is not the place to pursue it, but it would be interesting to trace how "one nation conservatism" seems to gain traction at the very times there is a widening gap between the rich and poor in Britain.

22. See, for example, Franco Moretti's (1982) reading of Frankenstein's monster as a representation of middle-class fears of the proletariat in a rapidly industrializing society.

23. As well as physical, this violence is also epistemic as Amis takes great pains to foreground Lionel's linguistic disruptions of standard English.

References

Agamben, Giorgio. (1995) 1998. *Homo Sacer: Sovereign Power and Bare Life*. Translated by Daniel Heller-Roazen. Stanford, CA: Stanford University Press.

Amis, Martin. 1978. *Success*. London: Jonathan Cape.

———. 1981. *Other People: A Mystery Story*. London: Jonathan Cape.

———. 1984. *Money: A Suicide Note*. London: Jonathan Cape.

———. 1989. *London Fields*. London: Jonathan Cape.

———. 1995. *The Information*. London: Flamingo.

———. 2012. *Lionel Asbo: State of England*. London: Jonathan Cape.

Anderson, Benedict. (1983) 2016. *Imagined Communities: Reflections on the Origin and Spread of Nationalism*. London: Verso.

Bachelard, Gaston. (1964) 1994. *The Poetics of Space*. Translated by Maria Jolas. Boston, MA: Beacon Press.

Bentley, Nick. 2007. *Radical Fictions: The English Novel in the 1950s*. Oxford, UK: Peter Lang.

Bergonzi, Bernard. 1993. *Wartime and Aftermath: English Literature and Its Background, 1939–1960*. Oxford, UK: Oxford University Press.

Braine, John. 1957. *Room at the Top*. London: Eyre and Spottiswoode.

Coppola, Francis Ford, and Puzo, Mario. 1972. *The Godfather*. United States: Paramount Pictures.

Derrida, Jacques. (1993) 1994. *Specters of Marx: The State of the Debt, the Work of Mourning, and the New International*. Translated by Peggy Kamuf. New York and London: Routledge.

Dickens, Charles. 1861. *Great Expectations*. London: Chapman and Hall.

———. 1838. *Oliver Twist*. London: Richard Bentley.

———. 1865. *Our Mutual Friend*. London: Chapman and Hall.

Disraeli, Benjamin. 1845. *Sybil, or The Two Nations*. London: Henry Colburn.

Edensor, Tim. 2008. "Mundane Hauntings: Commuting Through the Phantasmagoric Working-Class Spaces of Manchester, England." *Cultural Geographies* 15 (3): 313–33. https://doi.org/10.1177/1474474008091330.

Faragher, Megan. 2018. "Celetoids and the City: Tabloidization of the Working Class in Zadie Smith's White Teeth and Martin Amis' Lionel Asbo: State of England." In *Twenty-First-Century British Fiction and the City*, edited by Magali Cornier Michael, 103–29. Cham, CH: Palgrave Macmillan. https://doi.org/10.1007/978-3-319-89728-8_6.

Fisher, Mark. 2014. *Ghosts of My Life: Writings on Depression, Hauntology and Lost Futures*. Winchester, UK: Zero Books.

Foucault, Michel. 1986. "Of Other Spaces." *Diacritics* 16 (1): 22–27. https://doi.org/10.2307/464648.

Gąsiorek, Andrzej. 1995. *Post-War British Fiction: Realism and After*. London: Edward Arnold.

Gilbert, Jeremy. 2015. "Disaffected Consent: That Post-Democratic Feeling." *Soundings: A Journal of Politics and Culture* 60 (1): 29–41.

Hanley, Lynsey. 2007. *Estates: An Intimate History*. London: Granta.

Harvey, David. 1973. *Social Justice and the City*. London: Edward Arnold.

———. 2006. "Space as a Keyword." In *David Harvey: A Critical Reader*, edited by Noel Castree and Derek Gregory, 270–93. Maiden, MA: Wiley-Blackwell.

Hayward, Ian. 1997. *Working-Class Fiction from Chartism to Trainspotting.* Tavistock, UK: Northcote House.

Hewison, Robert. 1987. *The Heritage Industry: Britain in a Climate of Decline.* London: Methuen.

Hoggart, Richard. (1957) 1958. *The Uses of Literacy: Aspects of Working-Class Life with Special Reference to Publications and Entertainments.* Harmondsworth, UK: Penguin.

Johnson, Boris. 2019. "Election Results 2019: Boris Johnson's Victory Speech in Full." *BBC News*, December 13, 2019, sec. Election 2019. www.bbc.com/news/election-2019-50777071.

Jones, Owen. 2011. *Chavs: The Demonization of the Working Class.* London: Verso.

Knight, Steven, et al. 2015. *The Peaky Blinders.* United States: Warner Bros.

Lefebvre, Henri. (1974) 1991. *The Production of Space.* Translated by Donald Nicholson-Smith. Malden, MA: Wiley-Blackwell.

Linkon, Sherry Lee. 2017. "Narrating Economic Restructuring: Working-Class Literature After Deindustrialization." In *A History of American Working-Class Literature*, edited by Nicholas Cole and Paul Lauter, 392–405. Cambridge, UK: Cambridge University Press.

Lodge, David. 1979. *The Modes of Modern Writing: Metaphor, Metonymy and the Typology of Modern Literature.* London: Edward Arnold.

Lyle, Samantha A. 2008. "(Mis)Recognition and the Middle-Class/Bourgeois Gaze: A Case Study of Wife Swap." *Critical Discourse Studies* 5 (4): 319–30. https://doi.org/10.1080/17405900802405239.

Marsh, Huw. 2020. *The Comic Turn in Contemporary English Fiction: Who's Laughing Now?* London: Bloomsbury.

Massey, Doreen. (1984) 1995. *Spatial Divisions of Labor: Social Structures and the Geography of Production.* 2nd ed. New York: Routledge.

Moretti, Franco. 1982. "The Dialectic of Fear." *New Left Review* (136): 67–85.

Mornington, Alicia-Dorothy. 2020. "Was Boris Johnson's One-Nation Post-Electoral Pledge Sincere?" *Revue Française de Civilisation Britannique. French Journal of British Studies* XXV (3). https://doi.org/10.4000/rfcb.5693.

Mulvey, Laura. 1975. "Visul Pleasure and Narrative Cinema." *Screen* 16 (3): 6–18.

Nixon, Rob. (2011) 2013. *Slow Violence and the Environmentalism of the Poor.* Cambridge, MA: Harvard University Press.

O'Brien, Phil. (2019) 2020. *The Working Class and Twenty-First-Century British Fiction: Deindustrialisation, Demonisation, Resistance.* New York and Abingdon, UK: Routledge.

O'Shea, Gary. 2019. "How National Lottery Lout Blew £9.7m." *The Sun*, February 11.

Rabinovitz, Rubin. 1967. *The Reaction Against Experiment in the English Novel 1950–1960.* New York: Columbia University Press.

Raisin, Ross. 2011. *Waterline.* Harmondsworth, UK: Penguin.

Ritchie, Guy. 1998. *Lock, Stock and Two Smoking Barrels.* United States: Gramercy Pictures.

Rose, Arthur. 2018. "In the Wake of Asbestos: Ship-Building and Ship-Breaking in Ross Raisin's Waterline and Tahmima Anam's The Bones of Grace."

Ariel: A Review of International English Literature 49 (4): 139–61. https://doi.org/10.1353/ari.2018.0032.

Scorsese, Martin, et al. 1990. *GoodFellas*. United States: Warner Home Video.

Sillitoe, Alan. (1958) 1994. *Saturday Night and Sunday Morning*. London: Flamingo.

Skeggs, Beverley. 2005. "The Making of Class and Gender Through Visualizing Moral Subject Formation." *Sociology* 39 (5): 965–82. https://doi.org/10.1177/0038038505058381.

Soja, Edward. 1989. *Postmodern Geographies: The Reassertion of Space in Critical Social Theory*. London: Verso.

Storey, David. (1960) 1962. *This Sporting Life*. Harmondsworth, UK: Penguin.

Tyler, Imogen. 2013. *Revolting Subjects: Social Abjection and Resistance in Neoliberal Britain*. London: Zed Books.

Waterhouse, Keith. 1959. *Billy Liar*. London: Michael Joseph.

Williams, Raymond. 1976. *Keywords: A Vocabulary of Culture and Society*. London: Fontana.

———. (1973) 1985. *The Country and the City*. London: Hogarth Press.

Winter, Terence, et al. 2012. *Boardwalk Empire*. United States: Cold Front Productions.

9 "Paths That Lead Me Back"
Zadie Smith's Northwest London

Molly Slavin

In Zadie Smith's novel *NW*, one of the main characters, Leah, while attending a party for Notting Hill Carnival, overhears a television newscast about a young man's murder. Readers are told she only takes note of it because "it names a local road, one street from her own" (2012, 104)—the Albert Road in Kilburn, northwest London. The television newscaster says:

> The young man, named locally as Felix Cooper, was 32 years old. He grew up in the notorious Garvey House project in Holloway, but had moved with his family to this relatively quiet corner of Kilburn, in search of a better life. Yet it was here, in Kilburn, that he was accosted by two youths early Saturday evening, moments from his own front door. It is not known if the victim knew—.
>
> (104)

Leah, in frustration, shouts at the television set, "He was murdered! Why does it matter where he grew up?" (104).

This question of Leah's—why does space, place, location matter?—is a recurring concern of Smith's in her two novels *NW* (2012) and *Swing Time* (2016). In these two novels, Smith develops a common trope, depicting a friendship between two young working-class girls (later women) in northwest London, who grow up together, drift apart, but remain tied to each other and their neighborhood of origin throughout their adulthood (the neighborhood is, of course, where Smith also grew up).[1] In reading these two novels and their friendships (Leah and Keisha/Natalie in *NW*, an unnamed narrator and Tracey in *Swing Time*) together, it becomes clear that it is important to treat these novels as companion pieces to understand Smith's dedication to spatializing race, gender, and class through instances of mobility. In each pair of women, spatial difference underscores material distinction, and looking at each individual and pair's relationship to space and movement helps to clarify how race, imperialism, and gender regimes are themselves linked to space and location. In turn, this affects the way class is inscribed into space and gives

DOI: 10.4324/9781003119425-10

the reader a nuanced and complex understanding of Smith's relationship to the spaces of working-class London, as well as those of the African diaspora. By yoking together NW and *Swing Time*, we can see Smith as a writer particularly attuned to spatial formations and mobility regimes, using these tools to both advance her narratives and simultaneously critique twenty-first-century British culture.

NW is deeply concerned with the urban space of London, while *Swing Time* expands out to consider the wider locations of the African diaspora, from The Gambia to Harlem. As Smith considers the importance of space and its relationships to class, race, and gender, she helps to clarify Leah's question: "Why does it matter where he grew up?" Space matters a great deal, Smith argues consistently throughout these novels, and one of the most edifying ways we can understand *why* and *how* it matters is through considering the relationships of working-class women who are acutely tied to and inscribed in the spaces in which they reside. Borrowing from Kimberlé Williams Crenshaw's theory of intersectionality, which holds that we must understand how an individual's various identities intersect and combine with each other, this chapter will consider space by looking at these individual women and their friendship pairings through the lenses of all their identities and how these identities relate to space and positionality.

Henri Lefebvre argues in *The Production of Space*, "[A] space is not a thing but rather a set of relations between things" (1991, 83), making the case that space is a dynamic, intersectional process. It is the tension between different things—such as lived experience, perception of time, and everyday living—that elucidates space and makes it active, able to be shaped by those who inhabit it. In NW and *Swing Time*, Smith elucidates how relationships between things—identity markers such as race, gender, and class—help to define the spaces of London and the wider African diaspora, respectively, which in turn leads us to additional Lefebvrian principles: "We are confronted not by one social space but by many" (86) and "Social spaces interpenetrate one another and/or superimpose themselves on one another" (86). By considering how Kilburn, northwest London, and the spaces of the Black diaspora are not one space or one experience but instead many and various experiences superimposed onto each other, we can look at how Smith uses this figuration to illuminate the complex and multifaceted lives of each woman involved in one of these friendship pairings as well as reinforce Lefebvrian notions of tensions between and among race, class, and gender and how those work together to constitute space.

In recent years, the study of space and geography has become more central to the study of literature and the humanities generally. Edward W. Soja argues,

> For at least the past century, time and history have occupied a privileged position in the practical and theoretical consciousness of

Western Marxism and critical social science. . . . Today, however, it
may be space more than time that hides consequences from us, the
"making of geography" more than the "making of history" that provides the most revealing tactical and theoretical world.

(1989, 1)[2]

It is true that Smith plays around a great deal with time and history
in these two novels—after all, one is literally named *Swing Time*—and
these concepts will be explored in this paper, but I argue that space is
the central concern at hand and that exploring her use of location and
geography in these novels is in line with Soja's idea of "the 'making of
geography.'" By exploring the imaginative geography of these texts, and
how her characters move through that geography over time, we, as readers, gain a multi-layered and intersectional understanding of race, class,
and gender, as expressed through the spaces of Kilburn and Willesden.

Smith not only works to present her readers with a textured and tangible imaginative geography, she also commands us to comprehend the
importance of how her readers move *through* this geography, this space.
Each novel simultaneously makes use of and troubles Thatcherite conceptions of "success" that measure how far one is able to move away
from one's place of birth; if worldly success is achieved by moving up
and away from the "starting block" of one's birth, these novels and these
friendships interrogate and disrupt this conception of mobility. Mobility, or lack thereof, is of the utmost importance in breaking apart these
friendship pairings and the motivations and personalities of each woman
contained therein. How women can move through space over time is
inherently linked to historical regimes of power, capital, and imperialism,
and Smith urges her readers to consider how her characters might be able
to construct a more just world for the women living in her literary spaces.

Neoliberal conceptions of mobility are intrinsically tied to financial
and spatial ideas of success; the idea is that social mobility has to do
with economic standing and class and that social mobility necessitates
moving up or climbing a ladder, moving out of the space in which one
is born. Yet, these figurations of mobility and success are Eurocentric
and individualistic and rely in part on a willful ignorance of history, of
colonial conditions that make class mean different things in different
spaces. Smith's novels advocate for thinking our way out of mainstream
ideas of class and perhaps point the reader to a way to conceptualize a
different kind of space inhabitation. Mimi Sheller writes that, in order
to achieve what she refers to as "mobility justice," what is required is
"more sustained attention to aspects of colonial history and an understanding of the historical formation of contemporary forms and patterns of global im/mobilities" (2018, 21). Reading *NW* and *Swing Time*
with these historical formations of mobilities (and immobilities) in mind
helps us to also understand Doreen Massey's point: that it is important

to understand space as linked to the social relationship of class, but we also must acknowledge that "[g]eography matters to the construction of gender, and the fact of geographical variation in gender relations, for instance, is a significant element in the production and reproduction of both imaginative geographies and uneven developments" (1994, 2). NW and *Swing Time* tend to these concerns by investigating intersectional identities. We cannot understand space as linked to class alone—we must also consider race and gender and both of their relationships to past and ongoing imperialism and colonialisms.

NW (2012)

The first of Smith's novels in this pairing, NW, was published in 2012 and focuses on a friendship between Leah Hanwell, a white woman of Irish descent, and Natalie (born Keisha) Blake, whose parents are Jamaican. The novel is set almost entirely in the northwest corner of London, and specifically the neighborhoods of Kilburn and Willesden, two areas that are highly multi-racial, working class, and linked to the history of the British Empire. Doreen Massey writes of walking down the Kilburn High Road:

> It is a pretty ordinary place, north-west of the centre of London. Under the railway bridge the newspaper stand sells papers from every county of what my neighbours, many of whom come from there, still often call the Irish Free State. The postboxes down the High Road, and many an empty space on a wall, are adorned with the letters IRA. . . .
>
> Thread your way through the often almost stationary traffic diagonally across the road from the newsstand and there's a shop which as long as I can remember has displayed saris in the window. Four life-sized models of Indian women, and reams of cloth. . . . In another newsagents I chat with the man who keeps it, a Muslim unutterably depressed by events in the Gulf, silently chafing at having to sell the *Sun* . . . .
>
> (1994, 152–53)

This is just a sampling of a longer tour of the high road, but the reader understands the idea Massey is presenting; Kilburn and its neighborhood partner, Willesden, are distinctly urban spaces, part of the global city of London, and even if its residents rarely leave its environs, the world is still available to them at their fingertips.

Yet, this is not how Leah, one of the main characters of Zadie Smith's NW, experiences the neighborhood. NW is told in five interlocking parts, one from Leah's perspective, one from a young man named Felix's, and three from the point of view of Leah's best friend Natalie (born Keisha). There is no indication Leah and Natalie know Felix, or at least not beyond his being a familiar face in the neighborhood; rather, they are all tied together by the space of Kilburn and Willesden. Each of the sections differs greatly in narrative style, and Leah's begins in a kind of stream-of-consciousness that demonstrates her loyalty to her neighborhood:

> The fat sun stalls by the phone masts. Anti-climb paint turns sulphurous on school gates and lampposts. In Willesden people go barefoot, the streets turn European, there is a mania for eating outside. She keeps to the shade. Redheaded. On the radio: I am the sole author of the dictionary that defines me. A good line—write it out on the back of a magazine. In a hammock, in the garden of a basement flat. Fenced in, on all sides.
>
> (Smith 2012, 3)

This opening salvo sets the scene for the reader to understand Leah— she is hammocked, "fenced in," local, heat-dazed. Later, we learn that "Leah is as faithful in her allegiance to this two-mile square of the city as other people are to their families, or their countries" (6) and that Leah envies her Australian neighbor, Ned, who makes a point of going out and exploring London, because, "Leah, born and bred, never goes anywhere" (55). She grew up in a housing estate in the neighborhood and still "passes the old estate every day on the walk to the corner shop. She can see it from her back yard" (70). As Alexander Beaumont writes, "The estate—and housing estates in general—thus profoundly shape each of the characters' lives, and even though this particular form of determinism is never overstated in the novel, Smith insists on its significance in a number of ways" (2015, 199). One of these ways is by continually emphasizing the fact that Leah is local, completely of Kilburn and Willesden—her mobility is limited, and she is fully of the space of her neighborhood, her estate, her upbringing, this working-class area of northwest London.

Leah's immobility is reflected in her understanding of the neighborhood as well as her own personality. On the bus with her mother, she muses as "The window logs Kilburn's skyline. Ungentrified, ungentrifiable. Boom and bust never come here. Here bust is permanent" (Smith 2012, 52). Just as Leah stays still, locked into her space, so does her understanding of Kilburn as permanently working class, "ungentrifiable," locked into her understanding of the neighborhood from when she was a child. Leah, who is white and thus has the privilege of immobility in both her professional and her personal life,[3] is demonstrably working class and tied to the working-class space of Willesden and Kilburn—however, her race allows her to experience her space, and her gender, in a way very different from that of her Black best friend, Natalie Blake.

Natalie and Leah met as children, when Natalie saved Leah from drowning in a neighborhood pool.[4] As Natalie's mother recounts the story, "You rose up with these red pigtails in your hand. You dragged her up. You were the only one saw she was in trouble" (202). Immediately, from the start of their friendship as four-year-olds, the two women's relationship to space and mobility is established: Natalie is active, moving rapidly through space, while Leah is content to stay still, relax, and remain immobile, to the point of almost drowning.

This dynamic remains as the two grow up in their shared space of working-class Willesden and Kilburn. Unlike Leah's section, which is told through a stream-of-consciousness format over a time period of a few months when the two are already adults, Natalie's first and longest section covers the time from early childhood to the present day, when the women appear to be in their mid-to-late thirties. This structure allows readers to see how Natalie experiences space, as well as time, as we cover her chronological development over a time period of several years. We learn from Natalie's section that after she changes her name from Keisha in young adulthood, Leah and Natalie each go away for university but come back to the neighborhood, Natalie working as a high-powered barrister while Leah being content to work somewhere that does not offer much in terms of career mobility (see endnote 2 for further details). While they both live in the old neighborhood as adults, a space Leah understands as "ungentrified, ungentrifiable," Natalie lives in a different iteration of that space, one where she goes out to bougie brunches with her husband and another couple, where

> They were all four of them providing a service for the rest of the people in the café, simply by being here. They were the "local vibrancy" to which the estate agents referred. For this reason, too, they needn't concern themselves too much with politics. They simply *were* political facts, in their very persons.
>
> (300)

Natalie and her husband and their two friends are all people of color, a fact that she sees as defining them as "political facts, in their very persons." This understanding, and this brunch scene, also offers a clue as to how they experience their space differently than Leah, as a white woman. It is far more important to Natalie than it is to Leah to be viewed through outward markers of success—well-paying job, nice flat, good clothes, expensive brunches out, and so on. Natalie feels as though she has something to prove in a way Leah does not, and the way each experiences their childhood neighborhood reflects on that fact. Natalie propels forward, tearing through space and time—her section is marked by constant references to "that was the year" to help mark the passage of time,[5] and as she grows up, we see her develop in a way we do not with Leah. Her understanding of her social space and of the neighborhood reflects this type of mobility. Leah and Natalie's imaginative spaces, though occupying the same physical geography, "interpenetrate" and "superimpose" upon each other (Lefebvre 1991, 86), providing tension in space and accounting for the very different images of Kilburn represented in each of their narratives. Yet, for all of her initial mobility, her "sprint" from the starting blocks, Natalie seems to have some kind of tether that pulls her back to Willesden; even as she tears away from her origins in some kind of frenzy of propulsion, she gets drawn back, in a way that seems out of her control.[6]

In the present day, we see Natalie end her first section by getting into a fight with her husband over Natalie's registration on a dating website, and she exits her home to begin a nighttime wander throughout northwest London, an experience that further inscribes her understanding of her space into the reader's mind. The start of her walk makes it clear just how important mobility is to Natalie: "Walking was what she did now," Smith tells us, "walking was what she was. She was nothing more or less than the phenomenon of walking" (2012, 360). Tied as she is to forward motion, to mobility, she explores her space in a way Leah never does, continuing to need some kind of forward motion to make her feel real. She articulates her agency as she tries to use mobility to escape her life, brought back to the tangible space of the neighborhood in a way that makes clear how precarious her newfound class position always was.

As Natalie walks, she encounters an old classmate, Nathan Bogle,[7] who seems to have something to do with the murder of the young man, Felix, the newscast of which opened this chapter. Nathan refers to her as Keisha, which doesn't seem quite right, either; she's dethroned from her position as Natalie, but neither can she return to her starting place. Nathan joins her on her rambles, which take them through the neighborhood, to Hampstead Heath and eventually to Hornsey Lane, to a bridge known as the "suicide bridge," where Natalie seems to contemplate jumping; a kind of mobility that would lead to forever immobility. Even as she is on the verge of suicide, her narration reflects the importance of mobility and space:

> The view was cross-hatched. St. Paul's in one box. The Gherkin in another. Half a tree. Half a car. Cupolas, spires. Squares, rectangles, half moons, stars. It was impossible to get any sense of the whole. From up here the bus lane was a red gash through the city. The tower blocks were the only thing she could see that made any sense, separated from each other, yet communicating. From this distance they had a logic, stone posts driven into an ancient field, waiting for something to be laid on top of them, a statue, perhaps, or a platform. A man and a woman walked over and stood next to Natalie at the railing. Beautiful view, said the woman. She had a French accent. She

didn't sound at all convinced by what she'd said. After a minute the couple walked back down the hill.

(384)

It is impossible for Natalie "to get any sense of the whole"—her view of space is fragmented, cut through with symbols of mobility like bus lanes. The only things that makes any sense to her are the tower blocks where she grew up, which "had a logic," an organizing structure that lent the space meaning. This structure—a commitment to social housing that would be important to a working-class girl from northwest London—is what ultimately talks her out of suicide, and next we see her, she has woken up on the morning of Carnival, still in a fight with Frank, and to the news that Leah's husband has discovered Leah's secret stash of birth control pills. In response to him confronting her, Leah has ensconced herself in a hammock in the backyard and refuses to move or speak to anyone. Her husband, Michel, is distraught, and urges Natalie to come over right away to speak to Leah.

The stage is set for a final scene that reiterates the two women's understandings of space and time—Leah hammocked and uninterested in a baby, more interested in staying still, and Natalie, pushing forward through everything and choosing "propulsion" over "stasis" (390). However, when Natalie asks Leah why she is "sitting here flirting with skin cancer," Leah responds, "I just don't understand why I have this life" (399), continuing by asking Natalie why Felix was the one murdered, and not one of the two of them, for example. Natalie responds by saying:

> "Because we worked harder," she said, laying her head on the back of the bench to consider the wide-open sky. "We were smarter and we knew we didn't want to end up begging on other people's doorsteps. We wanted to get out. People like Bogle—they didn't want it enough. I'm sorry if you find that answer ugly, Lee, but it's the truth. This is one of the things you learn in a courtroom: people generally get what they deserve."
>
> (400)

This answer, much like Leah's question to the newscaster at the start of this chapter, is just patently offered in bad faith. Natalie, true, may have worked harder to get her job, but Leah has not: moreover, the idea that "people generally get what they deserve," especially considering Natalie's chosen framework of a court of law, is a callous and inaccurate reading of contemporary society. Much like Leah's, "Why does it matter where he grew up?" question, Natalie's claims here do not make any sense at all. Of course. it matters where Felix grew up, and Leah knows that better than anyone; of course, hard work does not necessarily translate into success, and Natalie knows that even though she was lucky, that one anecdote does not mean anything on a larger or grander scale. These Thatcher-inflected ideas and rhetoric of individual, bootstrapping success are deeply at odds with the experiences these two women have had in northwest London.

Space matters, and how one experiences it, and how different identities react to it, and how outside forces affect it: Nathan Bogle, as a Black man, has a much different experience of Willesden/Kilburn than either Leah or Natalie does. Of course, it matters where someone grows up, and of course, it matters how space affects their lives. But the two women, with their different approaches to that space, and to mobility within that space, choose not to recognize that at the most important possible moment.

NW ends with Leah and Natalie working together to report Nathan Bogle to the police on suspicion of involvement in Felix's murder (never mind they have no solid evidence whatsoever, rather, just a feeling on Natalie's part from her experiences the previous night). "First," Smith tells us,

> they sent an email. A police website for anonymous tips. But that was anti-climactic, not very satisfying, and once it was done they stared at the screen, and felt disappointed. They decided to make the call to Kilburn Police Station.
>
> (401)

When they make the call, they do so together as a kind of bonding exercise:

> [T]he whole process reminded her of nothing so much as those calls the two good friends used to make to boys they liked, back in the day, and always in a slightly hysterical state of mind, two heads pressed together over a handset. "I got something to tell you," said Keisha Blake, disguising her voice with her voice.
>
> (401)

What does it mean that this is the last act of the book and that Natalie reverts back to Keisha as she makes the call? What does the solidification of this friendship, based on two lies—Natalie's "because we worked harder" and an unverified report on a potentially innocent Black man—mean for the construction of the space of the city; their working-class neighborhood; and their classed, gendered, and raced identities?

The two, in the final pages of the book, further reify each of their identities as mobile or immobile in the space of their working-class neighborhood—it was Natalie's idea to call the police, and she puts it into action, while Leah remains in her backyard, along for the ride—and it highlights how each understands her placement vis-à-vis her other identities. Natalie, deeply interested in playing respectability politics to move out of the working class as the specter of Keisha consistently hangs over her head, must present herself as actively helpful in a police investigation, while Leah is happy to trail along behind but not take the initiative herself, because she does not feel the need to move up or present herself as respectable so urgently as a white woman. Nathan Bogle is collateral damage for the two working out their relationship against the backdrop of their childhood neighborhood. These tropes, first developed in *NW*, are expanded on further in *Swing Time*, in its related but divergent tale of space, mobility, and individual identities.

Swing Time (2016)

Swing Time, like *NW*, is the story of two young women who develop a deep friendship during their childhood in the working-class spaces of northwest London. But if *NW* is of Smith's earlier approach to the city and "celebrates dwelling rather than diaspora" (Upstone 2007, 336), *Swing Time* considers what happens when we move out from the city Smith treated with such complexity in the earlier novel. The unnamed narrator and her friend, Tracey, are both mixed-race (Black and white), though from opposite directions—the narrator has a white father and a Black mother, while Tracey has a Black father and white mother. This sets up the dichotomy for the rest of the novel, as Tracey and the narrator are mirror images of each other, linked in many ways but different in many (most) others. Both girls love to tap dance, though Tracey is unquestionably more talented, and the novel hinges on their friendship, much as *NW* does.

Unlike *NW*, however, *Swing Time* expands out past the spaces of working-class northwest London to explore the African diaspora more broadly, focusing on the medium of dance to do so. The two girls watch old Hollywood movies to explore their love of dance, many of which feature African American dancers; the narrator gets a job as an assistant to a mega pop star, Aimee, as a grown-up, which takes her to New York and West Africa (to a country implied to be The Gambia); and Tracey continues to try to dance professionally, attaining many roles in musicals that rely on patterns of African and African diasporic dance. In these global movements, *Swing Time*, taking its cues from Smith's earlier novels *White Teeth* and *NW*, "further explores the clash between individual identities and identity discourses" (Kürpick 2018, 331). These identities are similar to those explored in *NW* but with additional geographical and mobility valences.

The narrator gives the reader a sense of her understanding of how space, history, and life outcomes are tied together by musing, "And beyond personal luck, there is geographical and historical luck" (Smith 2016, 67).

This "luck" applies much more to the narrator, who is more of a Natalie Blake character than a Leah Hanwell. She achieves much more professional success than does Tracey, who never really receives more than bit parts in her stage roles and who eventually must stop dancing due to weight gain and having many children by different fathers. The two characters somewhat mirror those of Natalie and Leah—one thought to be an upwardly mobile "success story," one seemingly mired in the housing estate where both parties grew up—but the narrator acknowledges a certain amount of luck in her story, which Natalie, who espouses the bootstrapping ideology of hard work, does not really account for.

Kaitlyn Greenidge writes of *Swing Time* that it wrestles with the question of time and how it intersects with the experiences of Black people. "What do we do," she asks, "how do we respond, when we are violently shaken out of time, when we lose the thread of our own lives, when we are so certain of the narrative of our life and then are suddenly, jarringly, shaken loose" (2017, 196). It is a question about many things, from the transatlantic slave trade (which the geography of *Swing Time* mimics, moving as it does from Europe to West Africa to North America) to the experiences of two young biracial working-class girls in northwest London and their relationship and what it means to be a dancer. How does time work, and what happens when it breaks—in dance, in friendship, in metahistorical movements like imperialism, slavery, and colonialism?

Smith approaches this question through further exploring the dynamic between the narrator and Tracey. Tracey takes on the dominant role; she was, the narrator writes, "the choreographer: my only job was to dance as well as I could" (2016, 80). The narrator questions the power differential when she asks, "Did all friendships—all relations—involve this discreet and mysterious exchange of qualities, this exchange of power? Did it extend to peoples and nations or was it a thing that happened only between individuals?" (122). The narrator is "oppressed because of her gender, race, and class," which has led her to believe that she "is deprived of a self that could tell a coherent story. She has no self, no name, no voice: she only exists as a shadow of others" (Quabeck 2018, 462). The "mysterious exchange of power" the narrator alludes to simultaneously affects how space and time are interwoven, and moving into these different spaces allows Smith to put different emphases on markers of identity like class, race, and gender, through the same medium of female friendship as in *NW*.

When in West Africa with Aimee, who is there ostensibly to build a charitable school, the narrator watches a film dubbed over images of many different tribes from all across the world. The film narrator begins to

> [contrast] African time to the time of Europe and time as it is experienced in Asia. She said that a hundred years ago mankind was

confronted with the question of space, but that the problem of the twentieth century was the simultaneous existence of different notions of time.

(Smith 2016, 295)

Throughout the novel, time is explored through the rhythm of dance, the idea that New York is faster-paced than London and the notion that West Africa is somehow "behind" or "out of time" as compared to these two "First World" cities. By moving into the space of the diaspora, Smith touches on how power differentials have shaped the world and concurrently shaped how people in different spaces experience time. By extension, this raises questions about the way people of different classes, races, and genders experience the same. Tracey seems, like Leah Hanwell, to be "stuck" in both space and time, treading water in the old neighborhood and not wishing to "move forward"; the narrator, like Natalie, moves through space at rapid speed, achieving upward mobility and seeming to change class position. The friendship between the two maps onto historical dynamics put into motion by capitalist and imperialist formations; Tracey travels the diaspora imaginatively and over the course of many years through her dance while remaining locked into northwest London, while the narrator travels through space physically and becomes disconnected from the space of her birth in the process, leading her to a different relationship with time.

Yet, though the narrator covers a great deal of physical ground in the novel, she remains firmly rooted in the space of northwest London through her class and racial identity. As the movie she watched in West Africa guided her through a global tour of different tribes, her father works to remind her that "his tribe had always been defined by their labor, whether they wanted it to be or not. The importance of labor was a view he held as strongly as my mother held her belief that the definitions that really mattered were culture and color" (311). Even as she has new experiences in time and space, she has her same identity markers; to lightly paraphrase E. P. Thompson (1963), like Leah and Natalie in *NW* and like her own friend Tracey, those who inhabit the working-class spaces of northwest London create the city as much as the city creates these spaces.[8]

That inscription remains even as the narrator becomes more mobile through space. Malou Kürpick writes of *Swing Time*, "Spatial mobility maintains and extends the narrator's socio-economic privileges through the networks and resources she has access to" (2018, 339), noting in particular how spatial mobility makes the narrator "aware of colonial power structures" that "prompt[s] her to reflect on her own positions and actions" (338). Like Natalie Blake, the narrator compresses time and space into what Kürpick refers to as "spatial mobility" and what can also be understood as keying into colonially determined narratives of class and geographic mobility, while the corresponding half of her childhood best friendship does not attain the same kinds of privileged "networks and resources." In *NW* and *Swing Time*, Smith explores what time and space do in terms of class consciousness and how it intersects with gender and race, while considering what it means to remain linked to the space where all four women grew up, the space of northwest London. Even as the women imaginatively and literally explore different spaces of the African diaspora in *Swing Time*—a theme not directly covered in *NW*—northwest London is never far from their minds. As the narrator muses, "I can always find the Heath—all my life I've taken paths that lead me back, whether I wanted it or not, to the Heath" (Smith 2016, 106). Even though this friendship expands out to the diaspora, it never loses its focus on its space of origin.

Smith's goal in developing this trope of female friendship and its linkages to space, time, and identity markers such as class, race, and gender is to present her readers with a kind of textured geography that accounts for not just space, but the multi-layered dimensions of how individuals experience the world through an interlocking matrix of identities. Edward W. Soja argues that "the new, the novel, now must involve an explicitly geographical as well as a historical configuration and projection" (1989, 23). Smith gives her readers this in her novel, this "explicitly geographical" exploration of identity and experience, set against the historical backdrop of larger processes that inflect both space and an individual's identity markers. There is no way to understand space without time, class without race, race without gender, and so on.

What this means for the characters in Smith's literary northwest London is that there is absolutely no singular or objective way to experience the space of, say, the Kilburn High Road. Much as Doreen Massey noted that there is an Irish experience to the road set alongside the Indian experience set alongside her own as a white British woman, Natalie Blake, because of her experience of time and her identity as a Black upwardly mobile woman, experiences that same space differently than does her friend Leah Hanwell or *Swing Time*'s narrator or Tracey. Writing of geography, Henri Lefebvre asks,

> How many maps, in the descriptive or geographical sense, might be needed to deal exhaustively with a given space, to code and decode all its meanings and contents? It is doubtful whether a finite number can ever be given in answer to this sort of question.
>
> (1991, 85)

Edward W. Soja's theory of thirdspace, where reality and imagination exist alongside "the knowable and the unimaginable" (1996, 57) highlights the complexity of the space of northwest London, as the conceptual (social mobility) exists alongside the physical (spatial mobility or literally moving through the city). The sheer permutated number of experiences inherent in a given space is only hinted at in *NW* and *Swing Time*; these four women, and these two friendships, are only the briefest of beginnings.

The events of the 2020s remind us of this in very tangible ways. The global protests against police brutality and for racial justice after the murder of George Floyd in Minneapolis in the summer of 2020 were felt in London around a variety of issues, most visibly that of the call to tear down racist and imperialist statues. The #BlackLivesMatter protests are redolent of Smith's larger points about space and time, that they move together (who would have thought we would be arguing in 2020 about tearing down eighteenth- and nineteenth-century statues that take up city space, for example?) and are inextricably linked to how colonialism and imperialism have shaped race, class, and gender. If we are ever to achieve anything resembling racial, gender, and class-based justice, we must continually scrutinize how these fluid, dynamic concepts are all linked to how we all negotiate and navigate space and time.

This reminds us of Leah Hanwell's question that opened this chapter: "Why does space matter?" It matters on a number of levels, and Leah is fully aware of why. Space is a repository for these complex and thorny and knotted questions about the legacies of imperialism and racism, how they work across time to shape class and how we experience the world today. There is no way to understand the murder of Felix without understanding how he moved through the world—his race, his gender, his class—and there is no way to interpret the linked worlds and imaginative geographies of Zadie Smith's northwest London without understanding *NW* and *Swing Time*'s treatment of space and identity. These two novels, and the friendships of the women depicted in them, clarify concepts that are of a central concern to reading our world, and our cities, in the twenty-first century.

Notes

1. These novels are in sharp distinction to Smith's first novel, the very well-received *White Teeth* (2000). As Alexander Beaumont says, "There is an important distinction in tone between Smith's first and most recent novels [at the time, *NW*]" (2015, 202), arguing that if *White Teeth* is primarily optimistic, "*NW* represents an astonishing collapse of confidence in this optimistic vision" (205). The twenty-first century's hard pivot to austerity, especially in the decade-plus between the publication of *White Teeth* and *NW*, accounts for a large part of this shift in tone.
2. That said, these companion texts are also doing interesting things with the depiction of time. *NW* is broken into five sections, with Leah's narrated section coming first, but it becomes apparent as one reads that most of the events in Leah's section have actually happened after the events in the following sections. The second section is told from the perspective of Felix, a young man

who is murdered over a dispute on a tube train, yet Leah finds out about Felix's death in her own section. Similarly, Natalie and her husband, Frank, have an immense blowout fight prior to the Carnival party at which Leah learns of Felix's death, yet at that party, Frank acts as though everything is fine in their marriage: "We tell each other everything," he says to Leah (Smith 2012, 105), which the reader later realizes is patently untrue. *Swing Time* does something similar, in that it presents events and then "swings" back to the past to elucidate on them and give more context for the reader. Though the two novels share a treatment of time in some respects, this chapter will focus primarily on the overlaps they share as concerning space.

3. Leah works a dead-end job at some vaguely defined nonprofit and resists getting pregnant despite immense societal and personal pressure; even though Michel, her husband, very much wants to have a child, she steals birth control pills from Natalie and takes them because "She doesn't want to 'go forward'" (Smith 2012, 103).

4. At the time, Natalie was going by her birth name of "Keisha"—she later changes it to Natalie, for which an explanation is never provided, though readers can assume it has something to do with her professional aspirations as a Black woman in a racist world.

5. As in, "It was the year people began to say 'living the dream,' sometimes sincerely but usually ironically" (Smith 2012, 301).

6. This is in comparison to Felix, who attempts a kind of traditional bootstrap narrative, only to be cut down mid-pulling, and Leah, who is frozen in place and seems afraid of mobility entirely.

7. Though readers are never offered an explanation for why Keisha changed her name to Natalie, it is worth noting that by changing her name to Natalie, she shares initials with Nathan Bogle.

8. In *The Making of the English Working Class*, Thompson writes, "The working class made itself as much as it was made" (1963, 194).

References

Beaumont, Alexander. 2015. *Contemporary British Fiction and the Cultural Politics of Disenfranchisement: Freedom and the City*. Basingstoke, UK: Palgrave Macmillan.

Crenshaw, Kimberlé Williams. 1989. "Demarginalizing the Intersection of Race and Sex: A Black Feminist Critique of Antidiscrimination Doctrine, Feminist Theory and Antiracist Politics." *The University of Chicago Legal Forum* 140: 139–67. https://doi.org/10.4324/9780429500480-5.

Greenidge, Kaitlyn. 2017. "Shaken Out of Time: Black Bodies and Movement in Zadie Smith's Swing Time." *Virginia Quarterly Review* 93 (1): 196–99.

Kürpick, Malou. 2018. "The Cultural and Intersectional Politics of Nomadism in Zadie Smith's Swing Time." *Hungarian Journal of English and American Studies* 24 (2): 331–45.

Lefebvre, Henri. (1974) 1991. *The Production of Space*. Translated by Donald Nicholson-Smith. Malden, MA: Wiley-Blackwell.

Massey, Doreen. 1994. *Space, Place, and Gender*. Minneapolis, MN: University of Minnesota Press.

Quabeck, Franziska. 2018. "'A Kind of Shadow': Mirror Images and Alter Egos in Zadie Smith's Swing Time." *Zeitschrift Für Anglistik Und Amerikanistik* 66 (4): 461–77. https://doi.org/10.1515/zaa-2018-0038.

Sheller, Mimi. 2018. *Mobility Justice: The Politics of Movement in an Age of Extremes*. London: Verso.

Smith, Zadie. 2012. *NW*. New York: The Penguin Press.

———. 2016. *Swing Time*. New York: The Penguin Press.

———. (2000) 2001. *White Teeth*. New York: Vintage

Soja, Edward W. 1989. *Postmodern Geographies: The Reassertion of Space in Critical Social Theory*. London: Verso.

———. 1996. *Thirdspace: Journeys to Los Angeles and Other Real-and-Imagined Places*. Malden, MA: Wiley-Blackwell.

Thompson, E. P. 1963. *The Making of the English Working Class*. New York: Pantheon Books.

Upstone, Sara. 2007. "Same Old, Same Old." *Journal of Postcolonial Writing* 43 (3): 336–49. https://doi.org/10.1080/17449850701669666.

10 "Be Gone"

Escaping Racialized Working-Class Space in Bernardine Evaristo's *Mr. Loverman* and *Girl, Woman, Other*

Cornelia Photopoulos

While several contributors to this volume focus on the way identity is negotiated in working-class spaces, my chapter focuses more on the way Black characters *escape* racialized working-class environments. As a whole, this volume discusses how literature helps reveal strategies for and approaches to the articulation of classed identity in ways that gesture toward the utopian spirit of "the spatial turn." My chapter, by contrast, writes against such ideals, and instead explores how space—rather than being a site of new liberatory social formations—is imbricated in the materiality of the built environment and thus forms a site of domination by state and economic power. In particular, for those inhabiting BIPOC and queer identities, among others, additional limits to liberation persist that intersect with the boundaries of classed space. In her novels *Mr. Loverman* (2014) and *Girl, Woman, Other* (2019), Bernardine Evaristo represents Black British characters negotiating forms of ownership or control over spaces in which their identities are marginalized. By doing so, she offers an image of Black Britons not simply "making do" but insisting on, as David Harvey puts it, their "right to the city," which he frames as an explicitly anti-neoliberal reclamation of public space from the capture of capital and the privatization of property.[1]

I argue that in these novels Evaristo writes against the history of Black Britons' double dispossession as raced and classed "others" excluded from the space of the nation and centers them in the national narrative through their inclusion in privileged space as "subject[s] of value" (Skeggs 2004a, 6) in ways that, contra Harvey, work within capitalism and end up reinforcing the validity of the neoliberal regulation of classed space. First, I outline the way space regulates and reinforces social class. Second, I show how the intersection of race and class positions Black subjects in deprivileged class positions and restricts their access to privileged space. Third, I discuss the ways in which Evaristo's characters operate within a neoliberal framework, seemingly at odds with the kind of utopian potentiality associated with the "spatial turn" in the humanities. In doing so, the essay underscores Evaristo's representation of the limits

DOI: 10.4324/9781003119425-11

of social transformation under neoliberalism in a manner that echoes Mark Fisher's (2009) concept of capitalist realism—that it is impossible to imagine a society freed from the constraints of the current economic order. In such a society, the aesthetics and implicit moral value of class continue to shape how and if individuals can access privileged space, but the political valence of class has been evacuated and replaced by market logic. This is particularly evident in the primacy that private property ownership has in determining who can be read as a subject of value, and as a citizen, since, as Wendy Brown argues, the public, as a collective, participatory political entity, no longer exists under neoliberalism, having been replaced by economic metrics (2015, 155–61). While Evaristo's representations of Black British characters achieving social mobility and national belonging within classed space reads, on the one hand, as evidence of progress toward dismantling the systemic racism that has long excluded them, these representations simultaneously reiterate the class hierarchies that have deprivileged Black subjects (and other members of the poor and working classes). Though Evaristo represents Black characters' achievement of social mobility within the coordinates of classed space as a pragmatic strategy for coping with the dispossessions of racism at an individual level, such individual gains operate within neoliberal financialization and thus cannot provide collective solutions to systemic inequity. Evaristo's representation of the individualized "spatial fix"[2] thus comes at the cost of reinforcing the validity of institutions predicated on exclusionary classed space.

Social Exclusion and Spoiled Identity in the Built Environment

As critics have observed, the relationship between class and space is mutually constitutive: a metaphorical two-way street, which some individuals can traverse more freely than others. In my reading of Evaristo's novels, representations of classed space appear less as prescribed locations to which those in particular class positions must necessarily belong and more as discrete choices made by Black characters to assert identity and thrive within spaces and systems that have historically inhibited them. Pierre Bourdieu's theorization of "habitus"—the embedded patterns of daily life that constitute the relationship between a given locality and its inhabitants—provides a helpful starting place for discussing classed space. Bourdieu argues that "[t]aste classifies, and it classifies the classifier" (1984, 6): what we value, and what others see us valuing, locates us in a particular class position. Beverley Skeggs powerfully sums up the way that taste classes people in the built environment, describing how working-class women are not simply "positioned by their furniture and paint," but are taught to "doubt their own judgements" (1997, 90). This "emotional politics of class" is particularly salient to the domestic sphere: "[h]omes and bodies are where respectability is displayed but where class is lived out as the most omnipresent form, engendering surveillance and constant assessment of themselves" (90). As Skeggs shows, class and taste are not neutral: class positions described as lower or working class are perceived to be socially devalued positions. Skeggs's subjects recognize their lack of Bourdieu's four categories of capital—economic, cultural, social, symbolic—and they judge themselves for it in anticipation of being subjected to the judgment of those occupying more privileged social roles (2004a, 16).

Skeggs's approach is one of many scholarly contributions that demonstrate how the habitus of the working class and poor is judged to be socially deficient and in need of correction. But because what the poor and working class *lack*—financial capital, as well as cultural capital—largely informs their tastes, Zygmunt Bauman's concept of "social exclusion" is even more important to my argument than Bourdieu's "habitus." Though Bauman has discussed the concept of social exclusion in numerous contexts, I focus here on the socio-economic aspects of social exclusion and its relation to consumption. In *Work, Consumerism and the New Poor*, Bauman argues that the poor and working class are not just judged for their failures of taste (according to middle- and upper-class standards), but that their inability to consume the same quality and quantity of goods and services renders them "flawed" and "inadequate consumers" (2005, 38). In a late-capitalist society, where market logic catering to the individual replaces the collectivist, extra-market values supported by the welfare state (or other forms of communal networks for sharing resources), those unable to consume in the right way become "deficient citizens" (50): "The myth of the discriminating consumer and the myth of the market as the purveyor of free choice and the guardian of freely asserted preferences nourish and cultivate each other" (58). Consumerism thus underwrites citizenship and national belonging in the contemporary neoliberal era, presenting itself as the most viable option for existing in spaces that encode social class as marginal.

As Black subjects in a society that centers and valorizes whiteness as normative, Evaristo's characters negotiate racialized social positions as well as class hierarchies.[3] Being able to inhabit spaces marked as socially desirable marks one as a proper citizen-consumer—someone who belongs—versus one who does not belong, and both race and class positions inform belonging. Building on language disseminated by the IMF to unpack the ways that financialization regulates subject positions differentially, Skeggs argues that, under neoliberalism, an individual must become a "subject of value" (2004a, 6) to receive recognition from the state, a conception of personhood that relies on the concept of the "possessive individual" who is in a relation of ownership with the world around them (6). Individuals must formulate and perform "respectable subjectivity," which is "[t]he ability to accumulate different types of capital over time [that] enables bodies to move in social space with ease and a sense of value, or to become fixed in positions and ascribed symptoms of pathology" (2004b, 293). Performing in accordance with these "politics of recognition" is necessary because they "shape who is seen as a valuable citizen, and who can make a claim on the state"; those whose identities are "misrecognized as pathological" cannot make salient social claims (294). Reflecting what Skeggs elsewhere describes as the *"spatialized relation"* through which class constitutes *"culture as property"* (2004a, 15, emphasis in original), this differential social legibility of "the body as marked by and marking boundaries" entails differential claims to ownership: "property is experienced in and through the mobile, moving body [which] generat[es] entitlement to social spaces through distinction" (Moran and Skeggs 2001, 385). If individuals fail to inhabit space in the proper way and do not become legible as desired subjects of value, they will be socially excluded and marked as deficient. For Black British subjects, systemic racism—which, at its most explicit, positioned Black bodies *as* property—has historically intersected with class to differentially allocate social worth.

In her foundational essay "Whiteness as Property," Cheryl Harris (1993) articulates the interconnection between property ownership and race in ways that both show how property is embodied and reveal that whiteness is one of the most valuable properties one can own: such ownership makes available access to an array of other social goods, including property in the form of commodified space. Property is both embodied and possessed, and these two forms of property reinforce one another, their social value differentiated along racial lines. Sara Ahmed argues that such racialized differences in subject value are communicated through the circulation of embodied emotions that regulate belonging, illustrating how social exclusion operates through interpersonal and affective interactions in public space: "fear does not involve the defence of borders that already exist; rather, fear makes those borders" (2015, 67). In a passage that eerily evokes the racist rationale behind George Zimmerman's murder of Trayvon Martin, Ahmed describes the process by which neighborhood watch groups identify those whom they deem do not belong: "we recognise somebody *as a stranger*, rather than simply failing to recognise them" (2000, 21). The marking of Black bodies as "others" who do not belong perpetuates a conception of raced and classed spatiality in which the white, middle-class subject is, to return to Skeggs's terminology, the subject of value. If, as Ahmed puts it, "citizenship [i]s a technology for deciding whose happiness comes first," then the equation of whiteness with citizenship marks those excluded from that category as unhappy others who do not belong (2015, 225).

Given the intersection of racial and class hierarchies, and the legacy of white supremacy, thinking only about classed aspects of space is insufficient; space is also racialized in ways that reinforce class-based exclusion. As the above scholars note, in both the public and private sphere, racialized bodies are coded as belonging in lower-status class positions; likewise, spaces in which people of color predominate are marked as less desirable, or exoticized for white consumption. Winifred Curran observes that "neighborhoods become 'good' when they move toward [white] homogeneity and 'safe' when they become dangerous to their original inhabitants" (2017, 65). Bridget Byrne shows how white, middle-class parents who claim to value "multiculturalism and embrace . . . difference" in fact see schools that serve a majority of children of color as "sink schools" that would threaten their ability to inculcate middle-class belonging in their own children: "The presence of too many raced and classed 'others' appeared to threaten" the reproduction of classed and raced belonging and privilege that these women strive to maintain (2006, 1008, 1010). The terminology of "sink schools" alludes to the derogatory term *"sink estates"* and its explicitly racialized companion, *"concrete jungles,"* rhetoric that, along with police surveillance and pervasive unemployment, are some of the tactics of dispossession that Eddie Chambers argues have been formative of Black British culture (2017, xiv, xv, emphasis in original). These tactics of social exclusion, particularly the term "sink estates" with its vivid metaphor of collapse and downward mobility, are all mechanisms to regulate space along classed and raced lines, by effectively keeping Black Britons sequestered in deprivileged social positions. Housing estates have become, in the contemporary era, what Hans Skifter Andersen calls "excluded places" (2002), a point that leads Peter Malpass to observe that residents of such places bear the mark of "spoilt identity or less than full citizenship" (2005, 169).[4]

Housing Racism and Surveillance in the United Kingdom

Housing is the preeminent example of the way race and class combine in a society where citizenship is asserted through consumerism. The history of housing in the UK in the twentieth century is also a history of housing racism, stoked by white supremacist fears directed at Black migrants arriving from the colonies. The arrival of the *SS Empire Windrush* in June 1948, bearing around 500 Jamaican migrants (the exact figure is disputed), became an important origin story for future Black migrants arriving from the British colonies during the post-war decades of decolonization and imperial dissolution.[5] This event also spurred anti-Black racism that led directly to decades of changes to immigration policy specifically designed to exclude Black migrants.[6]

The exclusion of Black subjects from the space of the nation, through immigration policy, was reinforced at a local level through housing provision and policy—or the lack thereof. Those Black Britons who were able to settle in the UK were hard-pressed to find housing: the racial discrimination in the rental market was coupled with a lack of access to traditional lenders. Unable to obtain loans through banks, Black Britons pooled their resources in informal "pardner" arrangements, in which members would contribute to collective funds to be accessed by individuals as needed (Hiro 1971, 25). Up until the 1960s, it was also difficult for Black Britons to access public housing; families with the longest history of residence in the area were given preference, putting the newly arrived at a disadvantage.[7] When Margaret Thatcher became prime minister in 1979, she ushered in a new neoliberal era and sought to dismantle the achievements of the welfare state. Thatcher's introduction of the Housing Act 1980, commonly known as "Right to Buy," offered council housing residents the opportunity to buy their homes at a reduced price. The policy greatly depleted the stock of available public housing while valorizing homeownership. At the same time, it exacerbated preexisting inequity: those too poor to purchase their properties, even at a reduced rate, were unable to benefit financially from property ownership and were relegated to the status of second-class citizens.[8] These changes in how housing was perceived and distributed had a distinctly racialized impact. As Valerie Karn and Deborah Phillips note, "One feels that it is not coincidental that improved access for ethnic minorities to social rented housing has come at a time when the sector has lost status and desirability, becoming a 'residual sector' for 'residual groups'" (1998, 138). Once public housing had become a *"tenure of last resort,"* it became available to Black Britons (Fée 2016, 4, emphasis in original).

I have elaborated at length upon the various modes by which private and public spaces have historically been classed and raced in the UK in order to articulate how Evaristo's positioning of her characters within the coordinates of classed space rewrites the long history of Black subjects' exclusion from privileged spaces and from national belonging. In defiance of such discriminatory conditions, the characters of these novels leave or transform their places of origin, ascend to new social heights, and become property owners. Instead of being alienated or excluded, they achieve success, and some attain positions of privilege and authority, shaping the culture and spaces that once denied them entry. Evaristo even ends *Girl, Woman, Other* with a paean to familial and national lineage and belonging that writes Black belonging into the history of Britain. But the way that Evaristo's Black characters achieve their goals relies on the reinscription of exclusionary parameters of classed space and the reinforcement of the social mores that distinguish between those who belong and those who do not. Rather than breaking free of the power structures of classed space and the social institutions that support it—including capitalism, property ownership, and marriage—these characters seek inclusion within these spaces, contending with the racialized othering that excludes them by embracing social institutions that confer classed belonging.

This is the ideological landscape in which Evaristo's characters achieve their own individual successes. Viewing the possibility of collective action or the formation of alternative social structures as a non-option (as Amma, a Black lesbian playwright, explicitly describes in proclaiming her right to seek mainstream recognition), Evaristo's characters instead strive for success in a society that would otherwise deny them access to the classed spaces where the capitalist good life is lived.[9] That they can all access this supposedly good life depends on the perpetuation of social institutions that deny such access to others: rather than their success *actually* being the product of individual acts, it is, instead, imbricated in social and economic structures that regulate access to privileged spaces. Evaristo's representations of racialized classed space thus reveal the paradox at the heart of neoliberal narratives of individual "responsibilization," to use Wendy Brown's term (2015, 84): achievement is framed as the result of personal effort, when it in fact stems from the successful leveraging of entrenched social institutions that continue to mete out rewards sparingly. Faced with the double dispossession of race and class, Evaristo's characters strive for, and achieve, social mobility and leverage class power by claiming the right to belong in privileged space. Although this benefits them as individuals, it nevertheless relies on the inherently exclusionary nature of classed space.

Mr. Loverman and *Girl, Woman, Other*

Both *Mr. Loverman* and *Girl, Woman, Other* were lauded by general readers and literary critics. *Mr. Loverman* won two literary awards, and *Girl, Woman, Other* was awarded the prestigious Booker Prize, further establishing Evaristo's place of honor in British literature and culture. Both novels depict Black British characters making space for themselves in a nation that has historically been hostile to them, while charting the progress toward inclusion that they have achieved.

In *Mr. Loverman*, protagonist Barry, an Antiguan who immigrated to the UK as a young man and built a substantial real estate empire in circa 1960s London, is at a crisis point in his life: at the age of seventy-four, he is unwillingly outed as a gay man and finally forced to address his dysfunctional relationships with his family. *Girl, Woman, Other* is far harder to summarize; its expansive narrative encompasses a chorus of Black British women across space and time, spanning the turn of the twentieth century into the present day. I will focus on Carole, a successful banker in the present day, who grew up the child of an immigrant single mother in an under-resourced public housing development, and Grace, an orphaned girl in the early twentieth century, trained for service work, who rises above that station through marriage and becomes a property owner. More briefly, I discuss Amma, a successful playwright; LaTisha, Carole's friend, whose narrative provides a counterpoint to Carole's success; and Penelope, the discovery of whose Black ancestry Evaristo represents as a reenvisioning of British culture and space.

Class and Social Mobility in Evaristo's Work

Since being a neoliberal subject of value depends on the ability to consume, evidence of conspicuous consumption marks subjects as having value, as does inhabiting privileged spaces with ease: as Ahmed reminds us, being "at ease" in space is a sign that one's subject position is centered and valued (2015, 148). Evaristo references aspects of class through aesthetic signifiers that index wealth, taste, and sometimes even individual political affiliations but does not foreground class as such. In her work, classed aesthetics denote lifestyle choices rather than signifying the entrenched differential materiality, bolstered by systemic ideology, that locks individuals into particular social positions. Descriptions of "family homes that were privately owned" by people "with a preference for the old and decrepit" (2019, 137–38) signal landed old money in the English countryside; an ostentatiously appointed "huge house near Hyde Park" is inhabited by "obscenely rich" foreigners landbanking in London (69), but in neither case are the origins of wealth or the combined social effects of its hegemonic power (i.e., class) interrogated. At the same time, characters change their behavior to align with the dominant class structure: Carole in *Girl, Woman, Other* adopts the manners, language, food preferences, and personal style of her peers at university and learns to value what they do in order to fit in to the system that will further her career and allow her to transcend her class background. Class continues to shape how individuals inhabit space, and which spaces they can occupy, but it is not discussed explicitly as a social force.

Class in Evaristo's novels appears to signify identity and group affiliation rather than functioning as an opportunity for political analysis or a source of social change. Indeed, explicit political affiliation is relegated to the historic past and to individuals' youth. As a young woman in the 1980s, Amma and her friends inhabit a squat in London, making art and living communally, at once excluded by, and in defiance of, the capitalist system. However, they are only able to do this because the property owner, the descendant of industrialists, thinks back fondly on his own youthful sympathies for the Spanish revolutionaries of the 1930s (17); after his death, they are evicted by his profit-driven heirs. Rather than constituting legitimate alternatives to the capitalist status quo, such projects of reimagining interpersonal relations and modes of inhabiting space seem to be a phase one outgrows before inevitably embracing capitalist realism. Evaristo zealously parodies political posturing, whether that of the character Shumba in *Mr. Loverman*, a white Rasta who is actually a landed aristocrat and who later gives up his title and estate to fund philanthropic causes in Africa and run an organic farm

(2014, 279),[10] or that of Sylvester in *Girl, Woman, Other*, a white man who upholds the communist ideals of his youth and criticizes his friends for their success within the establishment, all the while receiving financial support from his well-off parents. That both these characters embodying leftist or antiestablishment beliefs are upper-class white men is significant: firmly ensconced in positions of social privilege, these characters have the luxury of discarding it and pursuing lifestyles that accord with their ideals. For others who have been denied access to such positions of power—female, non-binary, and Black characters—their social positions are quite different, and they understandably desire access to the privileges they have been denied. Evaristo represents both the critiques against those who seek representation within existing structures of power and the rejoinder to such critiques in an exchange between old friends Sylvester and Amma, a Black lesbian playwright whose latest play has gained mainstream success after decades of hard work. Sylvester, who runs a socialist theater company called The 97%, argues that Amma's *"sick-cess"* means that she has "dropped [her] principles for ambition" and is "establishment with a capital E . . . a turncoat"; Amma counters that "it was her right to be directing at the National" and that it is important to "make a difference inside the mainstream" (2019, 32–33). Amma's indignation at Sylvester's self-righteous critiques stands in for the finger-wagging of white leftists who criticize people of color and others in socially marginalized positions for wanting inclusion in the society that has excluded them.

Desiring success within the bounds of society as it is is not something that I am critiquing in and of itself, nor am I suggesting that representations of Black people are only valid if they portray unmitigated racial oppression (stereotyping that Evaristo excoriates and critiques academia and the publishing industry for encouraging).[11] What I do want to highlight is how Evaristo's characters are able to achieve social mobility in ways that belie persistent class hegemony and social exclusion and how the representation of such moves reaffirms the value and legitimacy of privileged, exclusionary locations within the matrix of classed space. The most optimistic reading of these representations of characters transcending the bounds of classed space would be that Evaristo is writing a new future into being rather than representing realities on the ground, a move that could be seen as "utopian." The Britain, and world, of Evaristo's novels could be read as a space of potentiality in which the individual can rise despite structural inequity: a revision of the "imagined community" of Britain, following Benedict Anderson's (1983) famous formulation of narratives of national belonging, in which Black economic and artistic success is the norm, rather than an exception.

I read these novels differently, as illustrating an essential neoliberal paradox: individual achievements, rather than entrenched class structures, are seen as determining life outcomes, but such instances of personal success are rooted in traditional social institutions that continue to perpetuate inequity. Displaying privileged class signifiers is one of the modes by which characters defy racialized social exclusion. Since racist policies in Britain have historically relegated Black subjects to lower class positions—as Hall et al. note, "[R]ace is the modality in which class is lived" (1978, 394)—race functions as a metonymy for class, even though the terms are not interchangeable, and important distinctions between them obviously remain. Rather than imagining liberation from classed space, the novels represent inclusion within classed spaces made possible by property ownership, late capitalism and financialization, and family inheritance: reproducing the inequities of classed space is the price of ameliorating racial inequity by opening up privileged spaces to Black characters.

Classed Spaces in Britain: Race, Property Ownership, and Being "at Ease" in Classed Space

Evaristo's characters are presented as neoliberal subjects who resource their individuality to become more than "respectable": they become *successful*. Through a combination of effort and luck, they escape the systemic racism that would otherwise have impeded their ability to leave impoverished and underprivileged spaces. For instance, Barry from *Mr. Loverman* amasses wealth by investing in London real estate at an opportune moment, whereas Carole from *Girl, Woman, Other* leverages academic success into a lucrative financial career. Though initially denied access to dominant social structures predicated on class and race positions they do not occupy, such characters attain financial freedom, social mobility, and access to national belonging. Evaristo's characters thus renegotiate their positions in classed space through individual achievements that defy the systemic racism that would exclude them from privileged space. In Evaristo's novels, class is malleable, and the borders that regulate classed space are represented as being surmountable through personal achievement and hard work.

Mr. Loverman explicitly addresses the imbrication of race, class, and property ownership in the UK; its plot tracks the sweeping developments in housing that transformed Britain from a majority-renter population post war to a majority-homeowner population by the turn of the millennium. For Barry, buying real estate both increases his wealth via rental income and is a way of asserting national belonging in the face of imperial and state racism by becoming a property owner and thus a subject of value. Defying housing racism, he declares that he will be the "exception to the rule" (2014, 113) in escaping from the deprivileged position that he would have occupied within the British class/race nexus.

In *Girl, Woman, Other*, Evaristo represents her characters' diverse array of personal narratives and experiences while recuperating and healing the injuries of the past. Rather than remaining fixed, Evaristo's characters transcend their class positions of origin and achieve upward social mobility, illustrated through changes in their relation to space: Amma becomes a successful playwright; Dominque leaves an abusive relationship and pursues a successful career in Los Angeles; Roland becomes a star academic; Shirley becomes a revered teacher; Bummi escapes patriarchal and sectarian violence and migrates to England; Carole overcomes sexual assault and endemic poverty and secures a lucrative career; Morgan rids themself of drug dependence and becomes a well-known activist; Hattie holds on to her family farm despite hardship, regional divestment, and the decline in agricultural production in England.

Even the one character who does not transcend her original class position aspires to a similar vision of success as a means by which to overcome the limitations of classed space, as we see in Evaristo's portrayal of LaTisha in *Girl, Woman, Other*. LaTisha invests great effort in a "smart and professional" appearance, as befits someone who is "on the move" and "stays focused on her goal" of job promotion (2019, 190–91). Though her success is not meteoric, as it is in Carole's case, LaTisha also ascribes to the neoliberal doctrine of self-improvement and continual striving.[12] The difference is that, in LaTisha's case, perpetual striving does not result in a change in physical or social location; she still lives with her mother and sister in the housing estate where she grew up. Individual ambition and hard work are insufficient to transcend classed space; LaTisha's striving, as a school-leaver, cannot propel her out of the housing estates in the way that Carole's academic success and entrance into university can, because LaTisha's ambition exists only within the limited purview that the housing estate and its milieu allow her to access. As Lynsey Hanley (2007) notes, housing estates circumscribe people physically, by sequestering them from desirable places of education and employment, while simultaneously limiting them culturally, by separating them from people who would model and teach them about opportunities outside their immediate experience. LaTisha's desire for success, and her failure to achieve social mobility, reveals the shadow side of ambition discourse that Evaristo otherwise does not depict. Hard work and "wanting it" is not enough, as the rewards for "success" in low-paying jobs are meager, and the scale of compensation for labor is insufficient to achieve any substantive upward momentum: LaTisha's raise of "only one pound per hour extra for a helluva lot more responsibility" (2019, 191) in her new role as supervisor is a far cry from the scale of success that Carole can achieve in finance.

LaTisha's lack of social mobility is a telling exception in Evaristo's novels. More typical are trajectories like Barry's: prophetically envisioning, in the 1960s, the future desirability of currently neglected properties in London, he purchases several buildings and builds a "wealthy property empire" (2014, 250–51). Barry frames his success as entirely due to the result of his own hard work and determination, undercutting the importance of the financial backing provided by his father-in-law, a successful business owner "expanding his Early Bird Empire" of grocery stores in Antigua, who "advance[s] [Barry] the working capital" to start his own real estate empire in London (114). Though marriage, a cultural institution that reproduces heterosexual patriarchy and regulates access to financial and cultural capital, provides Barry the needed funds, he frames his purchase as the work of a canny investor. Rather than acknowledging that he receives this financial beneficence from others, Barry boasts about "cajol[ing] … brainwashing" (114), and otherwise pressing his wife, Carmel, until she relents and asks for the money from her father. Though Barry occupies a working-class position in the UK, his marriage enables him to draw on his father-in-law's bourgeois social position and access to capital. Evaristo's narrative demonstrates that, despite his self-proclaimed entrepreneurial individualism, Barry's ability to capitalize on an incipient real estate boom is the direct product of bourgeois proprietorship, channeled through the heteronormative, middle-class institution of marriage that supports it.

Evaristo initially seems to complicate her representation of heteronormative bourgeois property ownership by locating the origins of Barry's property empire in his queerness. Barry first gets the idea to start buying property as a young adult, during what seems to be the late 1960s. He and his lover, Morris, are sitting in the park, surrounded by heterosexual couples kissing. Barry and Morris, however, abstain from expressing their affections and desires, inhibited by the social proscriptions against same-sex sexuality in an era when homophobic violence was normalized. Frustrated by his inability to inhabit public space freely, Barry begins observing the decrepit Victorian buildings that face the park, seeing their past glory and future potential:

> At some point I found myself paying proper attention for the first time to the three slummified Victorian houses on the walk opposite our spot. Vandalized windows, wrecked roofs, gardens being reclaimed by the forests of Ye Olde England. I said to Morris, "Look how huge they is, spar. Once upon a time, they must-a been built for the rich, and, you mark my words, one day the rich shall recolonize them. I, Barrington Jedidiah Walker, hereby predict the gentrification of Stoke Newington."
>
> (113)

These former dwellings of the rich will be home to the rich once again, and Barry will be the landlord who profits from their regained desirability. His inability, as a gay man, to inhabit the public space of the park on equal terms with the heterosexual couples who express their desire freely, leads to Barry's command of private property. Barry's disenfranchisement and social exclusion, produced by queerness (and Blackness), are trans-muted into control over capital and space.

Rather than overturn the classed, raced, and gendered conventions that control access to space—and, therefore, to capital and power—Barry eagerly replicates the aesthetics of the ruling classes of yore, just with a twist. He explicitly describes his property ownership as an act of "recolo-nization," and his aesthetic choices and domestic decor further emphasize that he intends to resist racial power dynamics by stepping into the role of ruler.[13] When Barry's relationship to Morris is finally revealed, he gets a divorce and remodels his flat to signal that his wife's reign over domestic space has ended. What Barry derides as a tacky, maximalist aesthetic— "Wifey is the Goddess of Bad Taste" (178)—is replaced with his idea of sophisticated "masculine" style. Sophisticated style, it turns out, is drawn from the visual vocabulary of empire, complete with "plantation-style furniture . . . a (parlor-palmed) conservatory" and "*master* bed-room," the added emphasis on the term "master" amplifying the imperial hierarchies alluded to in Barry's choice of furnishing (273, emphasis in original). Barry has imbibed these aesthetic preferences during his adult education art courses and subsequent relationship with an upper-class, white lover, Stephen, whose flat—strewn with relics of empire displayed as art objects—exemplifies how *"real men"* should live (179, emphasis in original). Barry's aesthetic choices, once he is living openly as a gay man, position him as a member of the master class, in his master bedroom. Possessing private space is a power move, attached to constructions of masculine authority derived from Britain's imperial past.

Barry's occupation of public space is likewise mediated by property ownership as a sign of occupying a position of power within classed space. Barry likes to stroll down "Queen Elizabeth's Walk, wherein reside my first three rental properties" (112), a narrative detail that emphasizes, through the double entendre of the term "queen," how his gay iden-tity and wealth are linked through real estate. But it is private property *ownership* that allows Barry to inhabit public space so freely and easily. A memory from the past resurges as Barry takes his walk: he recalls a Black man being beaten to death outside a club for his sexual relationship with another man. Fear of such backlash for being open about his sexual-ity in public has kept Barry closeted for seventy-four years.

Once he is outed, however, he finds that living openly as a Black gay man is not as perilous in the twenty-first century as it was in his youth. In part, this is because times have changed; in part, it is because he is financially secure and thus granted the social inclusion and access to privileged space that money confers. Evaristo represents Barry's awaken-ing to the public acceptance of his gay identity as a form of demographi-cally targeted consumerism rather than as a reclamation of public space. Barry's daughter, Maxine, takes him to a gay neighborhood and pub for the first time. His moment of public recognition, acknowledgment, and acceptance of his identity—"Ain't no fakery here. Lord, they *know* us" (231)—occurs in the context of consumerism: Barry is recognized not simply as a gay man, but as a gay *customer*, purchasing drinks in a gay pub, on a street that caters to gay men's tastes in commodities and services. Barry is, following Skeggs, the right kind of gay man— wealthy and gender-conforming; that is, "respectable" (2004b). Unlike the past scene in the park, where heterosexual couples were inhabiting public space freely—and for free—this scene in the pub illustrates how privately owned and operated spaces that provide alternatives to the private spaces of home and office are open only to a *paying* public. As a venue for consumers, rather than as a truly public space open to all regardless of financial solvency, the pub is not really "public." Barry's ability to inhabit the city as a Black gay man, without being subjected to censure or worse, is mediated by his access to capital and his status as a property owner and consumer. Though the novel represents Barry's character arc as one of coming into personal fulfillment, it also illustrates how classed (and raced and gendered) space continues to foreclose the possibility of truly public space by offering acceptance and belonging only to those who are financially solvent and addressable as consumers. The language of the market demographic is the only one that can be heard under global capitalism.

In *Girl, Woman, Other*, Evaristo also uses representations of control or ownership over space to mark characters' social mobility and escape from their class positions of origin. Though many characters in the novel—indeed, most of them—chart a similar trajectory, I focus here on the characters Carole and Grace. Carole is the character whose social mobility most explicitly figures as escape from, and transcendence of, her class position of origin. As a preteen, she is the target of sexual assault during a party in the tower block where she and her friends live. Evaristo represents Carole's rape as the product of the classed space that confines her. Even in the relative security of the flat she shares with her mother, Bummi, a Nigerian immigrant, Carole is subjected to an oppressively classed space: "in a tower block packed among hundreds of others packed together like rows of crates spread wide and stacked high . . . closer than they should be to the planes in the flight path of City Airport" (2019, 120). Evaristo's description both recalls the holds of slave ships, where Black bodies were loaded like cargo in closely confined spaces, while also evoking contemporary global shipping and the flows of international capital, in its proximity to the airport. By living in the tower block, Carole is marginalized even prior to the sexual assault she suffers at her friend LaTisha's party. The flattering attention of an older boy turns into a violent nightmare when he leads her to an isolated area of the housing estate, where several boys rape her. The tower block is depicted as a prison and place of social containment, while simultaneously operating as an unregulated space where violent crimes occur unchecked. Surveillance and neglect mark the space as socially undesirable and mark its residents as socially excluded.[14]

Carole shuts down emotionally after the attack, until one day, out of the blue, she decides to overcome her circumstances through sheer hard work and will. Evaristo represents Carole's epiphany and commitment to change her life as a desire to escape the space of the housing estate that confines her:

> [I]t was like she woke up from a bad dream, and she looked down the concrete bunker corridors of her inner-city comp on the anniversary of it. . . .
> [S]he saw their futures and hers . . .
> not me, not me, not me, she told herself, I shall fly above and beyond
> be gone from tower blocks with lifts stinking of piss
> be gone from rotten low-paid jobs or the dead-end dole queue . . .
> be gone from never being able to afford own my own home . . .
>
> (128, emphasis in original)

Carole suddenly experiences a vision of the future that shows her, and her friends, confined by the "concrete bunker[s]" of carceral poverty that she sees as condemning them to perpetual imprisonment in lives of desperate insufficiency. Carole's only way out is up: transcendence that will elevate her above the wretched materiality of the tower block. The image of the planes flying overhead echoes back differently, as an aspirational metaphor for Carole's commitment not to mere social climbing, but to soaring far above the class position in which she has lived her life.

Carole enlists the aid of the scariest teacher at school, Miss King, and becomes a studious pupil, going on to university and then a successful career in international finance. Evaristo portrays Carole's success through her representation of Carole's new relation to the spaces she inhabits. Instead of flying above the tower block, Carole the banker embraces her integration into the space of "the City," the terminology used in the novel to denote and emphasize the importance of London's financial center (117). Entering the train station,

> she passes under the timetable board listing departures and arrivals articulated through the medium of glowing alphanumeric . . .
>
> (113)

at home in the "cacophony of London's busiest station," one of those who, by virtue of their clothing and comportment, belong in this space:

"perfectly composed, so poised and in control, socialized to be out in public as reasonable members of society this Monday morning where all dramas are interiorized" (114). Carole has learned how to be the self-disciplined subject who knows how to occupy desirable public space "properly" and who is seen as deserving to do so. Emotional restraint is a mark of classed space that implicitly differentiates this space from the raucous emotionality that characterized the party at the tower block or the unruliness of Carole's friends at school. Inhabiting public space in prescribed ways is a form of classed behavior that both identifies who does and does not belong in a given space, while also functioning as a form of social reproduction that produces a particular area as a certain kind of space, bound by particular conventions.

Though teenaged Carole imagines the home she will one day own when she escapes the tower block, adult Carole is more interested in inhabiting "the City" in its concrete and abstract forms. Carole swims eagerly in flows of information that she accesses through her computer screen, "immers[ing] herself in a universe where fiscal cells split off to create gazillions of replicas of themselves spinning off into beautiful infinity" (115). Basking in the glow of blue light, which echoes that of the train timetable, Carole inhabits the space of abstract capital. Her ability to "live" in this disembodied space of financial transactions both accounts for her success as a banker and as a neoliberal subject, while also hearkening back to her rape, which she endured by attempting to distance herself from what was happening to her body by thinking of numbers and doing mathematical operations in her head (126). Evaristo represents abstraction and disembodiment as tactics that produce places of psychic refuge for Carole during and following the trauma of her assault, a point that I do not want to diminish. In terms of its connection to my larger argument about representing social inclusion through depictions of classed space, however, it is Evaristo's depiction of Carole's success in the world of finance, and her illustration of the incorporeality of global capital, that I focus on here. In portraying Carole's successful transcendence of the tower block's imprisonment, Evaristo illustrates how the abstract space of financial accumulation is tethered to, and regulates, the real space of the City and its mores. Becoming one with the abstract flows of financialization is how to survive the structural violence of racialized social exclusion and gain access to privileged classed space in the material world.

Evaristo illustrates a related, earlier iteration of the ways that global capital shapes classed space in her depiction of Grace. Grace, born to a white, working-class woman at the turn of the twentieth century, has grown up hearing stories of her father, a sailor from Abyssinia, whose ghostly presence conjures up images of "magical places" offering escape from the drudgery of daily life in the stories her mother, Daisy, tells her (373). But Daisy dies young of tuberculosis without ever escaping her life of misery and exploitation, and Grace is destined for an orphanage where she will be trained for domestic servitude. At the orphanage, Grace is the only Black girl among the white residents, both objectified and treated as a celebrity as she elaborates upon her mother's tales of an exoticized Abyssinia.

Grace learns that her racial otherness imposes particular demands in order to ensure that she will be socially accepted. She is told bluntly,

> [Y]ou are not like the other girls here, you have to be on your best behaviour at all times because life will be hard enough for you as it is, you will suffer much rejection from people less enlightened than we.
>
> (381)

Grace would rather be a shop assistant than a maid, but when she inquires about a job, the proprietor tells her that "she'd put his customers off" before "closing the door firmly behind her" (383). Already classed as a servant, even some forms of service work are unavailable to Grace due to her racial positioning.

The fairytale trope of escape from drudgery that reverberated throughout Grace's childhood becomes real when Grace catches the eye of Joseph Rydendale, a WWI veteran recently returned to his family farm, Greenfields. Grace, whom he calls "Queen Cleopatra" and "Lady of the Nile" (386) upon meeting her, becomes his wife and the mistress of Greenfields and thus a member of the petit bourgeois landowner class. When Grace now encounters overt racism, she wields her class position as a defense against it, flinging her coins on the grocer's counter after he has done the same to her, and "walk[ing] out with her Abyssinian nose in the air" (389). Grace can now inhabit the shop differently, despite her racialized otherness, because she has acquired the social status of her husband, a "local farmer and honourable ex-soldier" with a profitable farm and bank account, whose family has long-standing roots in the community (389). Greenfields, built in 1806 by Captain Linnaeus Rydendale, is a space in which Grace "play[s] at being the Lady of the Manor in the Long Room" (390), where she will hang a tapestry she is making, based on a painting of the house, as "a gift for her *husband*" (391, emphasis in original).

In these details, Evaristo compresses a wealth of associations about Englishness, class, gender roles, and domestic space. At Rydendale, Grace is torn between embracing and escaping history, and Evaristo represents this tension underlying the social inclusion that Grace seeks through her depictions of the way that Grace inhabits classed space. Though the Rydendales work the land themselves, rather than extracting rent from tenant farmers, they are landowners and are not subjected to rent extraction or wage slavery. Greenfields offers Grace the opportunity to "play" at gentility: making a tapestry reproducing the family seat (already represented in paint) is a form of cultural production that hearkens back to England's storied medieval era. In emphasizing that the tapestry is a gift for her husband, Grace also acknowledges the roles that the patriarchal institutions of marriage and gender roles play in distributing power and granting individuals differential access to classed spaces. At the same time, Grace takes "pride" in cleaning the house, "enjoy[ing] it as it was for herself" (391), and updates the decor. Although Grace hates working as a maid, the domestic labor of maintaining her *own* property is a source of satisfaction and worth: working hard as a mark of home ownership differs from servitude and occupying working-class space. Evaristo thus illustrates how classed signifiers of aristocracy intertwine with contemporary narratives of self-making to shape national belonging: in fetishizing the house and the family that owns it, Grace claims her place within the classed space of the landed gentry; in improving that space, she illustrates that she has earned her place within it as a subject of value.

Evaristo shows that Blackness was woven into the Rydendale family history, and the English nation, before Grace ever arrived. When Grace's daughter, Hattie, marries Slim, a Black American, he sees in the ancestral portrait of Eudoré, Captain Linnaeus Rydendale's wife, from Port Royal, Jamaica, something more than the "Spanish" origins attributed by rumor, asserting, "Hattie, she's one of us" (367). "[W]e people" were always here, Evaristo's narrative emphasizes, claiming nation space and belonging on the land, even as their presence went unrecognized by a white mainstream gaze unable to see the nuances of identity visible to Slim (367).

Evaristo ultimately rewrites the national imaginary in even greater depth. At its expansive conclusion, the narrative exceeds divisions of class and race, illustrating that they are contained within the capacious time/space of Britain as a shifting, mythic, historic, and contemporary location of lapidary shared cultures. Penelope and Hattie's meeting, at the novel's end, is a powerful homecoming that transcends time, space, and the merely personal to encompass all of Britain and its troubled history of racism.[15] Penelope, who had previously understood herself to be white, and who openly professed racist views, has received new information regarding her African ancestry and is "recalibrating" herself through an experience of biological and familial connection that teaches her that "anyone can be a relative" (452, 450). Evaristo's depiction of Penelope and Hattie's reunion is one of historical and personal—deeply physical and material, as well as emotional—homecoming. Penelope journeys to her centuries-old ancestral home in the North through an England that she now realizes "is made up of many Englands," a journey that takes her not only through space and time—"to the ends of the earth" (450), "stepping back to pre-civilization" (451)—but into her own origins, "returning to her beginnings . . . inside her mother's womb" (450). Healing personal loss and reclaiming family relationships happens through embodied knowledge and bodily proximity that transcends language and the cerebral, as the final lines of the poetically structured novel show:

> this is not about feeling something or about speaking words
> this is about being
> together

(452)

By juxtaposing Hattie and Penelope's reunion with the descriptions of Penelope's journey back through England's history, Evaristo gestures toward a parallel national healing that could be achieved if there were a more widespread coming together and recognition that "anyone can be relative" (450). The structures of racialized classed space can, seemingly, be transcended through personal connection.[16]

Evaristo's novels speak to a Britain where Black characters can achieve national belonging through individual initiative and personal effort and even write a landscape where the transcendence of structures of class and race through personal effort is not only possible, but normative. Winning within the capitalist system, rather than overturning it, is the goal that most of these characters achieve, and the successful command of property or financial capital grants them social inclusion and access to privileged classed space. However, the novels also imply that attempts to renegotiate marginalized identities in spaces demarcated by class and race have their limits. Though Evaristo's Black characters achieve individual success through tactics of social mobility that leverage hard-won class-based inclusion against racial dispossession, this strategy is seemingly at odds with ideologies of liberation that seek to dismantle class hierarchies. Some thinkers imagine possibilities for belonging that seek to decouple human interrelationships from property and the hierarchies of class and race that they enable. Joshua Bennett proposes a "vision of human personhood not rooted in the logics of private property ownership or dominion" (2020, 4), while Kathryn Yusoff argues that the materiality of dominion has been carved into the earth itself and that we must address histories of resource extraction and "redress *how* geology makes property relations and properties a relation of subjugation" (2018, 13). Here, domination is essential to property relations, leaving little room for the belief that, by claiming property for themselves, as owners, Black subjects (or any others excluded from belonging based on material possession) can achieve meaningful belonging in the nation state—the fact of property itself means that someone is being excluded. Instead, these scholars and many others envision a liberatory future in which domination as and through property ownership is replaced by new kinds of kinship and community. By contrast, Evaristo's novels illustrate what success looks like within the parameters of capitalist realism by valorizing property acquisition and depicting Black characters mastering the socio-economic institutions that historically oppressed them. In her reenvisioning of Britain as an imagined community, she rewrites the national imaginary in uplifting and aspirational ways that project the possibility of a better future, based on the necessity of recognizing, and reconciling, the past. Evaristo's work charts both the progress that her Black British characters have made in overcoming the legacies of structural racism and social exclusion, while also illustrating how the neoliberal horizon of possibility reinscribes economic inequities via classed space.

Notes

1. See Harvey's (2003) "The Right to the City," in which Harvey frames the term as denoting an explicitly anti-neoliberal project of reclaiming public space from capitalist capture. See also Peter Marcuse's (2009) "From Critical Urban Theory to the Right to the City" for an overview of the term's origins in Henri Lefebvre's foundational work in spatiality theory.
2. Here, and elsewhere, Harvey articulates capitalism's manipulation of space to create new markets and manage tensions by changing geographic location, a move that never truly resolves the problems it tries to solve (see Harvey 2001). Evaristo's representations of classed space likewise reposition inhabitants within spaces without resolving the tensions of class inequity.
3. See Kimberlé Crenshaw's important formulation of "intersectionality" for more on the interrelationship between multiple subject positions (1991).
4. For more specifics on Goffman's notion of the "spoiled identity," see Simon Lee's essay on class stigma in this volume.
5. See Matthew Mead (2009), "Empire Windrush: The Cultural Memory of an Imaginary Arrival" for discussion of the way that the *Windrush* arrival has become mythologized. Mike and Trevor Phillips's *Windrush: The Irresistible Rise of Multi-racial Britain* (1998) exemplifies the type of commemorative reckoning with the history of Black migration from the former colonies to the UK that proliferated in 1998 to mark the fiftieth anniversary of the ship's passage and to further establish the event's primacy of place in conceptions of Black Britishness. See also Photopoulos (2020), *"Home Is Where You Feel a Welcome": Homemaking as National Belonging in 20th and 21st c. Black British Novels*.
6. See Layton-Henry (1992), in particular: 1–9, 75–80, 188–92.
7. See Hooper (1965), who writes that "council housing today still goes to people who have had longest residence in a particular area" (51), and Layton-Henry (1992), who observes that "[a]ccess to council housing was initially difficult because of rules of residence and the points system which favored local families in need" (37).
8. See Malpass (2005), Chapter 8, "Housing, Wellbeing and the Market," which positions home ownership as a consolidation of inequity (145), as "the housing market is a way of sorting the population into socially distinct locations reflecting purchasing power. . . . It bestows different rates of capital appreciation and differential access to valued resources, thereby amplifying the differences in their starting points" (145); and James Meek (2014), "Where Shall We Live?" in *The London Review of Books*.
9. See Lauren Berlant's (2011) *Cruel Optimism* for their insightful theorization of the way that the pursuit of the capitalist "good life" will inevitably

disappoint those who seek it and increase their suffering because they are already excluded from accessing its supposed rewards.

10. It is only "Shumba's" Rasta phase that reads as parody; the philanthropic causes are presented as more genuine, at least in the eyes of Barry's grandson.
11. See Evaristo, "Beyond the Great White Male."
12. See Brown, as well as Salecl (2009), McGuigan (2017), and Photopoulos (2020) who (among many other scholars) discuss the neoliberal imperative of perpetual self-improvement (what I elsewhere call "neoliberal self-making").
13. Barry's choice of words alludes to Louise Bennett's (1966) poem "Colonization in Reverse," which humorously depicts the post-war migration of Black Britons to the UK and lampoons white subjects' fears of social change.
14. See Zygmunt Bauman, *Work, Consumerism and the New Poor* (2005). Bauman discusses the concept of social exclusion in Chapter 6, "Prospects for the New Poor."
15. The symbolic reference of Penelope and "homecoming" evokes comparisons to Homer's epic, but by making Penelope the one who leaves home, Evaristo emphasizes the centrality of Black women and maternal lineage and reimagines the original patriarchal narrative as one in which women go on journeys of discovery and create and maintain family structures.
16. However, this touching homecoming reinforces both the primacy of the biological family and the concept of bloodlines on which class structure, particularly that of the gentry and aristocracy, depends, while also centering biological conceptions of race and group belonging: it is a DNA test that connects Penelope to her new home and family and spurs her newfound self-conception of her Black identity. This representation of family and race as biological echoes the "one-drop rule" that characterized the Jim Crow era in the United States, in which, metaphorically, one drop of "Black" blood positioned an individual as Black. Such biological constructions of family stand in contrast to conceptions of belonging, identity, and family that are rooted in social relationships of affiliative—chosen—kinship. By framing social inclusion as biological, this depiction of family, race, and national belonging subtly reaffirms racial categories and taxonomies derived from enlightenment-era race "science" used as evidence in support of white supremacy. In the plot of the novel, however, a biological understanding of race and family is positioned as undermining white supremacy, by compelling Penelope to relinquish her previously held racist beliefs.

References

Ahmed, Sara. 2000. *Strange Encounters: Embodied Others in Post-Coloniality.* London and New York: Routledge.
———. (2004) 2015. *The Cultural Politics of Emotion.* New York: Routledge.
Andersen, Hans Skifter. 2002. "Excluded Places: The Interaction Between Segregation, Urban Decay and Deprived Neighbourhoods." *Housing, Theory and Society* 19 (3–4): 153–69. https://doi.org/10.1080/140360902321122860.
Anderson, Benedict. 1983. *Imagined Communities: Reflections on the Origin and Spread of Nationalism.* London: Verso.
Bauman, Zygmunt. (1998) 2005. *Work, Consumerism and the New Poor.* London: Open University Press.

Bennett, Joshua. 2020. *Being Property Once Myself: Blackness and the End of Man*. Cambridge, MA: Harvard University Press.

Bennett, Louise. (1966) 2005. "Colonization in Reverse." In *Jamaica Labrish*. Kingston, JM: Sangster's Book Stores, Ltd.

Berlant, Lauren. 2011. *Cruel Optimism*. Durham, NC: Duke University Press.

Bourdieu, Pierre. 1984. *Distinction: A Social Critique of the Judgement of Taste*. Translated by Richard Nice. Cambridge, MA: Harvard University Press.

Brown, Wendy. 2015. *Undoing the Demos: Neoliberalism's Stealth Revolution*. Cambridge, MA: MIT Press.

Byrne, Bridget. 2006. "In Search of a 'Good Mix': 'Race', Class, Gender and Practices of Mothering." *Sociology* 40 (6): 1001–17. https://doi.org/10.1177/0038038506069841.

Chambers, Eddie. (2016) 2017. *Roots and Culture: Cultural Politics in the Making of Black Britain*. London and New York: I.B. Tauris.

Crenshaw, Kimberlé. 1991. "Mapping the Margins: Intersectionality, Identity Politics, and Violence against Women of Color." *Stanford Law Review* 43 (6): 1241–99. https://doi.org/10.2307/1229039.

Curran, Winifred. 2017. *Gender and Gentrification*. Abingdon, UK and New York: Routledge.

Evaristo, Bernardine. (2013) 2014. *Mr. Loverman*. New York: Akashic Books.

———. 2019. *Girl, Woman, Other*. New York: Black Cat.

———. 2020. "Beyond the Great White Male." *The New Statesman* 149 (5541): 44–47.

Fée, David. 2016. "Housing and Citizenship in the UK: Towards a Conditional Right?" *Revue Française de Civilisation Britannique/French Journal of British Studies* 21 (1): 1–17. https://doi.org/10.4000/rfcb.770.

Fisher, Mark. 2009. *Capitalist Realism: Is There No Alternative?* Winchester, UK: Zero Books.

Hall, Stuart, Chas Critcher, Tony Jefferson, John Clarke, and Brian Roberts. 1978. *Policing the Crisis: Mugging, the State, and Law and Order*. Basingstoke, UK: Palgrave Macmillan.

Hanley, Lynsey. 2007. *Estates: An Intimate History*. London: Granta.

Harris, Cheryl. 1993. "Whiteness as Property." *Harvard Law Review* 106 (8): 1707–91. https://doi.org/10.2307/1341787.

Harvey, David. 2001. "Globalization and the 'Spatial Fix'." *Geographische Revue* 2: 23–30.

———. 2003. "The Right to the City." *International Journal of Urban and Regional Research* 27 (4): 939–41. https://doi.org/10.1111/j.0309-1317.2003.00492.x.

Hiro, Dilip. (1971) 1973. *Black British, White British*. New York: Penguin Books.

Hooper, Richard, ed. 1965. *Colour in Britain*. London: British Broadcasting Corporation.

Karn, Valerie, and Deborah Phillips. 1998. "Race and Ethnicity in Housing: A Diversity of Experience." In *Race Relations in Britain: A Developing Agenda*, edited by Tessa Blackstone, Bhikhu Parekh, and Peter Sanders. London: Routledge.

Layton-Henry, Zig. (1984) 1992. *The Politics of Immigration: Immigration, 'Race' and 'Race' Relations in Post-War Britain*. Oxford, UK: Blackwell.

Malpass, Peter. 2005. *Housing and the Welfare State: The Development of Housing Policy in Britain*. Basingstoke, UK: Palgrave Macmillan.

Marcuse, Peter. 2009. "From Critical Urban Theory to the Right to the City." *City* 13 (2–3): 185–97. https://doi.org/10.1080/13604810902982177.

McGuigan, Jim. (2015) 2017. *Neoliberal Culture*. Basingstoke, UK: Palgrave Macmillan.

Mead, Matthew. 2009. "Empire Windrush: The Cultural Memory of an Imaginary Arrival." *Journal of Postcolonial Writing* 45 (2): 137–49. https://doi.org/10.1080/17449850902819920.

Meek, James. 2014. "Where Shall We Live?" *London Review of Books*, January. www.lrb.co.uk/the-paper/v36/n01/james-meek/where-will-we-live.

Moran, Leslie J., and Beverley Skeggs. 2001. "The Property of Safety." *Journal of Social Welfare and Family Law* 23 (4): 379–93. https://doi.org/10.1080/09649060110083850.

Phillips, Mike, and Trevor Phillips. 1998. *Windrush: The Irresistible Rise of Multi-Racial Britain*. London: HarperCollins.

Photopoulos, Cornelia. 2020. " 'Home Is Where You Feel a Welcome': Home-making as National Belonging in 20th and 21st c. Black British Novels." PhD Dissertation, Tufts University, Medford, MA. https://dl.tufts.edu/concern/pdfs/4m90f7905.

Salecl, Renata. 2009. "Society of Choice." *Differences: A Journal of Feminist Cultural Studies* 20 (1): 157–80. https://doi.org/10.1215/10407391-2008-020.

Skeggs, Beverley. 1997. *Formations of Class & Gender: Becoming Respectable*. London, Thousand Oaks, CA, and New Delhi: SAGE Publications.

———. 2004a. *Class, Self, Culture*. London and New York: Routledge.

———. 2004b. "Uneasy Alignments, Resourcing Respectable Subjectivity." *GLQ: A Journal of Lesbian and Gay Studies* 10 (2): 291–98. https://doi.org/10.1215/10642684-10-2-291.

Yusoff, Kathryn. 2018. *A Billion Black Anthropocenes or None*. Minneapolis, MN: University of Minnesota Press.

11 "All I Need Is Myself"

Spatializing Neoliberal Class Consciousness in the Northern Millennial Novel

Chloé Ashbridge

In the acknowledgments of her debut novel, *Saltwater*, Jessica Andrews notes how so much of writing the book was about "making space in places where there is not enough" (2019, 297). The act of "making space" is political; it is about class position, voice and representation, and imbalances in belonging and the right to access and exist in space. These issues structure *Saltwater*'s spatial imaginary, demonstrating the novel's engagement with the interconnection between social relations and space, or what cultural geographer Edward W. Soja describes as the "socio-spatial dialectic" (1980, 207). The interplay between space and social relations is central to *Saltwater*'s exploration of twenty-first-century class embodiment. Moving between Sunderland, London, and Donegal in Ireland, *Saltwater* offers the coming-of-age story of Lucy, a young woman from the North East, who moves to London for university. Lucy struggles to discern how much space she is permitted to occupy in the cultural environment represented by the university. Throughout the novel, Lucy's mobility into exclusive social circles is experienced at the level of the body. Upon moving to London, Lucy is keen to "sandpaper her edges" and slip into the cultural and intellectual spheres of her peers, "whose parents were doctors and academics; people who fainted at the ballet and made oblique references to Christina Rossetti" (2019, 259). Yet, her sense of belonging in London remains limited by what Imogen Tyler describes as akin to "a moral economy of undeservedness" (2000, 192).[1] Lucy's experience is marked by simultaneous shame of her working-class roots and guilt at leaving her former identity and familial roots behind. Told retrospectively through Lucy's autodiegetic recollections, the narrative traces the internal conflicts wrought by two entangled forms of mobility: the social advancement initiated by university and geographic relocation from a former industrial estate in Sunderland to the metropolitan spaces of London.

    Saltwater's socio-spatial class imaginary might also be read in the context of persistent representational inequalities in British literary culture. In terms of Northern representation, *Saltwater*'s commercial reception positions the text as part of the garnering "devolutionary" momentum

DOI: 10.4324/9781003119425-12

throughout Britain's literary economy. In 2020 Andrews won the Manchester-based Portico Prize, which celebrates Northern England's "geographical, linguistic, and imaginative locations" and aims to destabilize London as the nation's cultural epicenter (Portico Prize n.d.). A recent letter from the regional publishing collective, the Northern Fiction Alliance, asked for the industry to change to better reflect its readers, noting how "white, middle-class and London-centric our industry still is" (Northern Fiction Alliance 2018). Such moves to decenter publishing from London have also coincided with increased literary production that challenges the association of Northern England with a particularly industrial form of working-class identity. Two recent examples that seek to provide more nuanced accounts of place and class identities are *Know your Place* (Connolly 2017) and *Test Signal* (Connolly 2021), both of which were published by presses within the Northern Fiction Alliance. The former offers a collection of essays by working-class writers, asking what it means to be working class from a range of intersectional social and geographical positions, while *Test Signal* provides an anthology of "Northern" writing that does not aim to locate a singular "Northernness" but capture a highly differentiated vision of the region and its varied demography.[2]

Likewise, *Saltwater* imagines a complex, fluid class identity within the spaces of Northern England. Lucy's individual experience of social mobility occurs within a regional history of structural inequality and socio-economic decline. The novel unfolds in non-linear vignettes, splicing the present with snapshots of the 1980s before Lucy's birth, recounting both her grandfather's life and the relationship between her mother and father in and around Sunderland. The first landscape introduced in the novel is the former coal-mining town of Houghton-le-Spring, which Lucy tells us now comprises a Kwik Save, a Greggs, and "derelict council estates waiting to be demolished" (Andrews 2019, 43). These accounts of formerly industrial space echo the post-war literary tradition of working-class masculinity and industrial labor.[3] The British New Wave films in the 1960s typically revolved around the scholarship boy and assumed that working-class life was something that must be escaped. Karel Reisz's *Saturday Night and Sunday Morning* (1960), Tony Richardson's *The Loneliness of the Long Distance Runner* (1962), and Lindsay Anderson's *This Sporting Life* (1963) are illustrative examples of this cultural movement, which focused on the lives of white, heterosexual, industrial male workers in the tradition of the "Angry Young Man" (Wood 2020, 9).[4] Stylistically, *Saltwater*'s bildungsroman form also prioritizes a voice that is rarely at the center of working-class fiction, but one that I argue raises important questions about how working-class identity is critically conceptualized in the twenty-first century—that of the socially mobile individual coming of age at the turn of the millennium. *Saltwater* challenges the masculinization of the "working-class North" (8), with Lucy admitting that she "did not know how much of my story I was entitled to take" (Andrews 2019, 12). Work and the industrial landscape are not what drive the novel; rather, it is the socio-economic implications of the Thatcher period occurring in the background. Much of the novel is dedicated to Lucy's attempt to erase her working-class identity and disidentify with her "Northernness." Lucy's regional vernacular is juxtaposed with the standard English of her colleagues. At university, she weakens her North-Eastern regional dialect, learning to push the " 'ewk' out of 'bewk' and say the kind of 'buck' that rhymes with 'fuck' " (216). This subtle linguistic modification forms part of Lucy's accrual and performance of what Bourdieu (1990) refers to as "embodied cultural capital," which includes accent, posture, and demeanor and the overall presentation of the body to others. *Saltwater*'s approach to regional dialect appears to recognize a broader cultural economy in which Northern England functions less as a geographical territory than as a metaphor for cultural bankruptcy. However, the novel utilizes the phonetic spelling for both "bewk" and "buck," refusing to present the common pronunciation in London with the standard written spelling. In doing so, *Saltwater* destabilizes a linguistic symbolic hierarchy in which the North is "subordinated to a London and South-East centric locus of national economic, governmental, media and cultural power" (Phillips 2017, 151), indicating an increasingly devolved literary culture in which there is space for marginalized places and voices.

Focusing on Lucy as an example of a "millennial" figure, this chapter examines social mobility as a politics of "taking up space."[5] Approaching "space" in both a symbolic and material sense, I suggest that *Saltwater* articulates an affective experience of mobility that is particular to the dematerialized conditions of class and labor under neoliberalism.[6] To do so, I draw on Rebecca Coleman's notion of austerity's "affective economy," which understands the financial instability as experienced through "bodily feeling" and "recognizes how affects and emotions work in and as relations of power" (2016, 84). Departing from Coleman's focus on the financial, I propose the notion of "affective bodily economy" to describe how the cultural conditions of class are experienced in and through the body and its relationship to space. In doing so, this chapter identifies the narrative function of the body for articulating affectively the transition from the stable conditions of Fordism to late capitalism's flexible relations of production. This shift signals the urgency for a complex, nuanced class vocabulary that is both attentive to the forms of labor and cultural conditions structuring neoliberal subjectivity—namely, incessant entrepreneurialism, self-sufficiency and self-interest, agency, and engagement in the kind of insecure work paradigmatic of "liquid modernity's" flexible labor economy (Bauman 2000). Paying attention to the body thus demonstrates an affective bodily economy specific to the dematerialized socio-economic relations structuring the twenty-first century. In sum, this chapter suggests an evolution in the relationship between space and class, linking these to matters of (dis)embodiment, mobility, and subject formation.

The relationship between class and the body has a long historical trajectory. Pierre Bourdieu's concepts of the class "habitus" and "embodied cultural capital" are particularly relevant here, referring to conscious and unconscious bodily significatory practices that construct and reinforce social distinctions. For Bourdieu, the cultivation of the body suggests disposable time and financial resources and was, therefore, a primary expression of cultural, social, and economic capital. As is explained, "bodily practices are incorporated into consumption patterns and everyday routines," and thus, they "contribute to the making of social position and schemes of social classification" (Bennett et al. 2009, 168). While Bourdieu was writing over forty years ago, his thesis on the relationship between social status and bodily practices is useful for tracing the evolution of class embodiment and identity markers that go beyond the purely economic. The laboring body has been a central feature of working-class literary representation and the establishment of a specific form of masculinity. In an economic and cultural context in which working-class identity has been related to manual labor, physical differences in skin texture and muscle tone have often distinguished depictions of the working and middle classes. As Sherry Lee Linkon notes, from the nineteenth-century industrial novel to the social realism of the post-war decades, the "physical prowess associated with manual labor has played a key role in defining working-class masculinities" (2014, 148). Conversely, the damage done to bodies by work has disproportionately affected industrial working-class communities. Health inequalities between the rich and poor are often played out on the body. The working classes have historically relied on physical capabilities to perform often unsafe and grueling manual labor. Poor working conditions, exposure to pollutants, and other workplace hazards, combined with unsanitary living conditions and inadequate diet, resulted in a range of stigmatizing bodily afflictions (i.e., occupational diseases) that signified an individual's social standing. Rebecca Gowland notes how "moral character was closely linked to physiology during this period," meaning that "social inferiority was considered to be a consequence of innate biological deficiencies rather than the institutional structures which subjugated the working poor" (2018, 157). The social classification of "working class" was thus written on and communicated through the body as part of a signifying system that equates bodily maintenance with cultural capital.

But while maintaining the body has often been understood as an act of middle-class leisure, the relationship between class and the body appears to work differently under neoliberal governmentality. Nikolas Rose, for example, pinpoints how the body has simultaneously become "the diagnostic object and clinical intermediary of a range of new holistic therapies, the means of access to and transformation of the alienation, repression, and fragmentation of the self in modern times" (1999, 217). Rose identifies how maintaining the body has come to operate as part of a broader governing logic between the individual and the state, wherein the subject evidences their commitment to the ideology of entrepreneurial individualism through self-care.[7] In this economy, the body is key to the signification of "successful" neoliberal agency. As Rose explains, through bodily surveillance and management practices, individuals become "entrepreneurs of themselves, shaping their own lives through the choices they make about the forms of life available to them" (230). Put simply, the body provides the material expression of an individual's productive worth in the neoliberal value system. The governmental incentivization of body surveillance and management explicitly revealed itself during the COVID-19 pandemic. The prescription from Boris Johnson's Conservative government for the public to lose weight and "save the NHS" neatly demonstrates a stigmatizing biopolitical discourse, in which body management is equated with civic value.[8] It also locates the way in which the neoliberal state can shoulder responsibility for welfare provision onto the individual while simultaneously preserving a political and economic system that systematically underfunds and privatizes public resources.

Conceptualizing Class in Twenty-First-Century Britain

In twenty-first-century Britain, the categories of "working class" and "age" have operated separately in the political sphere, even though the millennial generation has lived through the austerity measures of the 2008 financial crisis and the insecurity of modern wage labor. At her first party conference as prime minister, Theresa May harnessed class as part of a "culture war" between "elites" and "ordinary working-class people," avoiding discussion of material inequalities throughout the UK. May promised to: "put the power of government squarely at the services of ordinary working-class people," adding, "because too often that just isn't how it works today. . . . Politicians and commentators find your patriotism distasteful, your concerns about immigration parochial, your views about crime illiberal, your attachment to your job security inconvenient" (May 2016). May's account neglects how the "working class" is now just as, or more, likely to refer to young, precariously employed, and socially liberal people as to those who are middle-aged, socially conservative, with relatively stable jobs. Indeed, Sherry Lee Linkon pinpoints the generational "gap" in working-class representations. She argues that an industrial version of "traditional" working-class identity not only haunts individuals who "defined themselves through industrial labor" but that it "carries over to their children, who struggle to construct adult lives in an economy that no longer provides access to traditional markers of adulthood, such as stable employment or a living wage" (2018, 56). Consequently, younger generations' perceptions of themselves and the social worlds in which they live are filtered through the traditional image of the working class (2018, 56). This "filtering" erases the experience of working-class young people, effectively delegitimizing their claims to "working-class" identity and preventing class solidarity. The tendency to overlook young people's class struggles is particularly significant in the wake of the COVID-19 pandemic. Eighteen- to twenty-nine-year-olds were disproportionately affected by the forced closure of the creative industries during successive national lockdowns. Given that Britain is now entering the most severe financial crisis since the Great Depression, this group is likely to experience precarity long into the future'.

Despite evidence of the generational divide in disrupting class politics, literary representation of working-class experience has also been "filtered" through the "traditional image of the working class" (Linkon 2018, 56). As Ben Clarke and Nick Hubble note in their recent study of working-class writing, any substantive attempt to examine, disrupt, or extend existing understandings of working-class voices have been largely absent from recent discussions (3–4). Instead, there has been a tendency to either "celebrate" or "demonize" working-class individuals in stereotypical terms as "ordinary," hardworking` families or dysfunctional communities (4). *Saltwater*'s focus on the experience of the upwardly mobile millennial figure disrupts the dichotomy between "celebration" and "demonization" Hubble and Clarke identify, while also inserting a new image of what it means to grow up working class during the 1990s and 2000s. The narrative is partially set in the 1990s, making frequent cultural reference points familiar to those growing up in the era, including Woolworths, dial-up internet connection, Myspace, Top of the Pops, and S Club 7. *Saltwater* might thus be compared to other recent "millennial novels" published throughout the UK, including Sally Rooney's *Normal People* (2018), Eliza Clark's *Boy Parts* (2020), and Anna Glendenning's *An Experiment in Leisure* (2021), with the latter two narratives similarly centered on relocation from Northern England to the South East. Like *Saltwater*, these novels locate a coming-of-age narrative punctuated by warehouse parties and hedonistic alcohol consumption, sexual exploration, self-discovery, and social relations mediated by the internet. In all these texts, the socio-economic positions of their protagonists resist neat classification, demonstrating a class fluidity characteristic of capitalism's flexible relations of production. Coincidentally, like Andrews, Glendenning, Rooney, and Clark all focus their texts on arts graduates who engage in the precarious labor typical of what Richard Florida termed the "creative class." Florida notes one of the defining features of the creative class as engagement in low-paid flexible employment to support work in the creative industries, which itself is dominated by an insecure "creative economy" (4). Given this demographic's association with flexible labor and economic instability, we might think of these novels as providing insights into a current 'precariat figure' (Standing 2011, 7) marked by educational, spatial, cultural and class inequalities. As we shall see, in *Saltwater*, these inequalities are written on and experienced through the body. This chapter will demonstrate how an affective bodily economy signals a new evolution in the relationship between space and class, moving away from place-bound understandings tied to material labor toward an affective experience attuned to the various modes of precarity structuring neoliberal subjecthood.

Generational Class Inheritance and the Aspirational Self

The physiological fracturing of maternal connection underpins *Saltwater*'s exploration of class and the body. Lucy's mother is positioned as an embodiment of generational class inheritance to be escaped in the pursuit of social advancement. The novel's prologue describes the point of birth from Lucy's—at this point, fetal—perspective. Directing the narrative at her mother, she tells us that her story "begins with our bodies, skin on skin, my body burst from yours," noting the "spaces beginning to open" (Andrews 2019, I) when the singular pregnant body becomes two separate beings. This "splitting" (7) between Lucy's body and her mother's is central to Lucy's rejection of her familial class inheritance. Echoing the protagonist of Zadie Smith's *NW*, discussed by Molly Slavin in this volume—particularly, Smith's character's desire to become "the sole author" of her future—Lucy uses her body as a physical manifestation of her redefinition as a self-reliant, autonomous agent (Smith 2012, 3). Yet, while Leah fails to venture far beyond the four walls of her garden in *NW*, Lucy adopts the mantra "All I need is myself" (34) to the extreme. Some of the earliest scenes of the novel depict Lucy recounting her adolescence spent poring over magazines and trawling the internet, admiring images of independent young women in London:

> I was seduced by coloured lights hitting the river in the middle of the night and throngs of cool girls in chunky sandals who promised a future of tote bags and house plants. I thought that was the kind of life I was supposed to want. I worked in a bar every night while I figured out how to get there.
>
> (5–6)

Lucy's desire to live in London and leave Sunderland behind coincides with the mass rollout of the internet during the 1990s. This was a cultural moment of rebellion and rejection of the compliant femininity that dominated the post-war period and saw the circulation of alternative lifestyles and female role models. Lucy wants to be "rougher," "stranger," "skinnier," and "shake things up," referring to nineties' icons such as Kate Moss, Brigitte Bardot, Debbie Harry, and Courtney Love as her heroes—these women, Lucy tells us, "were more than the spaces they inhabited" (163).[9]

The freedom and autonomy Lucy associates with her feminist icons contrast sharply with the submissive femininity she experiences in Sunderland. The fracturing of Lucy's closeness to her mother locates what Linkon identifies as an emerging tension in contemporary working-class culture—that of the cultural and generational division between "the older model of industrial labor and an emerging but far from certain ideal of entrepreneurial creative self-expression" (2018, 79). Lucy's attempts to jettison her working-class identity are not centered on the accrual of economic capital, but through the modification of the body as a signifier of self-reliance and cultural capital. This quest for self-reinvention necessitates an abandonment of her familial background, a severance primarily achieved by rejecting a specific form of post-war working-class femininity associated with "respectability" (Skeggs 2004; Hanley 2016). Lucy comes from "a line of immaculately turned-out women" who were "experts in dusting makeup over their faces to conceal the tremors that ran through their lives" (Andrews 2019, 84). Here, the novel evokes a well-established notion of working-class femininity premised on the domestic sphere and maintenance of the body. Beverley Skeggs has written extensively on the pathologizing of working-class women and a damaging culture of "respectability" that emerged during the 1970s and 1980s. In this context, Skeggs suggests that working-class women's performance of value relies on strategies for self-improvement that indicate high levels of discipline and self-control. Similarly, domestic spaces provide the conditions for earning social and cultural capital. As Skeggs notes, regulating the body is heavily implicated in an economy centered on the " 'caring' labour expected of working-class women on their appearance . . . organization of their homes, childcare practices, and the control they are expected to exercise . . . over members of the family in order to earn respectability" (1997, 2–3).

The way in which Lucy's mother's generation is bound by adherence to a set of bourgeois domestic standards is particularly evident in the prominence of the beauty industry in Lucy's childhood and how these spaces operate as centers of gendered cultural currency.[10] Lucy's mother's reaction when she realizes that she has forgotten to take her makeup bag on holiday is particularly instructive here. She breaks down in tears and refuses to go out in public, with Lucy recalling that "it was as though she had forgotten her armour, and all the other families would be able to see how she was crumbling" (Andrews 2019, 84). Another influential maternal figure in this respect is Lucy's aunt, who works as a beauty therapist. Lucy recalls how her aunt waxed women's eyebrows and removed hair from their bodies "in an attempt to make them feel like they were in control of something" (18), evoking a gendered and classed environment of self-policing. This bodily economy informs Lucy's adolescence. As a teenager, she becomes aware of her body as a signifier of her place in the world. Journeys to school are marked by boys' eyes surveying her on the school bus, tugging her school skirt down over her thighs, and memorizing fashion rules so she might "wriggle into the sliver of space [she] was expected to occupy" (141). Directing the narrative at her mother, Lucy notes how she "did not know bodies were important until now" (127). This admission marks a turning point in the relationship between her psychological and physiological self—the body is no longer simply a vehicle in which Lucy exists; rather, it is crucial to carving out her place in the world.

Further, this pursuit of non-conformist images of femininity requires the external modification of the body. The development in Lucy's relationship with food becomes part of her "escape" from her parental roots:

> I started eating less, serving myself smaller portions and stopping before I was full. The internet forums I trawled through were covered with hip-bones and clavicles, and I wanted to give myself the best possible chance of becoming someone different.
>
> (154–55)

Lucy's disordered eating functions as a rejection of class inheritance from her mother. Her association of self-reinvention and bodily modification might be read as a form of Kristevean abjection, entailing a breakdown in meaning caused by loss of the distinction between object and subject or between self and other. In *Powers of Horror*, Kristeva forges a link between abjection and the severing of the parental bond; she suggests that "food loathing" is "the most elementary form of abjection" (1980, 2), signifying a rejection of parental care. As she puts it, refusal to eat "separates me from the mother and father who proffer it. 'I' want none of that element, sign of their desire" (3). Kristeva goes on to explain that, in psychological terms, food and nourishment are symbolic of the mother; "hence a daughter's refusal to eat can be seen as an attempt to escape a mother's control—a revolt against that which gave us our own existence or state of being" (3). Sociological studies of eating disorders also note the mother's influence in the development of restrictive eating habits. Kim Chermin, for example, argues that any attempt to change the body is also a way to set socio cultural boundaries within the mother–daughter relationship:

> When we attempt to determine the size and shape of a woman's body, instructing to avoid its largeness and softness and roundness

and girth, we are driven to the desire to expunge the memory of the primordial mother who ruled over our childhood with her inscrutable power over life and death.

(1994, 143)

In *Saltwater*, caloric restriction represents a threat to the symbolic order and the displacement of Lucy's mother as a beholder of biological life and sustenance. Lucy rejects her mother's description of her as "lovely" and, in contrast to the version of femininity typified by her mother, wants to be "spikey" (Andrews 2019, 163–64). In this regard, thinness operates as a physiological manifestation of the psychological urge to sever maternal attachments and abandon her working-class identity, while simultaneously positioning the body as a classed space to be harnessed in the project of social advancement.

Cultural Capital and Self-Sufficiency

Lucy's self-redefinition and rejection of her upbringing is consolidated during her time at university. While Lucy rejects the working-class femininity of her mother's generation, in London, she is faced with meeting the evolving standards and expectations for millennials located within twenty-first-century cultural tastes and lifestyles. In an economic and social system in which class distinctions based on Marxist categories of labor have lost their purchase, *Saltwater* documents less the aspiration for middle-class respectability (as typified by her mother), but a specifically twenty-first-century manifestation of the bourgeoisie. This demographic possesses little economic capital but boasts rich cultural and social capital, displayed by consumeristic and largely pretentious individualism with a "middle-class" subtext. Here, space takes on a new configuration, from the working-class, domestic spaces of Sunderland to the middle-class cultural space of the London university. In particular, student dinner parties present class-inflected cultural spaces that demonstrate Lucy's struggle to display necessary levels of capital. Sitting in a friend's home at a dinner party, Lucy tells us that she has tried to avoid these situations, recalling the nerves accompanying mealtimes in the surroundings of her peers in London:

> The potato smiley faces of my childhood are beige mush now. Dairy causes acne and gluten is the devil. Tapioca and soy milk and Maldon sea salt. Almonds are unethical and cheap beer causes migraines. If our bodies are defined by the things we put into them, then I am too afraid to put anything into mine. I am cheap things, sad things, small and unrefined.

(222)

The novel sets up a binary between the social spaces of Sunderland and London through dietary distinctions, with Lucy's recollections of her childhood marked by moralizing discourse regarding ethical consumption. The scene demonstrates how, in a society in which leisure has been invented as the domain of free choice, "the autonomous individual is obliged to construe itself in terms of choices regarding consumption" (Rose 1999, 230). The reference to gluten and dairy alternatives evokes a contemporary landscape in which identity and perceived social value are signified through dietary taste and the ability to make discerning choices about consumption. The potato smiley faces of Lucy's childhood no longer represent happy memories of her childhood but the shame of consuming processed "beige mush," indicating a fracturing of the relationship between the present self and the family home. Paralleling this familial distancing is the simultaneous disconnection between the psychological self and the body as the material site that renders dietary choices visible externally. Lucy's fear of making socially unacceptable choices regarding consumption pervades the scene: she is both afraid to eat the "rich," "delicate" meals of her peers and the "cheap," "unrefined" foods of her childhood, the latter of which she views as fundamentally incompatible with the life she has carved out in London. Here, then, diet carries a self-referential quality about class identity. Lucy's childhood meals also conjure up traits that ride against a governing logic of self-care—that of excess, indulgence, and unhealthiness—that she internalizes as working-class shame and a lack of self-restraint. Conversely, small portions of (often more expensive) food signify admirable levels of self-denial and sophistication. Lucy's food choices are ultimately a moral dilemma about not only class, but about self-responsibility performed through the virtuous pursuit of "health."

These pervasive, internalized dogmas about apparent "overconsumption" and individual responsibility register diet culture's neoliberal priorities, particularly the habituation of self-reliance as part of the performance of productive selfhood. The anxiety pervading social interactions elicits a psycho-social response, in which the subject distances themselves from physiological needs, including hunger. Perceiving herself as "not delicate enough" to appreciate the nuanced meals of her peers, Lucy does not permit herself to consume the foods that now accompany mealtimes, instead, dulling her hunger with coffee and wine (Andrews 2019, 222). More explicitly still, Lucy tells us that she is scared of "having too much" (47), directly linking caloric restriction to the will to demonstrate self-reliance. Fears of dependence and consumption can thus be read as an awareness of a social order that stigmatizes individuals who are not deemed financially productive. Her disordered eating is hence a kind of willed physical shrinkage, communicating a feeling of "undeservedness" of taking up social space in the university environment.

Lucy's commitment to self-reinvention takes on a further spatial configuration in her relationship to London's urban geography. The self-reliance enacted in her restrictive eating is paralleled by Lucy's compulsive exercise to pursue a sense of belonging in the city. On weekends, Lucy "traipsed the streets, seeking out a better version" of herself, which eventually develop into scenes of obsessive running and disembodiment. Lucy begins "pounding around the park for hours" to "get rid of the black smoke in her chest," but however hard she tries, she "could not stop" (273). Despite her apparent spatial mobility, Lucy cannot be considered a *flâneur* (Baudelaire 1964), or as Lauren Elkin (2016) would put it, a *flâneuse*. Rather than strolling aimlessly through the city as an observer, Lucy's movements are devoid of any agency; she circles the same area of space in a park near her apartment, desperately trying to "lose the sad pink shape" of herself (Andrews 2019, 273). In the absence of economic resources, the novel demonstrates how disciplining the body becomes a mechanism for signifying an individual's productive value and the possession of cultural capital. Lucy's compulsion to run is ultimately a process of disembodiment: just as she ignores the pangs of hunger at mealtimes, she also overrides the physical signs of her body's exhaustion. Lucy's inability to consume and take up space in the world is thus a symptom of a moral economy in which dependency is viewed as a social ill. Lucy herself appears to recognize such a context, applying dehumanizing language to her own longing for consumption. Her belief that it is "embarrassing, or entitled, or greedy to want things in a city where so many others are wanting" (223) signals the pervasiveness and internalization of a market logic that assigns value through extreme acts of self-discipline. Her disembodiment thus appears as a symptom of deeper psychological distress rooted in the internal conflicts wrought by social mobility and the will to assume "successful" neoliberal subjecthood. These conflicts are, in turn, exacerbated by the need to define one's identity in a society in which the individual must make visible their productive worth as part of a self-referential legitimacy. Just as, in the previous generation, the women visiting Lucy's aunt attempted to gain control and respectability through beauty treatments, Lucy's strategies of bodily self-discipline work to perform her own "sense of value" (Skeggs and Loveday 2012, 474).

Skin is also central to class embodiment in *Saltwater*, functioning as an inscription of cultural tastes and perceptions of differing levels of sophistication. Sara Ahmed and Jackie Stacy have previously examined the critical potential of skin as the boundary between self and society, suggesting a notion of *Thinking through the Skin* that moves away from "the body" as a privileged figure and posits skin as "the fleshy interface between bodies and worlds" (2001, 1). In *Saltwater*, class distinctions between Newcastle and London are articulated through differing approaches to modifying the skin. The act of fake tanning is particularly central to Lucy's working-class North-Eastern identity. Lucy reflects how her fake-tanned limbs were "shiny and lustrous" in Newcastle but, in London, they are "orange and sticky" (Andrews 2019, 212), gesturing toward the spatial dynamics of fake tan and as a class marker. Indeed, the practice of fake tanning—and, in particular, "orange" skin—evokes a regional, working-class stereotype of the "Geordie" who is often perceived as lacking in cultural taste and refinement.[11] As Emily Nicholls points out, Newcastle is renowned for the supposed performance of a particular type of "excessive" and "hyper-sexualized" femininity consisting of glamorous and revealing clothing (2018, 192). Within this dynamic, the "Geordie" is coded as white, working class and associated with "orange" fake-tanned skin (192). In a similar vein, Anne Graefer notes how heavily tanned "orange" skin has become "a metonym for bad taste and an 'improper' form of whiteness" belonging to the Northern working class (Graefer 2014, 108). Lucy's lack of belonging at university embodies these geographic class correlates; her "orange" and "sticky" skin... her "orange" and "sticky" skin evidences her lack of cultural capital compared to her peers and links Lucy's class shame to the pervasiveness of Northern working-class stereotypes. Here, then, skin does not simply contain the body but is "always open to being read" (Ahmed and Stacey 2001, 1) through a series of significatory practices.

The skin also inscribes the limits of social mobility. The ways in which Lucy inhabits her skin is crucial to her experience of class, but, unlike the size and shape of her body, she is unable to transform her skin to fit a glossy middle-class aesthetic: "There is another kind of skin that I did not know about. It is posh-girl skin. Expensive and gold. . . . It is lustrous and shiny where I am mottled. Look at my bruises, my scratches, my scars" (Andrews 2019, 218). In *Saltwater's* affective corporeal economy, the skin not only "records our personal biographies" (Ahmed and Stacey 2001, 2), but provides the surface for the experience of class shame. Lucy perceives her scars and bruises as *social* blemishes staining her character. Again, the novel returns to Lucy's belief that she is "undeserving" of taking up space in the university. We see a similar dynamic at work when Lucy reveals how she completed little reading for her degree program because she was too busy "changing the shape of my sentences, the texture of my skin and the weight of my skull" (Andrews 2019, 220). Paradoxically, Lucy's pursuit of a kind of bourgeois embodiment is also to the detriment of her university studies and, thus, her goal of social advancement. Her continual self-scrutiny and anxiety that her body will be "outed" as working-class counters the assumption that social advancement through the education system provides adequate levels of capital for the subject to make a stake for legitimacy and assimilation. Lucy's willingness to sacrifice educational tasks and behaviors in favor of acquiring cultural capital thus figures social mobility as an affective experience akin to "cruel optimism"—where attachment to the unobtainable "good life" locks the individual into a cycle of damaging behaviors

(Berlant 2011, 1). In other words, it appears that there is no space for the first-generation working-class student in the geographic and cultural spheres of the London university.

Despite her best efforts at self-reinvention, Lucy remains tethered to her working-class roots; she feels shut out by her privileged classmates and describes London as a series of "impenetrable shapes with fierce elbows" (Andrews 2019, 15). Lucy experiences the city as a space of simultaneous opportunity and alienation, with her relationship to London's architecture coding social mobility's psychological and emotional complexities. Again, the desire to assimilate into London's material and symbolic spaces is coded as a bodily sensation. Lucy "craved the speed and proximity to the centre" (15), describing her class aspiration as a hunger for geographic centrality. This connection between the body, social advancement, and spatial belonging is paralleled in exchanges between Lucy and an architect whom Lucy befriends while in London. Their relationship is depicted in terms of their unequal rights to space. While the architect has "so much proof of his existence," signified the physical presence of bricks and mortar of the buildings he designs, Lucy cannot claim a similar stake in the city. Instead, she gets "smaller everyday" (133). The physical spaces built in the architect's vision embody his privilege and serve as extensions of his identity: he would sit "up late at the kitchen table designing buildings on his laptop," as the couple grew "upwards and outwards night by night," while Lucy pulled pints in a bar and "turned in on [her]self, like an ingrown hair" (133). *Saltwater*'s association between social value and material space evokes a neoliberal class discourse that demonizes subjects who cannot perform their worth publicly. In particular, the psychological and physiological conflicts borne out of apparent social advancement that structure the novel echo neoliberalism's "call to individuality," with future-oriented investment in the self as a "project" signifying one's personal value (Skeggs and Loveday 2012, 474–75).

"The Answer Is Space"

Saltwater does not offer a neat solution to the alienating experience of class mobility in the present, nor does it propose a nostalgic return to the stability of the industrial past. However, the novel tentatively alludes to the ability to imagine life beyond the alienating experience of neoliberal subjectivity. For example, where we find glimpses of Lucy at ease with her identity and her body are the segments of the novel in rural Ireland. Utilizing the conventions of pastoral retreat, "Part 4" of the novel offers snippets of Lucy's convalescence when she returns to her grandfather's cottage. The relocation from London, a city home to 8.9 million—to Burtonport, a coastal town with a population of 304—triggers, for Lucy, a reconnection between the psychological and physiological selves.

Significantly, the return to the ancestral home coincides with her body "welcoming me back. I have missed you, she tells me" (Andrews 2019, 291). Burtonport's abundant landscape thus provides the conditions for a kind of psychotherapy, with the increase in material space reflected in sparsely populated pages of text:

> then
> later
> something
> different

(287)

In these closing vignettes, *Saltwater* provides a version of the aspirational narrative that complicates hierarchal approaches to class, with social mobility experienced less as "climbing the ladder" than a sidestep into a different world. In the end, it appears as if the socially mobile individual is frequently caught between two spheres and never fully integrated into either, rendering social advancement little beyond an ideological dream.

Lucy's return to Ireland is bolstered in her relationship with an unnamed man, who "smells of the factories and the warehouses, the cobbles and the terraced houses" Lucy associates with the North-East (104). Unlike Lucy's previous sexual encounters, which were often masochistic and self-demeaning, this relationship entails a return to the self in which she learns to exist in her body and acknowledge her ancestral past. Lucy recognizes that it is no coincidence that her choice of partner reminds her of life in Sunderland. Taxonomies of industry, manual labor, and Sunderland's former economy—all of which she associates with her family, particularly her father—dominate these exchanges. The man leaves traces of "oil" and "dirt" on her sheets, and his arms display muscularity from carrying "bricks and cement" (8, 96), indicating an opening up of space for Lucy's familial history in the present and the future too. In this sense, *Saltwater* appears to confirm what Hubble argues of working-class fictions that center on aspirational protagonists in a way that reflects Patricia E. Johnson's discussion of Ethel Carnie Holdsworth's characters in this volume. Hubble identifies the

> paradoxical nature of the process of "getting out" . . . whether in the form of London housing estates or the deindustrialized North. The individual means of gaining the agency to transcend the constraints of residual working-class communities is not by forgetting one's childhood past but in becoming fully aware of it.

(2018, 284)

The project of "becoming fully aware" of one's past is reiterated in the narrative's cyclical structure, which begins and ends in Ireland at Lucy's grandfather's cottage. The novel juxtaposes the speed and modernity of London as England's metropolitan center and the "gentle isolation" (Andrews 2019, 69) of Ireland's North-West coast: "Time passes differently here. The cliffs and the sea and the long, sandy beaches move infinitely slower than life in the city. The constant rhythm of the water makes the clatter of the tubes and the endless sirens seem trivial" (94). Here, the permanence of the coastal and mountainous landscape initiates a recalibration of space and time, a reversal of the "time-space compression" characteristic of capitalist modernity (Harvey 1989, 284). The natural pace of the tide, caused by the gravitational pull of the moon and the sun, renders London's accelerated speed enabled and urban infrastructure insignificant. Moreover, the permanency that Lucy associates with the landscape enables her to take up space and simply exist rather than constantly move in and through space in London, where even buildings are transient and "everything is fast and new or being knocked down and renovated" (Andrews 2019, 193).

The abundance of space and time in Burtonport is ultimately what triggers Lucy's process of re-embodiment as she rejects the relentless self-sufficiency and self-reliance structuring her life in London; she "must learn how to need, how to ask, how to want" (108). In a reversal of Lucy's previous assertion that "all I need is myself" (134), the end of the novel sees her learn to consume, be reliant on others, and attend to her bodily needs. Crucially, the scenes in which Lucy describes her life in Donegal entail her relearning the permission to eat plentifully as a source of pleasure. She is teaching herself how to cook "slow, careful meals" including "creamy curries and thyme-speckles vegetable bakes" (139), sharply contrasting with her "sad bowls of lentils and chickpeas" forming her diet in London (105). In this sense, Ireland represents a shift away from the speed of London and the meagerness and restriction that characterized her university years. Now, she is learning to "live with abundance" and work toward "a life that is full" (105). *Saltwater*'s ending on an emphatic rejection of the city and a move to a non-metropolitan space in rural Ireland destabilizes a linear temporality in which relentless forward progression is a foundation for social advancement. Instead, the novel communicates skepticism toward the reproductive potential of the city, prioritizing more meaningful attachments to place than economic value.

At the outset of this chapter, I proposed an "affective bodily economy" as a way of reading the experience of social mobility and class consciousness under neoliberalism. As we have seen, this attention to the body may include self-surveillance and regulation strategies, external bodily modification, familial detachment (especially from the mother), disembodiment, and a sensorial experience of place. What this notion helps demonstrate, then, is the centrality of the body in articulating the indeterminacy of contemporary life. It also positions the millennial as a key figure in twenty-first-century class experience, showing how class-conscious literature cannot simply be reduced to a set of socio-economic, geographic, political, or cultural issues. *Saltwater* gestures toward the potential of mobilizing "space" in new, productive ways, moving toward a literary registration of class that goes beyond material expressions of inequality. To pay attention to the body is thus to locate a new critical lens attentive to the neoliberal doctrine.

Notes

1. Tyler's notion of a "moral economy" is a central component of *Revolting Subjects: Social Abjection and Resistance in Neoliberal Britain* (2013). This idea is developed further in her more recent text, *Stigma: The Machinery of Inequality* (2000), in which "undeservedness" is cast as justification for austerity measures.
2. I have written elsewhere about the political implications of the continued association of Northern England and a specifically (de)industrialized version of working-class identity. See Chloe Ashbridge "'It Aye like London You Know': The Brexit Novel and the Cultural Politics of Devolution," *Open Library of Humanities* 6, no. 1 https://olh.openlibhums.org/article/id/4622/
3. There are exceptions to this tendency, however. As Simon Lee notes in his chapter, Shelagh Delaney, Nell Dunn, and Pat Barker have been crucial in inserting women's voices into post-war working-class regional representation.
4. Illustrative fictional examples specific to the North of England include Gordon Burn's *The North of England Home Service* (2003); David Peace's *Red Riding Quartet* (1999, 2000, 2001, 2002), and *GB84* (2004); and Philip Hensher's *The Northern Clemency* (2008).
5. In terms of defining the millennial, it is largely understood that this group refers to individuals born between 1981 and 1996. This generation was the first to grow up under neoliberal ideology and are said to experience more acutely than any other generation what Mark Fisher termed "capitalist realism" (Fisher 2009). In *Kids These Days: The Making of Millennials*, Malcolm Harris pinpoints the normativity of neoliberalism for millennials. He argues that the economic, political, and social actuality that the condition of neoliberalism fosters—economic precarity, self-interest, self-sufficiency—ultimately leaves the millennial unable to imagine alternative ways of structuring life or living it (2017, 163).
6. I understand "neoliberalism" as a particular economic, political, and social doctrine that has dominated British social and political life since the 1980s. My approach is informed by David Harvey's formulation of neoliberalism as a practice premised on the idea that "human well-being can be best advanced by liberating individual entrepreneurial freedoms and skills within an institutional framework characterised by private property rights, free markets, and free trade" (2005, 2). What is crucial for my discussion of class and social mobility in this chapter is the contradictory way in which the concepts of freedom and human agency are central to the neoliberal self. As Harvey puts it, the very assumption that these social outcomes are "guaranteed by freedom of the market and of trade is a cardinal feature of neoliberal thinking,"

with the pursuit of being the individual who is "free to choose" functioning as the lifeblood of neoliberal subjecthood (7).

7. For more on this topic, see also Skeggs (1997, 2004).
8. In July 2020, the Conservative Government's health secretary, Matt Hancock, advised the public to "lose 5lbs" to save the NHS £100million. See: www.telegraph.co.uk/politics/2020/07/26/lose-5lb-save-nhs-100m-says-matt-hancock-coronavirus-wake-up/, accessed August 12, 2021.
9. It is important to note, however, that popular constructions of assertive femininity in the 1990s (e.g., "Girl Power") were only partially subversive and largely operated within patriarchal gender norms in which women are judged by their sexual appeal and clothing choices. See Dibben (2002).
10. See, for example, Julia Prewitt Brown's examination of literary and cultural representations of middle-class domestic spaces: *The Bourgeois Interior: How the Middle Class Imagines Itself in Literature and Film* (Charlottesville: University of Virginia Press, 2008).
11. MTV's reality television series, *Geordie Shore* (2011–), popularized the stereotype of the Newcastle "Geordie" who displays "excessive" levels of glamour and a lack of cultural refinement.

References

Ahmed, Sara, and Jackie Stacey, eds. 2001. *Thinking Through the Skin*. London and New York: Routledge.
Anderson, Lindsay. 1963. *This Sporting Life*. Rank Organisation.
Andrews, Jessica. 2019. *Saltwater*. London: Sceptre.
Baudelaire, Charles. 1964. *The Painter of Modern Life and Other Essays*. Translated by Jonathan Mayne. London: Phaidon.
Bauman, Zygmunt. (2000) 2012. *Liquid Modernity*. Cambridge, UK and Malden, MA: Polity.
Bennett, Tony, Mike Savage, Elizabeth Bortolaia Silva, Alan Warde, Modesto Gayo-Cal, and David Wright. 2009. *Culture, Class, Distinction*. London and New York: Routledge.
Berlant, Lauren. 2011. *Cruel Optimism*. Durham, NC: Duke University Press.
Bourdieu, Pierre (1980) 1990. *The Logic of Practice*. Stanford, CA: Stanford University Press.
———. (1984) 2010. *Distinction: A Social Critique of the Judgement of Taste*. London and New York: Routledge.
Burn, Gordon. 2003. *The North of England Home Service*. London: Faber and Faber.
Chermin, Kim. (1981) 1994. *The Obsession: Reflections on the Tyranny of Slenderness*. New York: Harper Perennial.
Clark, Eliza. 2020. *Boy Parts*. London: Influx Press.
Clarke, Ben, and Nick Hubble. 2018. "Introduction." In *Working-Class Writing: Theory and Practice*, edited by Ben Clarke and Nick Hubble, 1–14. Cham, CH: Palgrave Macmillan.
Coleman, Rebecca. 2016. "Austerity Futures: Debt, Temporality and (Hopeful) Pessimism as an Austerity Mood." *New Formations: A Journal of Culture/Theory/Politics* 87 (87): 83–101. https://doi.org/10.3898/NEWF.87.5.2016.
Connolly, Nathan. 2017. *Know Your Place: Essays on the Working Class by the Working Class*. Liverpool: Dead Ink.

Connolly, Nathan. 2021. *Test Signal: Northern Anthology of New Writing.* London and New York: Bloomsbury.

Dibben, Nicola. 2002. "Constructions of Femininity in 1990s Girl-Group Music." *Feminism & Psychology* 12 (2): 168–75. https://doi.org/10.1177/09 59353502012002007.

Elkin, Lauren. 2016. *Flâneuse: Women Walk the City in Paris, New York, Tokyo, Venice, and London.* London: Chatto & Windus.

Fisher, Mark. 2009. *Capitalist Realism: Is There No Alternative?* Winchester, UK: Zero Books.

Florida, Richard. 2002. *The Rise of the Creative Class.* New York: Hachette.

Gledenning, Anna. 2021. *An Experiment in Leisure.* London: Random House.

Gowland, Rebecca. 2018. "'A Mass of Crooked Alphabets': The Construction and Othering of Working Class Bodies in Industrial England." In *Bioarchaeological Analyses and Bodies: New Ways of Knowing Anatomical and Archaeological Skeletal Collections,* edited by Pamela K. Stone, 147–63. Bioarchaeology and Social Theory. New York: Springer International Publishing. https://doi.org/10.1007/978-3-319-71114-0_8.

Graefer, Anne. 2014. "White Stars and Orange Celebrities: The Affective Production of Whiteness in Humorous Celebrity-Gossip Blogs." *Celebrity Studies* 5 (1–2): 107–22. https://doi.org/10.1080/19392397.2013.798913.

Hanley, Lynsey. 2016. *Respectable: Crossing the Class Divide.* London: Penguin.

Harris, Malcolm. 2017. *Kids These Days: Human Capital and the Making of Millennials.* London: Little Brown.

Harvey, David. 1989. *The Condition of Postmodernity: An Enquiry into the Origins of Historical Change.* Oxford: Blackwell.

Harvey, David. 2005. *A Brief History of Neoliberalism.* Oxford: Oxford University Press.

Hensher, Philip. 2008. *The Northern Clemency.* London: Herper Perennial.

Hubble, Nick. 2018. "Respectability, Nostalgia and Shame in Contemporary English Working-Class Fiction." In *Working-Class Writing: Theory and Practice,* edited by Ben Clarke and Nick Hubble, 269–84. Cham, CH: Palgrave Macmillan.

Kristeva, Julia. 1980. *Powers of Horror: An Essay on Abjection.* New York: Columbia University Press.

Linkon, Sherry Lee. 2014. "Men Without Work: White Working-Class Masculinity in Deindustrialization Fiction." *Contemporary Literature* 55 (1): 148–67. https://doi.org/10.1353/cli.2014.0003.

Linkon, Sherry Lee. 2018. *The Half-Life of Deindustrialization: Working-Class Writing about Economic Restructuring.* Ann Arbor: University of Michigan Press.

May, Theresa. 2016. "Theresa May's Conference Speech in Full." *The Financial Times,* October 5. www.ft.com/content/ffb25e84-8af2-11e6-8aa5-f79f5696c731.

Miranda, Veerle. 2021. "Young People's Concerns during COVID-19: Results from Risks That Matter 2020." *OECD,* July 6. www.oecd.org/coronavirus/policy-responses/young-people-s-concerns-during-covid-19-results-from-risks-that-matter-2020-64b51763/.

Nicholls, Emily. 2018. *Negotiating Femininities in the Neoliberal Night-Time Economy: Too Much of a Girl?* Basingstoke: Palgrave Macmillan.

Northern Fiction Alliance. 2018. "The NFA's Open Letter to the Publishing Industry." *Comma Press.* https://commapress.co.uk/news/the-nfas-open-letter-to-the-publishing/

Peace, David. 1999. *Nineteen Seventy-Four.* London: Serpent's Tail.

Peace, David. 2000. *Nineteen Seventy-Seven.* London: Serpent's Tail.

Peace, David. 2001. *Nineteen Eighty.* London: Serpent's Tail.

Peace, David. 2002. *Nineteen Eighty-Three.* London: Serpent's Tail.

Peace, David. 2004. *GB84.* London: Faber and Faber.

Phillips, Henrietta. 2017. "A Woman Like That Is Not a Woman, Quite. I Have Been Her Kind': Maxine Peake and the Gothic Excess of Northern Femininity." In *Social Class and Television Drama in Contemporary Britain*, edited by David Forrest and Sue Vice, 149–64. Basingstoke, UK: Palgrave Macmillan.

"Portico Prize." n.d. The Portico. Accessed August 12, 2021. www.theportico.org.uk/portico-prize.

Prewitt Brown, Julia. 2008. *The Bourgeois Interior.* Charlottesville, VA: University of Virginia Press.

Reisz, Karel. 1960. *Saturday Night and Sunday Morning.* Woodfall Film Productions.

Richardson, Tony. 1962. *The Loneliness of the Long Distance Runner.* Woodfall Film Productions.

Rooney, Sally. 2018. *Normal People.* London: Faber and Faber.

Rose, Nikolas. (1990) 1999. *Governing the Soul: Shaping of the Private Self.* London: Free Association Books.

Skeggs, Beverley. 1997. *Formations of Class & Gender: Becoming Respectable.* London, Thousand Oaks, CA, and New Delhi: SAGE Publications.

———. 2004. *Class, Self, Culture.* London and New York: Routledge.

Skeggs, Beverley and Loveday, Vik. 2012. "Struggles for Value: Value Practices, Injustice, Judgement, Affect and the Idea of Class." *The British Journal of Sociology* 63 (3): 472–490. https://doi.org/10.1111/j.1468-4446.2012.01420.x.

Smith, Zadie. 2012. *NW.* London: Hamish Hamilton.

Soja, Edward W. 1980. "The Socio-Spatial Dialectic." *Annals of the Association of American Geographers* 70 (2): 207–25. https://doi.org/10.1111/j.1467-8306.1980.tb01308.x.

Standing, Guy. 2011. *The Precariat: The New Dangerous Class.* London: Bloomsbury.

Tyler, Imogen. 2000. *Stigma: The Machinery of Inequality.* London: Zed Books.

———. 2013. *Revolting Subjects: Social Abjection and Resistance in Neoliberal Britain.* London: Zed Books.

Wood, Helen. 2020. "Three (Working-Class) Girls: Social Realism, the 'At-Risk' Girl and Alternative Classed Subjectivities." *Journal of British Cinema and Television* 17 (1): 70–90. https://doi.org/10.3366/jbctv.2020.0508.

Index

Tressell, Robert 2, 79–80; *see also*
Ragged Trousered Philanthropists,
The (Tressell)
Tuan, Yi-Fu: topophilia 8
Tyler, Imogen 157–158, 206; moral
economy 206, 222n1; stigma
production 133; *see also* abject;
social abjection

Uncommercial Traveller, The
(Dickens) 44
"undeservedness" 222n1; feeling of
216, 218; moral economy of 206
Union Street (Barker) 15, 127–130,
133, 136–143
Upstone, Sara 176
urbanism: architecture and 15; space-
class analysis applied to 9; urban
and rural, dichotomy between
147–148; urban anxiety 26; urban
apartheid 134 (*see also* Davis,
Mike); urban crime novel, emergence
of 150; urban development (cultural
forces linked to 135; gentrification
and 13; literary depictions of 21;
sight (vision) as trope of 21>);
urban imprisonment, house as site
of 38, 49; urban infrastructure
20–35 (Foucault on 20; social
order imposed via 31); urbanity,
modern 100; urbanization 142
(social novel and rise of 2); urban
landscape (1736 Edinburgh 32;
changing 153; deindustrialized 15,
154; imagined communities created
via 95, 1498; industrial 152, 154;
"lost futures" of 151; perceived
unhealthiness of 27; post-industrial
156; Regency anxiety. manifested
via 23); urban mixing, fear of chaos
tied to 32; urban planning 102,
134 (class differences expressed
through 96; fantasies of planners
rejected by Greene 102; middle-class
anxiety addressed by 94; Dickens's
representation of home as site of 38;
public health and 14, 22, 25; post-
war 97; propaganda promoting 15);
urban sociability 31; urban space
(London as 168, 170, 217; mapping
of 7); urban sprawl 29
Uses of Literacy, The (Hoggart) 3,
112–114, 148

value (economic) 221
value (socio-cultural), 190–192,
216–221; Braine's exploration
of the negotiation of 115–116,
124; British traditional 93, 95,
100; collective 78; communist
88; English 85; "exchange" 54;
hierarchies of 120; middle class 95;
performance of 213; racialization of
183–202; "sense of" 217; social 16,
54, 216, 219; Society 51; "subjects
of" 183, 190, 192, 200; surplus 39;
working class 123
value of everyday objects 115
value of possessions 72
value systems 73; neoliberal 210
Veenstra, Gerry 9–10
Victorian 105–106
"virtual" versus "actual" social identity
(Goffman) 132–133, 139, 143
vital heritages 131; *see also*
Habermas, Jürgen
Vodi, The (Braine) 114

Wacquant, Loïc: advanced marginality
134, 138; territorial stigmatization
15, 134, 136, 138–139
Wald, Priscilla 26
Waterhouse, Keith: *Billy Liar* 149
Waterline (Raisin) 15, 146, 150–157
Way We Live, The (documentary
film) 99
wealth and the wealthy: bourgeois
subjectivity and 46; class
segregation via space 31; class
status and 44; collective ideas
regarding 38; colonial hierarchies
of 57; conspicuous consumption
tied to 116; fantasies of 51; fear
of social mixing 25; fragility of
49; gay identity and 195–196;
illusions of 49; imagined 46–47;
middle class 40; new 52, 160–161,
192–193; psychological mobility
of 53; respectability politics of 119;
signifiers of 190; space connoting
26–27, 137; speculative 47;
suburbanization of 29
Weber, Max 10
welfare stigma production *see* stigma
We Live (Jones) 80, 84–85, 87, 89
Welsh, Irvine *see Trainspotting*
(Welsh)

Printed in Great Britain
by Amazon

38403476R00139